*What Was
Shakespeare?*

What Was Shakespeare?

Renaissance Plays and Changing Critical Practice

❖

EDWARD PECHTER

Cornell University Press

ITHACA AND LONDON

First published 1995 by Cornell University Press.

Library of Congress Cataloging-in-Publication Data
Pechter, Edward, 1941–
    What was Shakespeare? : Renaissance plays and changing critical
practice / Edward Pechter.
      p.   cm.
    Includes bibliographical references and index.
    ISBN 0–8014–3065–8 (alk. paper).—ISBN 0–8014–8229–1 (pbk. :
alk. paper)
    1. Shakespeare, William, 1564–1616—Criticism and interpretation—
History—20th century.   2. English drama—Early modern, 1500–1700—
History and criticisim—Theory, etc.   3. Renaissance—England—
Historiography.   4. Criticism—History—20th century.   I. Title.
PR2970.P43   1995
822.3'3—dc20   94–25366

Printed in the United States of America

♾ The paper in this book meets the minimum requirements of the
American National Standard for Information Sciences—Permanence of
Paper for Printed Library Materials, ANSI Z39.48-1984.

For Lesley, David, and Corbridge

Contents

✦

Preface

IX

Introduction: After "After the Carnival"

1

1 What Was Shakespeare?

13

2 The Rise and Fall of the New Historicism

49

3 Of Ants and Grasshoppers:
Two Ways (or More) to
Link Texts and Power

87

4 Teaching Differences

106

Contents

5 In Defense of Jargon: Criticism as a Social Practice
126

6 Against "Ideology"
142

Notes
167

Works Cited
179

Index
193

Preface

❖

This book proceeds from the belief (it may now seem self-evident fact) that the criticism of Shakespeare, like academic criticism generally, has undergone dramatic changes since the 1960s—in thematic interests, assumptions, and forms of self-understanding and -evaluation, even in the rhetorical protocols that tend to govern its expression. I am concerned not with a historical explanation of how or why these changes occurred but rather with the consequences of the current situation in which (to simplify) a variety of materialist practices have come to challenge a humanist critical tradition.

These challenges have considerably eroded the authority of traditional modes of Shakespeare criticism, but neither totally displaced nor replaced them. On the contrary, traditional critical concerns substantially survive even (maybe especially) in the work of critics for whom such residual presences are the least welcome. I am interested in the continuities that underlie the transformations and in the resulting situation of critical disagreement—not just between traditional and innovative critical modes but among the various modes of contemporary criticism competing against one another.

For one version of the problems inherent in this situation, consider the pained questions Aleksii Antedilluvianovich Prelapsarianov asks at the beginning of *Perestroika*, Part 2 of Tony Kushner's *Angels in America*: "And Theory? How are we to proceed without Theory? What System of Thought have these Reformers to present to this mad swirling planetary disorganization, to the Inevident Welter of fact, event, phenomenon, calamity? Do they have, as we did, a beautiful Theory, as bold, as Grand, as comprehensive a construct . . . ?" The absence of theory? For the many people who believe our current problems arise rather from an excess of theory, Aleksii's lament may seem perverse. The proper question from their perspective is not how we can get along without theory but how we can hope to proceed in its wake.

Theory, however, either too little or too much, is not the cause of our problems; it is a symptom. The golden time in Aleksii's memory (or imagination) was one when there was not just Theory but a single predominant theory—when there was a "we" effectively united in a shared faith. (Aleksii conveniently ignores the element of coercion involved in sustaining this community, but Kushner—who gives him his ironic name and also describes him as "unimaginably old and totally blind"—does not want us to forget this fact, and I have tried not to.) We have not lost the beautiful-grand-comprehensive Systems of Thought Aleksii mourns. We have them in abundance, and it is this abundance that generates the contrary view that our problem is caused by an excess of theory. But this view too confuses cause and effect. The problem with theory is not that there is too much of it but that there are too many of them, or rather that belief is fragmented among a variety of professional academic constituencies, all of them significant, each with its own totalizing explanatory narrative, but none of them strong enough to be determining. Behind both complaints, too much theory and too little, is the same anxiety: what we are lacking now is an effective consensus. Now that poststructuralism (not the absence but the proliferation of competing explanatory narratives) has established itself in the academy, what do we do?

How is it possible for us to talk to each other, and what should be the terms of the academic conversation? I cannot answer these questions (or I have different and contradictory answers—which amounts to the same thing), and I do not think anybody can. The differences among Shakespeareans are beyond resolution. But they do not need to be resolved—or so I argue in this book. Dissensus is not new to Shakespeare studies; it is the normal condition for our work, as I think it is for all work in the humanities. Contemporary disagreement is abnormally intense and wide-ranging, but the current situation does not prevent us from writing useful critical commentary about Shakespeare, and can even enable us to write it—a proposition this book aspires both to argue for and to illustrate.

The argument is set out and developed in the Introduction and Chapter 1. The subsequent chapters furnish the illustrations by accommodating the argument to a variety of occasions. Versions of some of the material in these chapters have appeared elsewhere. Chapter 2 is based on "The New Historicism and Its Discontents: Politicizing Renaissance Drama," *PMLA* 102 (1987): 292–303, and on a review of Stephen Greenblatt's *Learning to Curse* in *Modern Language Quarterly* 53 (1992): 250–56; Chapter 3 is based on "Of Ants and Grasshoppers: Two Ways (or More) to Link Texts and Power," *Poetics Today* 9 (1988): 291–306; Chapter 4 is based on "Teaching Differences," *Shakespeare Quarterly* 41 (1990): 160–73; Chapter 5 is based on "In Defense of Jargon: Criticism as a Social Practice," *Textual Practice* 5 (1991): 171–82; and Chapter 6 is based on "Against 'Ideology,'" in *Shakespeare Left and Right,* edited by Ivo Kamps (New York and London: Routledge, 1991), pp. 79–97. I am grateful to the original publishers for permission to draw on these materials here.

For encouragement and suggestions, my thanks go to Maurice Charney, Stanley Fish, Terence Hawkes, E. A. J. Honigmann, Gerald Graff, and Russ McDonald.

Edward Pechter

Montréal, Québec

What Was
Shakespeare?

Introduction:
After "After the Carnival"

"SHAKESPEARE" IN THE TITLE of this book does not refer to the
glover's son from Stratford, still less to the Earl of Oxford or
any of the other pretenders to the Bard's title. It does refer to the
plays and poems collected in the Riverside edition (from which I
have taken all quotations), but not always and exclusively so.
Although Shakespeare's plays figure more or less prominently in
the following chapters (history plays at the end of Chapter 1, *A
Midsummer Night's Dream* in Chapter 4, *Hamlet* in the middle of
Chapter 5), so occasionally do non-Shakespearean plays as well—
Marlowe's *Doctor Faustus* and Webster's *Duchess of Malfi* in Chapter
3, for instance. So "Shakespeare" can serve as a synecdoche for
Renaissance plays, but even this turns out to be misleading if the
plays are understood primarily as objects of critical study. It is
rather the study itself that most interests me—what we say about
the plays of Shakespeare and his contemporaries, and how, and
why. In other words, this is a book about criticism.

There are limitations here that should be confronted at the outset. Criticism, especially academic criticism, is a small space within
which to confine discussion of Shakespeare, and an even smaller

one if "Shakespeare" is taken for Shakespeare rather than for the plays of his less esteemed contemporaries. Unlike Homer, Dante, Wordsworth, and other classics whose works thrive almost exclusively in university classrooms and in the writing of university professors, Shakespeare is still vital beyond the institutions of academic criticism and pedagogy. The major difference is the existence of a healthy theatrical tradition. Theatrical Shakespeare has lots of connections to academic Shakespeare, especially in Britain, but theatrical Shakespeare has its own institutional space and energy as well. To make matters more complicated, there are versions of Shakespeare outside both the academy and the theater—in the streets, so to speak. In "William Shakespeare in America," Lawrence Levine describes the gradual process that led to the separation of low and high culture, including the elevation of Shakespeare to the latter category. But Shakespeare still has a substantial authority in the popular culture of the English-speaking world, in music, television, and the movies (a comparable claim probably could not be made for Goethe, Racine, and Calderón, say); so popular culture exists as a third version, itself many different versions, to take into account, as Derek Longhurst reminds us. But nobody can do everything; limitation is inherent in all work, and a manageably small area allows for a certain clarity of focus. Besides, even with the qualifications I have acknowledged, academic criticism clearly remains, no matter where you stand, one of the most important of all the various social practices by which we produce Shakespeare; and if you are an academic critic or student, as I assume most readers of this book to be, it is the most important.

But then, it may be asked, why bother to write about Shakespeare criticism when you can write about Shakespeare's plays themselves? The problem with this question is that it assumes the plays to exist in a stable, original, and retrievable form, unmediated by interpretation. If we understand Shakespeare in theatrical terms, this assumption makes no sense. Since meaning in the theater depends on a large number of variables unique to each performance, most of which (like the physical space of the theater itself) are at best only partially subject to control by the author, director, actors, and audience, the idea of a retrievable textual stability is an illusion. We can, of course, choose to examine Shakespeare as a literary rather than a theatrical text (most of us do), but the idea of textual autonomy remains no less problematic. Shakespeareans still committed to the idea are likely to distinguish the plays themselves from various forms of current critical practice (Marxism, feminism, deconstruction, new historicism, cultural materialism) which are said to be imposed arbitrarily on the plays. But the topics apt to fall into place on the other side— unity of action, richly interesting characters, elegant and powerful language, genre—are themselves equally constructions produced by various forms of critical activity developed over the long history of Shakespeare criticism. It is just that these forms are familiar ones. (They are more likely to seem familiar if you are closer to fifty than to thirty, but for reasons developed in Chapter 1, I do not consider this short-term focus to be the decisive factor.) The relevant distinction, then, is not between the texts and their critical mediations but between different kinds of mediations, some relatively strange and new, others so familiar that they may seem like emanations from a naturally existing pre-interpretive entity. Though the Shakespeare text may seem to be such an entity, placed somewhere behind the criticism conceived of as an activity dependent on and referring to it, it makes more sense to say that Shakespeare has no existence apart from the various forms constructed by our critical practice. From this angle, Shakespeare and Shakespeare criticism turn out to be like Nature and Homer in Pope's supposition about Virgil—"*Nature* and *Homer* were, he found, the *same*": not a relationship but an identity.

The claim that criticism is an active way of making sense rather than a passive way of finding it should not seem daringly innovative these days. The various arguments that stand behind the claim ought to be familiar: about the beholder's share; about the arbitrariness of the sign and textual indeterminacy; about gender and social distinctions and political power as influential factors in the production and reception of texts; about the contingent rather than necessary distinctions between disciplines; and about how the categories of literature and texts in themselves have come into being and been developed through history. As a result of their familiarity, I have not felt it necessary to reproduce such arguments in any systematic way; except for the beginning of Chapter 1, which is devoted to unpacking the assumptions of the state-of-the-art Shakespeare criticism in place around 1970, I do not engage in any sustained negative critique. The fact that criticism has changed profoundly since the 1960s isn't the point of this book; it's the starting point.[1] For as George Dillon says, if " 'it's all rhetoric' " (1)—basically the same claim I am making here, that it's all criticism or interpretation—it is not clear where we are or what we ought to be doing next.

According to Dillon, writing in a chapter significantly called "After the Carnival," the "repeated polemical and by now ritual slaying of positivism, foundationalism, correspondence theories of truth, and Methodology" has left us in a state of "confusion" about "what new distinctions and oppositions are likely to emerge." For although "the conception of an enlarged study of discursivity in general is an attractive one, arising as it does from the awareness that academic and scientific discourse is woven out of human actions and is as rooted in human desire as a love letter or a legal complaint, . . . there are profound differences that cannot simply be swept away with a wave of the hand" (2). Dillon's point about the continuities that persist despite changes in criticism is something I want to emphasize in the following chapters, and it is worth considering here, if only in passing, why this state of affairs obtains: now that so many distinctions have come to seem irrelevant or unsustainable or maybe even just plain wrongheaded, why is it that they nonetheless either refuse to go away or keep coming back in similar forms?

The simplest way to answer this question is to apply the basic premise of orthodox materialism: our ideas are determined by the social relations and institutional sites, such as university departments and the academic publishing industry, where they are generated and circulated; and these, though changing all the time, indeed "cannot be swept away" by a wave of the hand, still less by an announcement of the birth of a new paradigm. We can prove satisfactorily (at least to ourselves and our intellectual allies) that there is no essential difference between philosophy and literary criticism, for example, and we can argue convincingly (to the same audience) that both should now be seen in terms of a containing unity (discourse, rhetoric, criticism, interpretation); but while philosophy has become more literary critical and literary criticism more philosophical, any reader minimally familiar with these disciplines, given some excerpts from unidentified journals recognized as reputable in either field, will be able to identify which of these two fields she is inhabiting. Philosophy and literary criticism are still different—in tone, mode of argument, choice of subjects, and frames of reference. They are different even in the way they designate their practitioners: philosophers are not called philosophy critics, and we are not called "*littérateurs*" or "writers" or "culture critics" or just plain "critics." Maybe we should be, since such new designations would tend to eliminate the (arguably) invidious distinction the absence of such a word seems to have created; and maybe we will be, since as Horace said in the *Ars poetica*, and many others have said before and since, words are always being born, reborn, and dying. But the emergence and general acceptance of our new name, if it happens at all, will not happen overnight. The resistance to its happening is not limited to traditionalists anxious to reaffirm the primacy of literature itself. Even those convinced that we ought to have a new word for our practice will have to make do with what language and history have provided us. So far they have provided us with different kinds of discourse, and until such time as we have come to inhabit offices in the Discourse Department in the Discourse Building, and journals with names such as *Social Text* and *Textual Practice* have proliferated to such an extent that they have driven journals with names such as *Modern Language Quarterly* and *Mind* into oblivion—until then, the differences in our discourse will continue to remain crucially determining.

So the distinctions return or remain after all, including the one between Shakespeare criticism and Shakespeare's plays. At least in practical terms, this distinction should serve to alert readers that the following chapters tend to focus more on such topics as jargon and ideology than on colonialism in *The Tempest,* or the cultural work of gender norms in the tragedies, or indeterminacy in the comedies. But there is an even more important kind of practical continuity, concerning the investigative norms and evidentiary protocols that govern our activity. In the days when texts were discussed as self-contained formal objects, our job was to see the objects as in themselves they really were. Textual objectivity is no longer self-evident and is in many quarters taken as a risibly naive notion, but to a perhaps surprising extent, our obligation to get things right seems still to be in place. In an essay on literary history, Lee Patterson quotes Huizinga's dictum that "the utterly sincere need to understand the past as well as possible without any admixture of one's own is the only thing that can make a work history," and adds that "as literary historians move into a postmodern age, it is by no means clear that they can afford to jettison Huizinga's difficult imperative" (261–62). What Patterson says about historians and the past is exactly transferable to literary critics and texts: almost all of us accept the obligation to do our best to get them right. The trouble is that the obligation seems to depend on beliefs that are no longer generally acceptable, dating back not just to 1950s-style New Criticism but to nineteenth-century-style positivism, "*wie es eigentlich gewesen*" and "seeing the object as in itself it really is," and all those other slain dragons Dillon mentions. When we say we have to get it right, what can we possibly mean by *right* (what constitutes validity in interpretation?), by *it* (what is the text?), and by the neat separation between us and it (critical interpretation vs. the text itself)? And perhaps most important of all, at least for the view I am trying to promote in this book of criticism as a social practice, what do we mean by *we?* In view of such questions, Huizinga's imperative, or its equivalent for literary criticism, is liable to seem not just "difficult" but impossible.

Like the still-strong residual respect accorded to the literary text, the continuing authority of objectivity can be understood in terms of historical inertia: this is the way we were trained to work, this is the way we are used to working, we would not know how to work any other way. This kind of explanation manages to satisfy nobody. For the kind of critic who thinks we ought to have a new name, objectivity feels like the dead hand of the past; we ought to have a new theory and methodology to go with our new name. On the other hand, even those who are glad that the felt need to get it right still governs our practice believe that we ought to be able to explain why. The explanations, however, are not easy to come by; and if you look at them long enough, they come to seem more like anxious threats than grounded arguments.

When Patterson says "it is by no means clear" that we ought to jettison objectivity, for instance, he means to suggest that it is by all means clear that we mustn't do so. The implicit warning derives from his sense of the negative consequences of such an abandonment, the chief of which is an anything-goes interpretive arbitrariness and totalization. Thinking about models associated with cultural anthropology, systems of symbolic representation, and Foucauldian discursive formations, Patterson complains that "any single item of cultural practice can serve to represent every other item, so that a *geistesgeschichtliche* probe at any point in the cultural matrix will reveal the principle that organizes the whole. This results . . . in large claims resting on very little evidence" (261). But the people who make these claims understand them to be substantiated by irrefutable masses of evidence; it is just that Patterson, who is working out of a different set of assumptions from the critics whose methodology he questions, cannot see the evidence to which they are pointing. The issue here is "precisely what counts as evidence and what does not, how data are to be constituted as evidence, and what implications for the comprehension of the present social reality are to be drawn from the evidence thus constituted." Thus Hayden White (*Metahistory,* 284), a historian with a richly deserved reputation for substantial learning and meticulous argument, who has never been given to traveling what R. S. Crane called the "High Priori Road"—and who was writing, it might be added, long before the carnival had come to town, at least in the postmodern form we know it.

Dillon is another case in point. Among the confusions he sees in our present situation, "after the heady spirit of carnival has passed," is uncertainty as to "where the new insights into language are to be found"; for with the disappearance of foundations ontologically prior to language (reality, truth, even thought), there is nothing we can say about language that is not itself in language ("it's all language"), and we seem to find ourselves trapped in an infinite regress where nothing can be validated and anything valorized. Dillon characterizes this situation as "a nasty hangover of cynicism, passively contemplating the workings of unlegitimated power" (2). Like Patterson, Dillon does not like this prospect, and like Patterson's "by no means clear," Dillon's "cannot be swept away" has an evaluative as well as a descriptive function—not just about what is practically possible (you can't make a silk purse out of a sow's ear) but about what is ethically desirable (you can't make love with every willing partner who happens to turn you on). But why not? That is, what is wrong with contemplating the workings of unlegitimated power? There are critics who think that the workings of unlegitimated power need to be not just passively contemplated but actively analyzed, interrogated, problematized, deconstructed, unmasked, and laid bare. For such critics, this activity is not a "cynical hangover" (license, he means) but an empowering endeavor (they cry liberty), wise and good, arguably (these critics can and often do make the argument) the only right, true end of all our learning.

Dillon is concerned with postcarnival confusions, but the situation seems to be even more complicated than what he describes.

For one thing, our revels are not quite ended. There are still carnival types in our midst, and although they have shifted their attention from the arbitrariness of the sign and the pleasure of the text to the arbitrariness of power and the effects of subjection, they constitute an active and significant constituency on the present scene. To make matters yet more complicated, there are critics currently at work who never joined carnival to begin with, and although some of them may be dismissed as ostriches or consigned, like the prelate who refused to peer into Galileo's telescope, to the dustbin of history, this constituency includes many critics doing interesting and useful work. We have now moved to a tripartite distinction, among carnivalesque and pre- and postcarnivalesque critics, but this augmented model is still a gross oversimplification. "The differences are spreading," Catherine Stimpson tells us ("Nancy Reagan" and "Are the Differences Spreading?"), thinking of feminism where the process is most conspicuous. Not merely has feminism eroded the consensus of a male profession, but now the earlier consensus of feminism has itself disintegrated into a variety of competing points of view— French and American, first-wave essentialists, new-wave historicists of gender, Marxist feminist materialists, anti-Marxist feminist materialists, identity politics lesbians, women of color, and so on. Furthermore, this process of apparently endless subdivision is not unique to feminism; it exists throughout literary studies. As a result, we would probably need dozens of categories to be able to map the field, and we would wind up (as I did listing the varieties of feminism just now) sounding like Polonius on the literary kinds ("tragical-comical-historical-pastoral," etc.). To make matters yet more complicated, there is considerable movement across the various categories, so that the class identification of individual workers is hard to define. At the same time, the various classes themselves seem not only different but antagonistic; and although we can more or less adequately account for the class war in materialist terms as the result of "uneven developments," the contradictions do not seem to be resolvable in any logical or theoretical way. Whether it is license or liberty, for instance, depends on where you stand, but the position where you stand will have already been determined by your beliefs as to whether it is license or liberty.

This book is about the problems that arise when we try to write criticism in such a situation. In Annette Kolodny's memorable phrase, it is like "dancing through a minefield." She was thinking about feminist criticism, but you do not have to be a feminist to know what she is talking about. Many Shakespeare essays read as if their authors believed that criticism began with Stephen Greenblatt or ended with C. L. Barber, but that is just the end product; criticism is supposed to sound self-assured and internally consistent, and who knows what shadows have fallen in the process between the conception and the action? Some critics are no doubt more self-conscious than others, proceeding on the basis of a carefully strategic response to the current fragmented scene, targeting some audiences and avoiding others—segmenting to get market share. I have problems with such a description, not chiefly because it suggests the commodification of academic culture, but because it exaggerates the extent to which our critical practice is governed by a sovereign self-knowledge. We do a lot of what we do without thinking about it, probably without even being able to think about it (how can we know the dancer from the dance?) But this point works the other way around as well. Even the most blandly insouciant critic we can imagine, though he may be blissfully ignorant of the problem, is going to be caught up in it anyway. For one thing, how will he find an audience these days? For another, such ignorance will eventually exact a cost in the return of the repressed. My general point is that there is no way any of us can avoid the problems of fragmentation and irreconcilable differences. Whatever our beliefs as individual critics, to whatever extent we are blessed or cursed with self-awareness, criticism is a social practice, and the disputes and contradictions in the subject of academic criticism are bound to be reproduced in our practices as individual critics.

In the face of all this, it might seem we have moved beyond mere confusion and achieved chaos with the consequence that the process of criticism can no longer be sustained. Kent's question seems relevant here: "Is this the promised end?" I do not think so. Except for the possibility of huge royalties, I have not been tempted to call this book *The End of Literary History and the Last Critic*. On the contrary, one of my main points is that the problems we have at present do not add up to a crisis, and that there are ways to understand our current situation as even a positively enabling one.

I can introduce the point here in two ways, one concerning individual and the other institutional practice. If we need to ground our practice in a solid theoretical foundation, then we are indeed in an impossible situation. But we don't. Knowing that all knowledge is situational does not prevent us from being securely situated in our knowledge. To quote Richard Rorty, who stands behind a lot of what I have to say in this book and who, if he did not exactly put this argument on the map, seems to be the main creator of the current map on which to put it: "A belief can still regulate action, can still be thought worth dying for, among people who are quite aware that this belief is caused by nothing deeper than contingent historical circumstances" (*Contingency*, 189).

Rorty makes my point as well for the institutional question with his idea of "keeping the conversation going." Academic criticism is fiercely contentious these days, and it is increasingly clear that these contentions are not resolvable—at least not in the sense we so often crave, of being subject to adjudication from some position *au dessus de la mêlée*. But when were they ever? Shakespeareans and other literary critics have always been arguing with each other. Humanists are not scientists. As Thomas Kuhn argues, the productive norm for work in the humanities has always involved not the supersession and erasure of old paradigms by new ones, but rather the proliferation of contending paradigms. If this is so, then critical action in our post-postcarnival world is far from impossible. In fact, life after "after the carnival" begins to look like business as usual.

This may sound overly sanguine. For one thing, many of us, probably most, are committed to consensus as a professional desideratum; we think we should be trying to reach agreement. The same commitment probably underlies the craving I mentioned just now to reach a neutrally adjudicating perspective. I think it is still hard to exaggerate the power of the scientific model to shape our assumptions of how we work, even when we know better.[2] But I must acknowledge finally that "business as usual" may not only sound too sanguine, it may be too sanguine. The range and intensity of dispute have varied significantly through the history of study in the humanities, and we may nowadays have too much of a good thing. As Blake says, you never know enough until you know too much; and by then, unless we have reached the Palace of Wisdom, it is too late. Maybe this *is* the end: of literature and criticism, if not of man and history and (in Douglas Adams's phrase) "life and the universe and everything." I do not think so, and my primary aim in the following chapters is to persuade readers to share my conviction that the current situation is not just sustainable but potentially productive. However, since it is impossible to be on top of history while being inside it, I cannot say for sure.

What Was Shakespeare?

"**W**AS?" The past tense looks perverse. The plays continue to flourish in the theater. In the academy, the odd voice here and there—Malcolm Evans's, say, or Cary Nelson's—cries out that we are spending too much time and energy on the Bard,[1] and Shakespeare may well have conceded some curricular turf to new writers, new kinds of writers, new areas of writing. But any such retrenchments have probably been compensated by the reinvigorated extension and expansion of Shakespeare into the same new kinds of critical concern and new areas of writing that seemed to constitute the threat to begin with.[2] Moreover, the production statistics indicate an almost unabated growth. In 1964, working from the *Shakespeare Quarterly*'s annual bibliography, Norman Rabkin reported an annual output of 1,159 works (ix). Six years later James L. Calderwood and Harold E. Toliver, working from the same source, came up with "well over 3,200 items" (v). The figures from the most recent *SQ* bibliograpies are as follows:

1985	3,871	1987	4,541
1986	4,069	1988	4,846

| 1989 | 4,495 | 1991 | 4,587 |
| 1990 | 4,925 | 1992 | 5,597 |

The downturns for 1989 and 1991 are interesting but equivocal. They may indicate market correction or profit taking; or perhaps they are the anomalous results of different reporting procedures.[3] In any event, the returns to record growth for 1990 and again for 1992 seem to make it clear that we are not witnessing the beginning of the end of Shakespeare Studies as We Know It. Even in the gloomiest scenario (or perhaps the rosiest, from Evans's and Nelson's point of view), it would be premature to claim that Shakespeare is fading—let alone has faded—into the past.

I mean the past tense, though, to indicate not the cessation or even abatement of Shakespeare criticism but rather its transformation. Juxtaposed with the work of the last generation, today's Shakespeare commentary looks different to the point of such radical discontinuity that we may indeed be at the end of Shakespeare Studies as We Know It, with "As We Know It" as the operative phrase. To put this another way, the earlier critical construction of Shakespeare looks as if it may have become obsolete. I take the word from the title of a research seminar directed by Herbert Weil for the 1990 meeting of the Shakespeare Association of America: "Is the One-Volume Anthology Obsolete?" In his statement to the participants, Weil recalls a time when a single volume seemed adequate to represent current Shakespeare criticism not just to students but to "those non-specialists—in universities and the public—who love Shakespeare, who frequently read and attend performances, and who want to know something of the best that we have done" as professional Shakespeareans. Weil's reminiscence is not nostalgic, nor is it based on imaginary memories. Most of us in the seminar knew from our own experience that the one-volume anthology was the normal medium (in North America, anyway) to introduce Shakespeare criticism to students; and given hiring patterns during recent times, many (if not most) current Shakespeareans still have access to the same or similar memories.

Memories from when, exactly? If we want a date when the consensus represented by the one-volume anthology seemed most secure, I would suggest 1970. In 1970 six anthologies were available, any one of which might have seemed adequate to represent modern Shakespeare criticism. I have already mentioned the editors of two of them: Rabkin and Calderwood-Toliver; the other four are Edward Bloom, Leonard Dean, Alvin Kernan, and Anne Ridler. Not that these six volumes are identical. They have their differences from one another, and their internal differences as well; but such differences, disguised rather than acknowledged, did not seem at that time to fracture the containing structure, or prevent us from understanding modern Shakespeare criticism as a more or less unified discourse. Its mavericks and marginal figures could be acknowledged, even appreciated, without displacing the center, let alone erasing it. In retrospect, it is easy to see that this center was not really holding (the same year, 1970, saw the publication of the 1966 Hopkins conference "The Languages of Criticism and the Sciences of Man" [Macksey and Donato]), and that this sense of unity was illusory; but no matter. Like the fantastic joys in Donne's "The Dreame," if we thought we had them, we had them, and the one-volume anthology existed to represent and even reify our sense of that unity.

In the same spirit of misplaced concreteness, I offer 1985 as the year by which this consensus had incontrovertibly disappeared. The old anthologies had of course gradually lost authority during the intervening years (not to mention, in some cases, their in-print status), but 1985 seems crucial in that it saw the publication of three anthologies that not merely were new but in their very titles aggressively asserted contestation (Drakakis's *Alternative Shakespeares*), innovation (Dollimore and Sinfield's *Political Shakespeare: New Essays in Cultural Materialism*), and interrogation (Parker and Hartman's *Shakespeare and the Question of Theory*). These three anthologies, especially when added to the 1980 feminist collection called *The Woman's Part* (Lenz et al.), must have made it self-evident to even the most oblivious or resistant Shake-

15

spearean that the old consensus had disappeared. Confirming events occurred in each of the next two years: in 1986 Stanley Wells came out with a new *Cambridge Companion*, including a transformed and greatly expanded representation of modern criticism,[4] and in 1987 a fifth anthology appeared (Howard and O'Connor). By 1991, non-Shakespearean Renaissance drama criticism had caught up with a revisionary anthology of its own (Kastan and Stallybrass).

What happened between 1970 and 1985? It is not just the one-volume anthology that became obsolete; the conceptual message of that medium disappeared as well. Shakespeare criticism as a unified discourse, a totality that transcended its different constituents, now seems to inhabit the dark backward and abysm of time. Whether we celebrate or mourn its passing, we are now in a unique position to perform an anatomy of the still freshly dead corpse. If nothing else, a certain curiosity ought to be sufficient motive to make "What Was Shakespeare?" a question we should try to answer.

WAS

Leonard Dean's anthology is the place to start. It was the first published in North America, the only one to be revised, and the most popular, and it is still in print. "The purpose of this volume," Dean tells us in his preface,

> is to bring together some of the good modern essays on Shakespeare, as many as could be reprinted in a single volume at a reasonable price. I looked for essays offering a fresh and thoughtful interpretation of the plays; and I had in mind the general reader as well as the student, teacher, and critic. The plan was to include a few general essays, at least one on each of the major plays, and as far as possible several essays on a play or group of plays in order to represent contrasting or complementary critical views.

16

It turned out that almost all of the essays finally selected and available for reprinting had been written rather recently. It is likely, therefore, that this volume has some value as a sampling of contemporary Shakespearean criticism, even though no effort has been made to represent systematically whatever schools of criticism may exist. Good literary criticism is to some extent a creative act, a lucky thing which cannot quite be explained by circumstances; but luck takes different forms at different times and places, and perhaps it is not surprising or altogether accidental that many of the essays in this volume reflect contemporary interest in poetic language, the aesthetics of drama, the Elizabethan theater, and Renaissance modes of thought. Furthermore, critics are sensible people who find it dull to do over again what has already been well done, and this fact, too, helps to account for recent emphasis on patterns of imagery, the structure of ironic drama, and other topics somewhat neglected by earlier critics.

Except for one additional paragraph of acknowledgments, this is the whole of Dean's preface. The brevity is conspicuous, and it is not unique to Dean. The average for prefaces and introductions of these six anthologies is only four pages (hence I will not bother providing page references when I quote them), in striking contrast to the newer anthologies, which average sixteen pages. Something in the situation of the old anthologists made Shakespeare criticism seem, as it evidently doesn't to us, like the visiting lecturer whose work is so familiar and self-evidently interesting that it "needs no introduction."

One way of getting at this "something" in the old situation is to notice another area in which Dean did not need to agonize, the process of selection. In fact in one important respect, the vintage of the essays, the selection process seemed to work independently of the selector's own intentions: the book, Dean says, "turned out" to be a contemporary selection—"wrote itself," as we might say. Sometimes Dean seems genuinely oblivious of any need for effort, at other times resistant to it, as when he acknowledges that "no effort has been made to represent systematically whatever schools of criticism may exist." Why announce the absence of this effort unless in response to some cultural or internalized voice that is urging it upon him—making a claim, in other words, that criticism is precisely a systematic and analytic kind of discourse whose value depends on the selection from among conflicting opinions? In any event, Dean will have nothing to do with any such implicit claim. Indeed, he seems benignly indifferent to the very fact of conflict, let alone its systematic representation: schools "may exist," he tells us, but then again they may not. This indifference seems to sort oddly with his claim earlier "to represent contrasting or complementary critical views," but Dean's very indifference to the meaning of difference (which is it, contrast or complement?) is completely consistent with his later disclaimer. Apparently it does not matter whether differences are ultimately resolved or not, and this in turn means, I think, that they *are* resolved, because they are looked down upon from a position of amused detachment, like Troilus's at the end of the Chaucer poem.

Like his brevity, Dean's insouciance is characteristic of the old anthologies. Calderwood and Toliver too renounce any obligation to work at determining their selection principles: "Rather than force essays into groupings based on method, which would imply the division of criticism into certain well defined sects, we have thought it better to let the organization of the selections derive from the plays themselves, bginning [sic] with essays on some general issues, then focusing on the natural unit of Shakespearean criticism, the individual play." As in Dean, critical conflict seems inconsequential, maybe even nonexistent: "would imply" leaves it up in the air whether the "well defined sects" of criticism exist or not. But Calderwood and Toliver can help us see more clearly than Dean why such an avoidance can be justified. The crucial point is that "the selections derive from the plays themselves." Once criticism is understood as a secondary discourse, dependent on the primary existence of the literary text, Calderwood and Toliver can afford to be indifferent to questions of selectivity because the principles needed to guide selectivity have already been determined for them. Since the individual play is "the natural unit of Shakespearean criticism," all an anthologist needs to do is cover "the major plays," to recall Dean's phrase. Calderwood and Toliver follow the same course of coverage, simply adding genre to the great individual plays. "Each of the major comedies, tragedies, and histories is represented by at least one essay." Further, the relegation of criticism to a position of dependence on the Shakespearean text also solves any potential problem arising from critical disagreements. "The literary work of art," according to Calderwood and Toliver, "is polysemous and hospitable to a variety of interpretations," especially when the author is the "infinitely generous Shakespeare." Since the unified space of the primary Shakespearean text can accommodate infinite differences, then differences in the secondary critical texts just do not matter: "Which of the various critical methods calls forth the most meaningful and enduring responses from Shakespeare it would be difficult, and not especially profitable, to establish."

Edward Bloom makes the same decisions, for the same reasons. His introduction begins in the familiar mode of renouncing selectivity: "The editors agreed that no attempt should be made to assign subjects or limit approaches." The plural ("approaches") serves to acknowledge and then forget difference, but a few pages later the question returns, like a bad penny or the repressed, when Bloom has to acknowledge that his selection includes "disagreements about certain fundamental issues." Not to worry, though; the disagreements are "amicable," and the essays "can be read not only as individual pieces but as parts of a unified whole. The constant image in Shakespeare's world is man, but man himself is variable and ambiguous; it is thus that he is portrayed and thus that we are called upon to understand him. To apprehend the art of Shakespeare, then, is a way of coming to terms with ourselves." There's an interesting circularity here, in which difference is resolved by being referred to a unity that is itself constituted out of difference. A similar move occurs at the end of Bloom's introduction: "The various approaches may be heterogeneous, but even seemingly contradictory attitudes may be reconciled when they are committed to a common purpose, a better perception of Shakespeare's meaning and art." Here the facts of difference are turned into mere appearances when bathed in the transcendent light of the unified object to which the differences are reaching. Such is the power of "Shakespeare's mind and art," in whose body we are all members.

Kernan's and Rabkin's anthologies are more or less exceptional, yet they prove the rule. The subtitle reflects Kernan's difference: *Essays on Style, Dramaturgy, and the Major Plays.* "The major plays" takes us back to Dean and the others, deferring selectivity to the plays themselves, and most of the essays in Kernan "deal chronologically and by genre with the major phases of Shakespeare's career as a playwright." But the remainder, and even those covering the major plays, are chosen on the basis of formalist principles of style and dramaturgy, designated at the beginning of Kernan's subtitle, the "belief that Shakespeare's plays are most usefully and properly approached, not as realistic imitations of human nature and affairs, but as symbolic structures, elaborately intertwined and interworking parts that combine to create, not a photographic representation of the world, but an image of reality as it is perceived by the imagination." These principles make explicit the assumption implicit in the other anthologies: the literary text is a unified discourse that contains and absorbs any and all contradictions within it. Hence Kernan's chief criterion in choosing essays dealing with individual plays is that "they provide a coherent and complete view of an entire play," that each "grapples with an interpretation of the whole and tries to see how the beginning relates to the end, how the individual parts fit together to create a unity." Moreover, Kernan's selectivity allows him to come even more confidently to the conclusion that modern Shakespeare criticism is unified as a whole. Where the others stumble upon differences (which, to be sure, they then sweep under the rug), Kernan consciously excludes potentially conflicting approaches, especially historicist ones.[5] No wonder that as a consequence "the critics represented in this volume are in remarkable agreement about the fundamental tenets of Shakespearean criticism, about the ways in which the plays are to be approached and understood."

We come finally to Rabkin, by far the most interesting and thoughtful of the older anthologists. He alone will not have his selections determined for him by the "major plays and modes." On the contrary, about a third of the essays concentrate on the same play (*Macbeth*), a disproportion designed to serve precisely as "a recurring point of comparison among critical methodologies." And not just comparison, but contrast; hence we get L. C. Knights engaging with Bradley, Helen Gardner with Cleanth Brooks, R. S. Crane with monists of any sort, Roy Battenhouse's Christianity played off against Sylvan Barnet's limits of Christianity, and so on. And added to this is a variety of distinct approaches—psychoanalytic, Marxist, anthropological. Alone among the old anthologies, Norman Rabkin's tries to engage with modern criticism in terms of its contradictions and differences.

And yet for all his richer understanding, Rabkin finally arrives at the same conclusion: that the differences do not matter. "Most of the controversy which flourishes so vigorously, though it is nowhere near being reconciled, centers about a surprisingly small number of issues" and does "not represent as much theoretical disagreement as their authors believe." Although modern Shakespeare criticism "may seem, in the turmoil of a moment populated by hundreds of cantankerous writers, to be the work of antagonists fruitlessly engaged in a chaotic and wearisome set of struggles to the death," these conflicts turn out to be merely family battles, contained within a unified structure. The reason is that all the different approaches

add up to the pluralistic and rich approach to Shakespeare that can and should be cultivated by twentieth-century readers. We are lucky to have so many avenues. . . . each time a new approach is developed, Shakespeare turns out to be the chief exemplar of the virtues which that approach recognizes for the first time. Like his continual popularity, this fact is testimony to his enduring greatness. The criticism of the twenty-first century will invent methods of which we have not yet dreamed, and again it will be discovered that Shakespeare preeminently has achieved what his critics are learning to perceive. This is in the nature of literary art, which flies while analysis, conceptual, rational, and selective, marches on the ground. But the more marches we take the more we understand of Shakespeare's flight. The controversy is exciting and we are the richer for it.

A powerful sense of teleological history is at work in this argument. Shakespeare as infinitely inclusive text or person (*"pananthropos,"* as Bloom calls him) now functions as a kind of Hegelian *omnihistoria*, the figure in whom the ongoing tradition gradually reveals its ultimate unity of differences. Irving Ribner, one of Bloom's contributors, develops the same argument, writing about "the great tradition" of Shakespearean criticism "extending from Coleridge down to our own times, and behind Coleridge back to Samuel Johnson and John Dryden," and he too ends with a Sabbath-sight revelation of future harmony: "The twentieth century has developed and amplified this great tradition. . . . Often the critics have tended to be partisan and acrimonious, but a new generation just ahead of us may recognize that even in seemingly contradictory approaches there has been room for reconciliation in terms of a common larger tradition" (208).

The same assumption is implicit in Calderwood and Toliver's claim that "criticism since 1950 has been able to draw on the rich methodological reserves built up in the past while investing in its own portfolio of interests." (This gives a very specific inflection to Rabkin's claim that "we are the richer for it": invest in shares of the history of Shakespeare criticism, a guaranteed high-yield mutual fund.) Even Dean's bland assurance that "critics are sensible people who find it dull to do over again what has already been well done" seems to constitute the history of Shakespeare criticism as a cumulative commodity, a growth stock whose dividend is interest itself, or perhaps pleasure, or whatever is opposed to "dullness."

Rabkin's other assumption in this passage is the familiar one in which critical disagreement is contained within the generous unity of the literary text. Although critical disagreements are "nowhere near being reconciled," those disagreements belong to the analytic march of criticism, not to the imaginative soaring of Shakespeare's flight. Though Rabkin alone recognizes his own dependence (and the general dependence of his contemporaries) on Coleridge, in particular on Coleridge's conception of the "imagination—which is the source and domain of literature— as the ability to reconcile 'opposite or discordant qualities,'" Rabkin's ability to speculate about the Coleridgean space as it were from outside does not prevent his being finally positioned very securely within it.

In these anthologies, the primary status of the literary text does not so much solve as displace and disguise the critical problems to which it is addressed. Hence though the question of selectivity is decided by deferment to the shape of the canon, this deferment succeeds only if the canon is assumed to exist as a natural fact (which we locate presumably by following our own noses to the smell of greatness issuing out of "the major plays") rather than seen as the product of the very decisions that are being deferred. In the case of critical differences, the primacy of the literary text seems to solve a problem at the cost of raising a worse one. Critical differences are said not to matter; but inextricably attached to this reassurance is the consequence that criticism itself does not matter, for as a dependent or secondary discourse, it seems either parasitic or useless, a kind of handmaiden to a being who, without any "defects of loneliness," is entirely self-sufficient.

Ridler is probably the most overtly embarrassed by this scandal. "There is now," she tells us in evident dismay, "a book or article on Shakespeare published for every day of the year. . . . Shakespeare has condemned the world to the everlasting torment of explaining his masterpieces." Ridler's figure, derived from a contemporary *Shakespeare Survey*, may seem laughably small compared to the more recent *Shakespeare Quarterly* numbers I furnished at the beginning of this chapter, but the same implicit self-justification is at work: we've culled the best for you. How much of a justification is it, however, to reduce a phenomenon to manageable size when the thing itself is one for which we have no apparent need? Maybe it is an inkling of this question that provokes Ridler to add an immediate justification for her own—and our own—endeavors:

> And yet, to read and think about Shakespeare is to draw life from an inexhaustible store, and each man has his report to make on what he has found there. This book is intended as a useful companion to the general reader in his own excursions, and I have kept this test in mind—that each essay chosen should send its reader back to the original with his power of understanding strengthened. There has been no attempt to include essays, however brilliant, which are substitutes for reading the plays, or those which require a complex technique of understanding, as does the work of Professor William Empson.

But even if we all have to make our report on Shakespeare, what public consequences follow from this private obligation? Why as readers of Shakespeare do we need to trouble ourselves with the reports of others, or how as critics ourselves can we presume to make any claim on the attention of other Shakespearean audiences? Excluding the unclubbable Empson is common sense: we certainly do not want such a difficult companion on our "excursions." But since it is in the nature of excursions to be purposelessly pleasurable, to include even an easy companion seems at best a matter of indifference. Just how would such an essay be "useful," how "strengthen" the reader's understanding of the primary text?

Current anthologists abide such questions; Ridler and her contemporaries are free. But freedom in this sense is empty—"just another word for nothing left to lose." Hence Dean: "The purpose of this volume is to bring together some of the good modern essays on Shakespeare." But what is the purpose of this purpose, the function of criticism? Maybe Dean implies an answer in his assertion that "good literary criticism is to some extent a creative act, a lucky thing which cannot quite be explained by circumstances." For a moment criticism assumes the status of the literary text, a mysterious self-sustaining unity that transcends the "circumstances" of history and defies analysis. But if the critical act is justified by its dependence on the creative act, how can criticism itself be creative? Or put it the other way round: How can creativity survive as the source of value when it inheres in the secondary objects on which value must be conferred? These days we are likely to recognize creativity and criticism as an easily deconstructable binary opposition, and from this perspective, Dean looks like Wile E. Coyote just beyond the edge of the cliff in the Saturday-morning cartoons, bicycling his legs fiercely in the air to keep from plunging into the abyss. Dean himself, however, probably does not experience the giddiness of the moment. All that is required is some genial blather, a sort of gentlemanly *sprezzatura* that hedges his beliefs about with qualifications ("to some extent," "cannot quite," "perhaps . . . not surprising or altogether accidental," "somewhat neglected"). Such insouciance now looks less like *je ne sais quoi* than *sauve qui peut.*

At the end of her Introduction, Ridler invokes the authority of H. D. F. Kitto to assert that " 'drama [is] like music' ":

"its real 'meaning' is the total impact which it makes on the senses and the spirit and the mind . . . when we reduce it to the logical formulae of prose, as the critic must, we are gravely attenuating it, we are making a kind of translation; and translations can be poor ones." But the "translations" in this book are not poor ones: so long as the reader is aware of their nature, they can do him nothing but good.

With its scare quotes around "meaning," Kitto's assertion takes us back to Pater (poetry aspires to the condition of music) and ultimately, as Rabkin points out, to Coleridge, but also to Rabkin himself, for whom the prosaic march of criticism is a *sermo pedestris* that can never reach the heights attained by poesy's viewless wings. Translation is the best to be hoped for. But why, when we have access to the original, primary, and privileged language of Shakespeare's plays, should we bother with any translation, even a good one?

One final way to get again at the shaky (or absent) foundations of such criticism: it concerns professionalism and specialization on one hand, common sense and the general reader on the other. With the interesting exception of Rabkin again, who has no use for "the belletristic charm—and often vapidity—of critics of an earlier day," these anthologists are worried about what they sense as the increasingly specialized and technical nature of Shakespeare criticism. According to Edward Bloom,

> the best writing on Shakespeare . . . is less ecstatic and more exacting, less impressionistic and more insightful [than fifty years ago]. It is informed by painstaking knowledge of dramaturgy, history, psychology, philosophy, language, textual matters, as well as the *sine qua non*, literature. Shakespeare today is largely managed by the specialists, but the specialists are giving him back to the general public with discrimination and enhanced import.

Specialized knowledge gets a moment of respect here before deference to the needs of the general public, to whom, as the apparently legitimate owners, Shakespeare is restored. This is the same audience to whom Ridler defers in whole ("a useful companion to the general reader") and Dean at least in part ("I had in mind the general reader as well as the student, teacher, and critic"). But just who is this general reader? It is hard to talk about the general audience except in negative terms. They are the people who are not defined by parochial interests (Empson's "complex technique," for example), but by the time you have eliminated all these particular specialized interests, nothing seems to be left (unless, as so many critics since 1970 have been relentlessly hammering home, it is male gender, white race, heterosexual preference, Christian religion, and bourgeois politics). In this context reconsider Dean's casual remark that "critics are sensible people who find it dull to do over again what has already been well done." This is presumably intended as reassurance: critics are motivated by the same down-home common sense as ordinary people and are therefore effectively identical to the general audience. But again, the desire to elide or deny difference—here between critic and general reader—has the consequence not of anchoring criticism but of eroding its foundation, for why do the general readers need critics if the critics are themselves just plain folks?

The general reader functions as an equivalent to Bloom's *pananthropos,* or to the polysemous and infinitely generous unified text in the others, or to the history of criticism as a Hegelian unfolding of the unity of differences. This unity is always elsewhere, tantalizingly beyond our grasp. Or if it is internal, as Bloom suggests in his claim that "to apprehend [Shakespeare] is a way of coming to terms with ourselves," then it still remains inaccessible, though now in temporal rather than spatial terms, like Irving Ribner's "new generation just ahead of us" who will see the wholeness of history. For as Catherine Stimpson remarks about this "lovely gift of Western humanism," this "belief in a conscious self that generates texts, meaning, and a substantial identity," it remains forever just beyond our grasp. As in the Koren birthday-party cartoon she describes, this magical unity is always only "about to" be realized:

> Around a table sit eight little girls, some in paper hats, staring at a happy Birthday Girl and her cake with six candles. Smiling watch-fully and sweetly, Mother holds the back of Birthday Girl's chair. Holding a tray full of glasses and bowls of ice cream, Dad stands at

attention. Ah, sighs the Birthday Princess, "I'm about to experience the totality of who I am!" ("Nancy Reagan," 236)

WAS AND LARGELY REMAINS

Good-Bye to All That: Robert Graves's autobiography provides a
good working title for the narrative that has brought us to this
place, a story in which past beliefs—in this case the sustaining
assumptions of an immediately antecedent formalist and humanist tradition of Shakespeare criticism—are scrutinized from a position of critical detachment. The plot is a very familiar one in
current criticism, where it is routinely announced by titles that
include "new," "beyond," "after," and "against." Here is one such
version by Stephen Greenblatt:

> One of the more irritating qualities of my own literary training
> had been its relentlessly celebratory character: literary criticism
> was and largely remains a kind of secular theodicy. Every decision
> made by a great artist could be shown to be a brilliant one; works
> that had seemed flawed and uneven . . . were now revealed to be
> organic masterpieces. . . . Behind these exercises was the assump-
> tion that great works of art were triumphs of resolution, that they
> were, in Bakhtin's term, monological—the mature expression of a
> single artistic intention. When this formalism was combined, as it
> often was, with both ego psychology and historicism, it posited aes-
> thetic integration as the reflection of the artist's psychic integra-
> tion and posited that psychic integration as the triumphant
> expression of a healthy, integrated community. (*Learning to Curse*,
> 168)

For Greenblatt, the collapse of this exhausted formalist humanism creates the possibility of vital critical innovation. "New historicist critics," he continues, "have swerved in a different direction,"
and he thereupon proceeds systematically to fill the spaces
vacated by receding tradition with its critical contraries: conflict in

place of resolution; ideological critique in place of celebration; materiality for ideality; margins for a center; and so on. As a result, we can see Greenblatt's synoptic history as representing a triumphant renewal in the heroic-vitalist mode: *Look! We Have Come Through!*

But this is not the story I want to tell here, and if you look more closely it is not the story Greenblatt is telling either. "Was *and largely remains* a secular theodicy," he says, acknowledging the scandalous persistence of an apparently outmoded formalist humanism on the current scene. "And largely remains" tends to get lost not just because of subordination, probably, but because the main point, in its suggestion that we are free to rise from the ashes of our own exhausted past, is such a reassuring one. The same reassurance may be behind the various expedients developed of late whose consequence is to trivialize those humanist residues, chiefly by trying to seal them off into isolated compartments. Humanism survives in the classroom, it is sometimes claimed, but not in our publications; or in undergraduate but not graduate classes; or among the old troglodytes hanging on but not among the young insurgents busily shaping the future precisely in the domains of publication and graduate school from which formalist traces have been eliminated. But this cannot be the whole truth; the separations are not absolute. Teaching and writing or graduate and undergraduate teaching are not usually experienced, or constituted, as totally disconnected activities; only a psychopath would see the world that way, or maybe a Vice Rector Academic. The generational separation does not work so neatly either; some of the most radical-sounding insurgents are over fifty, and lots of recent academic recruits seem to be attached to the authors of the traditional canon in respectful and even affectionate ways.

The bizarre academic life we have at present must be connected with the collapse of the job market in the 1970s and 1980s and the effective loss of almost a whole generation. But our situation can be understood in nonmaterial ways as well, or rather in terms of the ideas and intellectual dimensions that make up so much of the material conditions of our professional lives. From this perspective the heroic-vitalist narrative I may have seemed to be telling in the first section of this chapter is fundamentally misleading. Without backtracking to the defense of the old criticism's now empty-sounding celebrations, I want to spend the rest of this chapter, and many of the chapters that follow, arguing against the view of recent criticism as a triumphant innovation. Such a view seems to me wrongheaded, not just about Shakespeare criticism but about the way we work generally in literary criticism and the humanities. The argument is one I can only begin to make here, but as a kind of prospectus, consider the following claims: (1) that we have *not* come through; (2) that we are still there ("there" being the definite past tense to which I have relegated the old anthologies); (3) that the very idea of a there-and-was and a here-and-is as radically discontinuous domains is misleading; (4) that the idea of an unconstrained productive capacity for inventing new modes of critical activity is self-deluding; and (5) that this state of affairs is not such a gloomy one as might be supposed.

Consider the argument John Drakakis makes in the Introduction to *Alternative Shakespeares,* one of the new anthologies I referred to earlier. Starting from the belief that "the existing dominant paradigm of literary studies" is now experiencing "a crisis" (1), Drakakis concludes that alternative modes of criticism are now well positioned "to break the dominant paradigm of Shakespeare studies" (23). Drakakis offers two main contentions to support this claim about the triumph of alternative criticism—first, its heightened theoretical self-consciousnessness and second, its radical difference in method and purpose. Neither of these contentions, as I understand them, sustains scrutiny.

To begin with theoretical awareness: Dominant-paradigm critics are repeatedly accused of lacking such awareness—"unable to develop some of the theoretical implications . . . fails here to theorize clearly . . . naive empiricism . . . no clear theoretical awareness" (6, 9, 11)—a litany culminating in an assertion of "the resounding failure of successive traditions of humanist criticism to articulate critically the ensemble of assumptions upon which their perceptions rest" (24–25). In contrast to the "unexamined assumptions and traditions . . . naively . . . generated from within essentialist individual critical consciousness," contemporary materialists are said to be "thoroughly self-aware" in their production of "theoretically informed modes of criticism" (25).

But is humanist criticism as theoretically uninformed as Drakakis keeps asserting? These assertions sort oddly with the other main theme that recurs with similar persistence throughout his Introduction—namely, the resilience with which the dominant paradigm, basically in place at least since Coleridge, has managed to maintain its dominance against all earlier threats. Drakakis runs through a variety of topoi that have interested Shakespeareans over the centuries—character, the social makeup of the audience, the politics of the history plays—and discovers the same thing: "minor changes" have done "little to disturb the epistemological foundations" of a critical tradition "firmly committed to the idealistic assertion[s] of liberal humanism" and "cling[ing] doggedly to an organicist view of culture" (10–11, 14, 15). Even now, though twentieth-century critics have chipped around the edges, the Bradleyan (which is to say Coleridgean) edifice remains fundamentally intact: "apparent movements forward . . . surrender to a ubiquitous tradition the very ground which they seek to occupy," with the result that "the dominant critical discourses . . . remain committed to idealist constructions" (22–23). How, we might wonder, can such a naive set of assumptions have survived fundamentally intact for so long in the face of so many challenges?

The charge of theoretical self-ignorance becomes even more dubious when you look at Drakakis's supporting evidence. After quoting J. W. Lever's characterization of *The Elizabethan World Picture* as a " 'manifestation of universal *caritas* . . . whose natural or metaphysical aspects served mainly to ratify the social-political *status quo*,' " Drakakis comments that "Tillyard was groping towards the concept of an ideological apparatus, but he did not perceive in the analogy a strategy of coercion, nor could he comment on the mechanisms whereby this coercion might be internalized psychologically as a system of rules governing behaviour" (15). Drakakis represents Tillyard as "groping towards" a materialist kind of explanation, but Tillyard is not a materialist manqué; he is an idealist. His interpretations come out of the assumption (among others) that shared affection is better than social conflict as a position from which to understand Shakespeare and the world. Far from being naive, idealist assumptions have unlimited explanatory power. In their variously systematized manifestations (Kantian aesthetics, Augustinian ethics and theology, Platonic ontology, etc.) they can accommodate anything and everything within their scope. This absorptive power extends to critique: any competent idealist could easily dismiss charges of misrecognition as cynicism, or even sin (this in the old days before Christian humanism decayed, as many saw it, into liberal humanism). In the same way, an idealist could simply reverse the charge of theoretical self-ignorance and claim that such charges are themselves theoretically uninformed. From this perspective, as an inverted mirror to Drakakis on Tillyard, materialist thought looks like idealism manqué; Bakhtinian dialogism or heteroglossia, say, like a "groping towards" the meaning of pluralism or even (the really good old days again) God's redemptive grace.

In contrast to claims about theoretical self-awareness vs. theoretical naiveté, this infinite reversibility should suggest that the relation between alternative and dominant paradigms is rather a symmetrical one. This was Kuhn's point about paradigms (if you look under the word to the argument that sustains it)—their incommensurability. There is no way to demonstrate (in the sense of mathematical proof) the superiority of materialism to idealism, no way to choose (logically) between them. As with the competing narrative structures Hayden White discusses in *Metahistory*, "there are no apodictically certain theoretical grounds on which one can legitimately claim an authority for any one of the modes over the others as being more 'realistic'" (xii). The immediate access to the real which would be required in order to claim such authority is simply unattainable. As a result, "it is fruitless," as White argues,

> to try to arbitrate among contending conceptions of the nature of historical process on cognitive grounds which purport to be value-neutral in essence, as both Marxist and non-Marxist social theorists attempt to do. . . . The Marxist view of history is neither confirmable nor disconfirmable by appeal to "historical evidence," for what is at issue between a Marxist and a non-Marxist view of history is the question of precisely what counts as evidence and what does not, how data are to be constituted as evidence, and what implications for the comprehension of the present social reality are to be drawn from the evidence thus constituted. (284)

From this angle, Drakakis's reasons for preferring materialism go round in circles. Materialism is bound to look like a better theory (in elegance, economy, range and power of explanation, etc.) so long as you are a materialist; and so long as you are a materialist, idealism will look naive. Drakakis is stating a preference rather than arguing (logically) for it: he rejects idealism not because it is less adequately theorized than materialism but because it is *differently* theorized—that is, made up of beliefs about texts and about the world different from the ones he subscribes to.

All this brings us to the second claim for the new materialist criticism—difference itself. According to Drakakis, difference offers two distinct sorts of virtues. On the one hand materialist critics share a common opposition to tradition, but on the other this shared opposition is made up of a "diverse body of alternatives" (2) that are opposed to each other:

> The 'alternative' Shakespeares which emerge resist, by virtue of a collective commitment to the principle of contestation of meaning, assimilation into any of the dominant traditions of Shakespeare criticism. That contestation takes place both in relation to established views and *between* individual contributions, each of

which is written within a position which engages critically with specific areas of theoretical concern (24).

Alternative criticism, then, is characterized by both internal and external differences. The question is whether these different kinds of difference, either one or both, justify the claims Drakakis makes on their behalf.

We can begin with the internal differences. In pointing to the disputes among his contributors, Drakakis calls attention to a situation very often remarked in current criticism—in feminist commentary, in Gerald Graff's program of "foregrounding conflicts," and in all the recent Shakespeare anthologies.[6] This widespread eagerness to proclaim internal conflict suggests that such conflict is conceived of as somehow empowering. At the beginning of their Introduction, the editors of *Shakespeare Reproduced* tell us why: "Differences became very obvious" at the seminar that generated their anthology, and these "tensions and contradictions," Howard and O'Connor explain, demonstrate our progress from the "political activism of the 1960s [which] remained relatively untheorized and was often premised on notions of autonomous, unified, and wholly volitional selves acting as agents of change within social formations assumed to be responsive to such agency" (2). But why is conflict theoretically sophisticated? Howard and O'Connor's claim is made from inside the same loop as Drakakis's: if you are a materialist—that is, committed to a conflict-based model for understanding the world—conflict will look good to you and consensus naive. Materialists like materialist theory, but their preferences do not constitute a persuasive argument for idealists, who are committed with equal and opposite conviction to the belief that consensus-based models are theoretically sophisticated and in touch with reality.

The fact of internal conflict, then, does not constitute evidence for the superiority of current criticism, merely evidence for its difference. Current critics tend to hold beliefs (about human nature and identity, social organization, literature, theater, what have you) different from those of traditional critics. We come back then to external differences, the resistance shared by all alternative critics to established views. It seems clear that such differences can change and in fact have changed the way we all work. (However incommensurable, paradigms are different, and they do change.) Drakakis's claim, though, is not just for difference but for "radically alternative strategies and objectives" (23); not just for change but for "radical transformation," or indeed "a series of radical transformations" (24)—permanent revolution, as it were. "Radical" is not a vague intensifier, like Ed Sullivan's "*really* big show." Drakakis believes that alternative criticism is bringing us to a different order of being: that it "will, in the final analysis, liberate" us from traditional modes of understanding, and that "when the record is scrupulously and disinterestedly examined these traditions will not be found to contain covert radical sensibilities [but will be shown as] wholly inadequate to the challenges now proposed" (25). The promise here is not just transformation but revelation. Interest melts away; we see face to face; materialist sheep are definitively separated out from idealist goats. Behind such a strong claim stands, probably, the painfully long history of the dominant paradigm as an infinitely assimilative structure. When L. C. Knights asked about Lady Macbeth's children, and when G. Wilson Knight jettisoned plot for spatial form, they understood themselves to be engaged in meaningful change; yet as Drakakis argues, their revisions have been absorbed into an unruptured tradition. Will alternative critics suffer a similar fate? Will future generations look back on them as they do on Knight and Knights (or as Irving Ribner looked back, though more in pleasure than in anger, on "the great tradition" of Shakespearean criticism "extending from Coleridge down to our own times"), all saying, "Plus ça change, plus c'est la même chose"? The stress on "radical" is a form of reassurance: no more co-optation. This time we are leaving the exile of tradition forever behind us, crossing over Jordan into the promise of an altogether new future. Radical alternative criticism will give us, in the Monty Python phrase, "something completely different."

The first thing to say about such hopes is that they have not materialized. By way of demonstrating their unfulfilled promise, let us go back to the internal differences among current critics, not the mere fact of such differences but their substantive nature, with an eye to their discontinuities and (more important) continuities with traditional critics. What are contemporary materialists arguing with each other about? For Shakespeareans, "Feminism vs. New Historicism" is a convenient place to begin. This was the name given a special session at the Shakespeare Association meeting in Boston in April 1988. It was organized to carry on a debate from earlier conferences (SAA in 1986 at Berlin, MLA in 1987 at San Francisco), but even the non–*Small World*ers in the overflow plenary crowd in the Oval Room at the Copley Plaza would have felt at home, for the debate had already begun to take up space in the journals Shakespeareans read (Boose, Erickson, Neely). In dispute are questions about textuality and history, and about subjectivity, agency, and political effectiveness. Such as: If all knowledge is mediated, what is the purpose of historical study? And if as historical subjects we are constructed by our culture, then what position is available to engage critically with that culture?

The dispute between feminism and historicism is not limited to Shakespeare studies (Fox-Genovese, Newton, Jane Marcus, Waller); furthermore, the dispute exists within each of the projects whose opposition is designated. The historicist position is itself split between the new historicism and cultural materialism, at least in Jonathan Dollimore's 1985 construction—that is, between an apparently functionalist view summed up in Greenblatt's tendentious phrase that "authority produces transgression" and Dollimore's own insistence on appropriation as allowing for the conception of counterhegemonic forces (Dollimore & Sinfield, 1985, 12). The *locus classicus* within feminism for this dispute is probably Toril Moi's *Sexual/Textual Politics*, but the sides had been clearly drawn at least three years earlier in the exchange between Peggy Kamuf and Nancy K. Miller in the feminist issue of *Diacritics*. In opposition to Kamuf, who would be rid of "the signature" as the metaphysical baggage and totalization of a unified self, Miller complains about the consequences of such a jettisoning for women whose history has never included the luxury of this illusion. "Only those who have it," she says, "can play with not having it" (53). The dispute, in recognizably similar terms, continues today.[7]

To see the common ground of these various disputes, consider the poignant epilogue often cited from Greenblatt's *Renaissance Self-Fashioning*: like William Hurt in *The Accidental Tourist*, on a plane to—or in his case from—Baltimore, Greenblatt finds his space violated by the passenger in the adjacent seat ("I want to die"). The anecdote serves Greenblatt as a means to refashion his authorial identity not once but twice. The first is retrospective. He had inaugurated his project as an attempt "to understand the role of human autonomy in the construction of identity," but was impelled to conclude that we are imprisoned within and constructed by "the relations of power in a particular society." But then in a surprising volte-face the author returns to a qualified reaffirmation of his original faith, "because I want to bear witness at the close to my overwhelming need to sustain the illusion that I am the principal maker of my own identity" (257).

What is Greenblatt acting out here? (The question is not meant to imply insincerity, since the values and meaning we attach to sincerity are themselves in dispute.) One answer is that he is dramatizing the conflict between alternative conceptions of the subject in the new criticism and the old: a constructed or postmodern subjectivity on the one hand, and on the other that "lovely gift of Western humanism," to recall Catherine Stimpson's phrase from the end of this chapter's first section, the "belief in a conscious self that generates texts, meaning, and a substantial identity." ("Lovely" in Stimpson acknowledges attraction as well as repulsion, a mixture similar to Greenblatt's of nostalgia and detachment, a mind self-consciously beset with an ironic contrariety of desires.) But another answer is that what Greenblatt dramatizes for us here is the alternative conceptions of the subject *within* contemporary criticism (Kamuf vs. Miller, textuality vs. social change, historicism vs. feminism, theory vs. politics, etc.), in which the discovery of constructedness corresponds to the figures on the left side of the opposition, and the will to keep the original faith to those on the right. My point is that both of these answers are right. The differences within current criticism seem to reproduce the differences that mark off current criticism from that of the last generation. These internal differences, then, are a sign not of radical transformation but of continuity.

Such continuity is entirely predictable. Again "paradigm" is the key word here, provided we examine the argument underneath the word. Kuhn developed the concept of paradigm and of paradigm shift specifically for the history of science. In science, because of the basic need to reduce the field of study to a single paradigm, older paradigms are ruthlessly relegated to oblivion; hence Whitehead's assertion that "a science that hesitates to forget its founders is lost" (quoted in Kuhn, 138). If you want radical change, as much and as quickly as possible, in order "to break the dominant paradigm of Shakespeare studies," then the Kuhnian scheme for understanding the history of science is enormously attractive. But as Kuhn keeps saying, science is a special case, and the notion of paradigm shift is not transferrable to the humanities. Even in their most quiescent and consensual moments, even when they are closest to "normal science," the humanities are never given over so thoroughly to "problem solving." Theoretical conflict is even then a significant presence. In humanist study it is not the reduction to a single paradigm but the coexistence of different paradigms that is the productive norm.

Norms can and do change, but this one looks solid and permanent. The continuity I have been concerned with here describes not only the way things happen to be working out but the way they have to work out. It is not just that the hopes for radical change expressed by Drakakis and so many materialist critics of Shakespeare on the current scene have not been fulfilled, they cannot be fulfilled; for radical difference in the sense of total discontinuity makes no sense. Perception depends on familiarity ("looks 'a not like the King?"), without which the strange would be neither wonderful nor horrible—it would be invisible. (Hence Freud's insistence on the connection between the uncanny and the familiar—*das unheimlich* and *das heimlich.*) Difference is not a pure, free-floating energy; it is a relational predicate. You have to be different *from* something, alternative *to* something. The first question alternative criticism has to answer is, Alternative to what? (Bartender to Marlon Brando in *The Wild One:* "What are you rebelling against?" Brando: "What have you got?") But this means that the "what" continues to occupy a position at or near the center of the discursive space. When Drakakis says that "the objective common to all of these essays is the demystification of the 'myth' of Shakespeare" (24), he is willy-nilly acknowledging that the topoi of the Shakespeare Myth continue to determine critical discussion. The very act of resisting the dominant paradigm helps to guarantee that what was the dominant paradigm *largely remains* so.

TIME'S SUBJECTS

"Was and largely remains" is a hard place to describe. As a short-hand for "both alienated from and inside our own history," it should seem like a familiar place, for when are we not there? But there are times when our location inside of an intolerably strange past feels like paralysis. Hamlet's Denmark is the *locus classicus* for this feeling in the tragic mode, and *Hamlet* will serve as a source for much of what I want to suggest in the rest of this chapter. But it is the historical mode that is closer to my needs here, and in the historical mode the place of "was and largely remains" is Gaultree Forest.

Gaultree Forest is where the rebels under the Archbishop of York meet to encounter the royalist forces led by Prince John of Lancaster. Before any battle is joined, Westmoreland enters from the King's side to initiate the conventional parley. His speech is a long one (2 *Henry IV*, 4.1.30–52), as such speeches usually are, culminating in a seven-line demand for York to explain his behavior. York begins his reply by reiterating the predication of Westmoreland's peremptory last question: "Wherefore do I this? so the question stands. / Briefly, to this end." It is a spirited beginning, cutting through the extraneous detail to focus imme- diately on the essence of the matter. Not that we expect brevity: the Archbishop is called upon to explain behavior of national political significance, and as a rebel ("opposite . . . against" the King; an "alternative critic," so to speak), he bears an explana- tory burden heavier than the loyalist Westmoreland's. Nothing less than a full historical analysis would be appropriate—that "large discourse, looking before and after." But if the length of York's response (53–87) is predictable, the surprise comes when York reveals his total inability, despite the energetic purposeful- ness with which he begins, to explain and apparently even to understand the circumstances that were and are "the question of these wars."

"We are all diseas'd": The opening words are a disheartening sequel to York's forceful introduction, more so his subsequent admission that "I take not on me here as a physician." As if sensing the inadequacy of such a response, York abruptly signals a return to rhetorical mastery, "Hear me more plainly," and seems to get back on track:

> I have in equal balance justly weigh'd
> What wrongs our arms may do, what wrongs we suffer,
> And find our griefs heavier than our offenses.

Like Claudius ("In equal scale weighing delight and dole"), York exercises a purposive rationality, carefully discriminating between alternatives as a way to decide on meaningful action. It is just the sort of energetic will promised by his opening words, but his "spark and fire" suffer an immediate "abatement . . . and delay":

> We see which way the stream of time doth run,
> And are enforc'd from our most quiet there
> By the rough torrent of occasion.

An old emblematic tradition equips the personified Occasion with a forelock to be seized by the ambitious entrepreneur, but the dominating metaphor here disallows any place to active heroic energy. If you are immersed in the stream of history, it does not seem to do any good to know which way it runs; York feels himself "enforc'd"—without choice, a victim of circumstances.

In this respect, York is in the same situation as his chief antagonist. In an earlier scene, Henry confronts the loss of historical meaning: "how chance's mocks / And changes fill the cup of alteration / With divers liquors" (3.1.51–53). Warwick tries to console Henry with assurance about "a history in all men's lives, / Figuring the nature of the times deceas'd, / The which observ'd, a man may prophesy" (80–82), but the predictive power of such observations turns out to be nearly worthless, an awareness only of "the necessary form" of the future (87). "Are these things then necessities?" Henry asks. "Then let us meet them like necessities" (92–93). Henry does manage to rouse himself from his doldrums; but since necessities remain necessary, inevitable whether met or unmet, his renewal, lacking the belief in any effective consequences for his actions, is bound to seem artificial and defeated—will doing the work of reason.

As York's speech continues, the syntax seems to act out the erosion of purpose.

> The dangers of the days but newly gone,
> Whose memory is written on the earth
> With yet appearing blood, and the examples
> Of every minute's instance (present now)
> Hath put us in these ill-beseeming arms.

York and the others have become the objects, not the subjects, of action. Behavior is rendered not as a response to circumstances but as their effect. These circumstances are themselves indefinite: past and present ("dangers gone" and "examples present now") collapse into one another and become indistinguishable—like the "thoughts and memory fitted" of Ophelia's madness. The singular verb "hath," instead of "have," while not technically wrong in Elizabethan English, remains anomalous; it allows us to understand "the dangers . . . and the examples" as a meaningfully integrated structure—History, rather than change—but also makes us suspect that the understanding is illusory (like trying to distinguish among the diverse liquors filling up the cup of change), based merely on nominal artifice, like a mixed metaphor that cannot really articulate practical purpose: how can you take arms against a sea of troubles, say, without becoming "native and indued unto that element": "Drown'd? Drown'd, drown'd."

With the completion of York's speech, the scene shifts rhythm; the speeches become shorter and sharper, and Mowbray enters the quarrel. The question centers on the rebels' grievances, real or imagined, redressed or not. Speaking to Mowbray, Westmoreland justifies the King:

> Construe the times to their necessities,
> And you shall say, indeed, it is the time,
> And not the King, that doth you injuries.

The words have the ring of truth. "We are time's subjects": Hastings' words early on (1.3.110) belong as much to the King as to the rebels. But the claim hardly constitutes a strong justification of Henry, and Westmoreland moves quickly, before Mowbray can respond, to a different kind of argument: "were you not restor'd / To all the Duke of Norfolk's signories?" Mowbray replies with bitter resentment at the unjustified loss that necessitated such a restoration to begin with: "What thing, in honor, had my father lost, / That need to be reviv'd and breath'd in me?" As in a really good marital quarrel or an ethnopolitical dispute (Israelis vs. Palestinians, Serbs vs. Croats, Québecois vs.

Canadians—examples are legion), the discourse has turned backward as each side ransacks memory for the justifying point of origin.

Mowbray finds this originating point in the banishment of his father during Richard's reign:

> The King that lov'd him, as the state stood then,
> Was [force] perforce compell'd to banish him;
> And then that Henry Bullingbrook and he,
> Being mounted and both roused in their seats,
> Their neighing coursers daring of the spur,
> Their armed staves in charge, their beavers down,
> Their eyes of fire sparkling through sights of steel,
> And the loud trumpet blowing them together . . . (113–20)

The speech is an extraordinary exercise in the building of tension. The chivalric combat between Mowbray's father and Bullingbrook is brought to the point of climax, and then sustained there by means of gerundives and absolute clauses for half a dozen lines. When the tension has become intolerable, "and" at the beginning of the last line seems to transport us at last into an action—a sense based on both syntax ("and" signals the last of a long list) and meaning (the trumpet signals the onset of combat). In the event, however, nothing happens:

> Then, then, when there was nothing could have stay'd
> My father from the breast of Bullingbrook,
> O, when the King did throw his warder down
> (His own life hung upon the staff he threw),
> Then threw he down himself and all their lives
> That by indictment and by dint of sword
> Have since miscarried under Bullingbrook. (121–27)

The subordinate clause ("when there was nothing") turns out to be followed not by an independent clause describing the engagement but by *another* subordinate clause ("O, when the King did throw") which postpones the engagement yet again—indefinitely, as it turns out.

In a way this postponement redirects our attention back to the original point, Richard's action in banishing Mowbray's father. It was the battle itself that was disgression—or at least secondary—in Mowbray's description of the particular circumstances surrounding Richard's action of banishment. But the problem with Richard's action is that it was not an action—not the authoritative, self-knowing intervention of human will in the processes of history. Richard "was [force] perforce compell'd to banish him"; it was political circumstance, "as the state stood then," that dictated Richard's action. As now with Mowbray *fils*, so it was with Mowbray *père:* the time and not the King did him his injuries. Given these circumstances, Mowbray's diversion of attention from the banishment to the battle is not a deflection from his original purpose but a way of focusing attention, of achieving his purpose. Maybe the combat is not "what really happened," but at least it almost happened. It offers Mowbray the illusion of an event, a decisive beginning, without which a historical understanding seems to be impossible.

You can argue that the speech offers something more substantial to the audience than it does to Mowbray. Mowbray's desperate quest for a beginning takes us back to the originating action of the first play of the second tetralogy, and may therefore be said to confirm a perception of historical-cum-theatrical unity. But is this perception any less illusory than Mowbray's? There is no evidence that the plays sometimes called "the second tetralogy" were presented to Elizabethan audiences as a group; the concept of tetralogy is a retrospective construction, and from a position in the middle of 2 *Henry IV* it has not yet achieved the closure on which even later critics can look back. This is not a problem for totalizing critics from Tillyard to Harry Berger, who claim that everything is answerable to the Great Idea of a tetralogy that is always already complete. But the main obstacle to reaching this position is not the unattained closure; it is at the other end, in the origin that has never been satisfactorily established. For to look back from Gaultree in the middle of 2 *Henry IV* to the lists at Coventry at the beginning of *Richard II* is to find not a beginning but just an earlier middle itself looking for a beginning. *Richard II* is characterized by endless (or beginningless) deferrals—a syntactic and dramatic habit whose frustrating consequence, as Stephen Booth wittily observes, "pushes each member of its audience toward being his own Pierce Exton" (89). The play refers ceaselessly back into a past that seems to be both crucially determining (the figures of deceased times shaping the necessary form of the future) and indeterminate—something to do with Woodstock and Calais, with the Black Prince, with a lost garden, maybe even with "Julius Caesar's ill-erected tower" or "the model where old Troy did stand" (5.1.2, 11). The play draws its energy from such shadowy remembrances at the inaccessible peripheries of consciousness, actions and feelings that cannot quite be spoken or known. Like the Queen's grief, without antecedent, for "nothing hath begot it," and without prospective form, for it is "not yet known," motives remain "nameless," hidden to the mind (2.2.34–40). This is what it means to be time's subject: you are reduced either to a condition of dumb, grieving inertia or to futile exertions in quest of a purposive mastery as a result of which—in Westmoreland's words when Mowbray finally sinks into silence—"You speak, Lord Mowbray, now you know not what" (128).

Gaultree Forest is not a heroic narrative about a triumphant insurgency smashing the authority of the dominant paradigm with an innovative one of its own. Quite the opposite. I offer Gaultree not just as an antithesis to the Drakakisian version of literary history but as an antidote. It looks to me like a more accurate representation of our current situation. Part of this situation is the inaccessibility of a clear point of origin. Where, after all, do our problems as Shakespeareans (if they are problems) effectively begin? With Bradley? With Coleridge? What if they originate in— are coterminous with—Shakespearean drama itself? Another part of the difficulty we have is in the recurring crossovers between authority and insurgency, as a result of which traditional and alternative projects bleed into one another and lose their shapes as distinct forms of thought. And finally, how can we know where we are going? Drakakis presumes to such future knowledge, but his vision of a "disinterested final analysis" is just eschatological rhetoric. As Lear's Fool says about his own apocalyptic prophesy, "who will live to see" such a thing? The "final analysis" is inaccessible, like the Marxian "last instance" or, for that matter (so long as "this muddy vesture of decay doth grossly close us in"), the totalized unity in the dominant paradigm of the old humanist criticism. Keynes gives us the only thing we are entitled to say for sure about the final analysis: In the long run we are all dead.

A gloomy prospect, to be sure, and maybe the gloom helps to explain why impossibly grandiose claims for the power of insurgent criticism are so much a part of today's scene. Is it really true that the academic left represents a threat to traditional American pieties equivalent to Saddam Hussein's (he's got the SCUDS, but we're the belief-shapers)? Or that preferring Shakespeare to Middleton is tantamount to complicity in the murder of Salman Rushdie's Japanese translator?[8] It is hard to believe that even the authors of such claims believe them. But then maybe, like Othello's last speech in Eliot's heartless description, the purpose is to cheer us up. Well, why not? If the situation is so bleak, after all, some kind of upbeat dallying with false surmise may be the best we can muster.

But it is not so bleak; I have come to my final point, that this state of affairs is not so gloomy as might be supposed. The subjection to time imposes powerful constraints, but it does not mean that we are necessarily in Othello's situation, or Emma Bovary's, or York and Mowbray's (neither of whom will survive Gaultree Forest and, like Mowbray's father, without even getting the chance to fight that apparently imminent decisive battle). That there are no "apodictically certain theoretical grounds" for our beliefs does not mean that we are necessarily paralyzed or trapped in a dithering indeterminacy. We do not need such grounds, only "massive historical and immediate experience" (the words are Raymond Williams's in a passage discussed at length in the last chapter of this book), and we have got plenty of that. In arguing that radical change is conceptually incoherent and impossible in practice, I have not been trying to suggest that there is no alternative to what we may construe as an illegitimately established authority, or that contesting such authority is necessarily futile. I have been arguing against the possibility of radical change, but not against change itself, which, for reasons developed in Chapters 5 and 6, is not only possible but inevitable.

At the beginning of *The Eighteenth Brumaire*, Marx says that people "make their own history, but they do not make it just as they please; they do not make it under circumstances chosen by themselves, but under circumstances directly encountered, given and transmitted from the past. The tradition of all the dead generations weighs like a nightmare on the brain of the living" (15). There is nothing fundamentally inconsistent with this position and the equally familiar eleventh thesis on Feuerbach: "The philosophers have only *interpreted* the world in different ways; the point is to *change* it" (*Selected Writings*, 69). Though their emphases vary, both statements express a commitment to change without idealizing the instrument of change as the free and self-knowing consciousness. Both are materialist statements in acknowledging that any understanding we may achieve of history is determined by our position within it.

Marching under Marx's banner at this point may be misleading, since so many who do so are given to making the kind of implausible claims I described earlier about the political (or, on the right, the ethical) consequences of critical activity. I make no such claims here, at least not in the way they are usually made, though again deferring fuller explanations until later chapters. My own ambition is more modest, simply to suggest that the limitations associated with being one of time's subjects do not preclude our going on to write interesting and useful criticism, where these adjectives are understood primarily in the professional and disciplinary sense: engaging the interest of other critics in making use of our work. The immodest part is that I offer the following chapters not only as arguments for this claim but as illustrations of it.

The Rise and Fall
of the New Historicism

"A SPECTER IS HAUNTING CRITICISM—the specter of a new historicism." At least so it seemed to me when I wrote a draft of
the first part of this chapter, under circumstances to be described
shortly. Circumstances have changed; they always do. Although
"the new historicism" remains a phrase to conjure with, still powerful as the designation for a strange new presence on the cutting
edge, it has been thoroughly domesticated as well, comfortably
ensconced within conventional critical practice (as in the Bedford
Case Studies in Contemporary Criticism) and confirmed in its
secure position by the popular press ("his 'new historicism,'"
according to a 1993 *New York Times Magazine* feature on Stephen
Greenblatt, is "at the red-hot center of lit-crit" [Begley]). Both
avant-garde and orthodox, the new historicism is also old-fashioned. From a perspective inside the profession, the *Times*'s red-
hot center is apt to seem like dying embers, and even the
relentless and unabating expense of sensibility devoted within
academic criticism to defining and evaluating new historicism
may be evidence not for an achieved but for an eroding intellectual power—Minerva's owl flies at dusk. Is the new historicism

"emergent," "dominant," or "residual"? All three of Raymond Williams's terms seem to fit. Unlike the usual phenomena comprehended by the cliché in the title of this chapter (Silas Lapham, say, or the Third Reich), the new historicism seems to be rising and falling at the same time.

From a different angle, these claims look exaggerated. Individual academic critics usually have clear and definite beliefs about what new historicism is and where it fits into the shifting patterns of current critical practice. And they will (without invitation) tell you so—during conferences, after guest lectures, in fine detail, at great length, over and over again. The problems I describe above, however, pertain not to the beliefs of individual academic critics but to their ensemble, to the fact that these particular beliefs differ dramatically from and frequently contradict one another. Where do we start, with individual beliefs or the ensemble? If it is the former, then the ensemble can be conceived of as merely a gross aggregate, and our job is to describe the new historicism as we see it—aware, certainly, of the ebb and flow of fashion and of critical disagreement, but from a fundamentally stable position that allows us to sort out and evaluate the fiercely contested claims and counterclaims. This is basically what I try to do in the first part below. But then it might be argued the other way around, as many people do argue these days, that the ensemble of critical practices substantially constrains and even determines our particular beliefs. In this case, trying to define new historicism seems less interesting than speculating why so many people are trying to define new historicism. Such speculation is the subject of the second part of this chapter.

The relationship between the individual and the ensemble is a frequently debated topic in recent criticism and a matter of central concern to new historicists. Indeed, according to Perry Anderson, writing about theory since World War II, "it is clear that there has been one master-problem around which *all* contenders have revolved[:] the nature of the relationships between structure and subject in human history and society" (33, Anderson's emphasis). The existence of a master problem does not release us from responsibility for seeking out master solutions, but such solutions are bound to seem wrongheaded to a significant constituency, because it is fundamental disagreement about the nature—let alone the solution—of a problem in conjunction with general agreement as to its importance that makes for a master problem in the first place. I do not have a master solution and in fact am trying to warn readers that the two-part discussion below is more of an embodiment than a resolution of the problem.

THE NEW HISTORICISM AND ITS DISCONTENTS: POLITICIZING RENAISSANCE DRAMA

A specter is haunting criticism—the specter of a new historicism. As Jean Howard puts it, "Suddenly indifference to history has been replaced by avid interest. Renaissance journals are full of essays placing the works of Milton, Donne, and Spenser in historical context." And not just Renaissance journals: the trend evident there is "part of a much larger critical movement in the post-structuralist period to rehistoricize literary studies" (236). This movement stems from the belief that poststructuralist criticism in its earlier textualist or deconstructive phase was essentially a continuation of formalism. However interesting at the peripheries, it retained the central impulse of formalism to focus on the text in isolation from human will and from the particular social formation within which will and desire are produced, directed, controlled, satisfied, frustrated. The new historical criticism aims at putting the text back into the context from which it was generated.

This emphasis on the cultural production of texts extends to their reception as well. Audiences themselves have will and desire, which also develop in connection with social or cultural authority. Hence the new historicization of literary studies is equally a new politicization, with interpretation judged as an expression of the political interests of the audience—sometimes the contemporary audience, sometimes the modern one, sometimes both. And here again the phenomenon is by no means unique to Renaissance studies. David Simpson points out that in 1983 at least five books focused on "the politics of Romanticism" (81). Moreover, the major theoretical journals have taken a similar course, publishing special issues with such titles as *The Politics of Interpretation* and *Nuclear Criticism.*[1] One final example: When Wayne Booth tells us in the pages of *Critical Inquiry* that he is trading in his reliable and efficient "implied reader" for a powerful new vehicle called the "real reader," we may be sure we have turned a corner. But do we know where we are going? And are we sure we want to get there?

Putting the text back into history sounds like something we might all want to do, but we should be certain we know what history means and what the practical consequences of such a program are. It also sounds like a good idea to acknowledge the political needs of real audiences, instead of mystifying those needs with some formalist, neo-Kantian Myth of an Audience—as long as we can be persuaded that the real audience is not another myth, another hypothetical construct, and that the politics of literature are not, as Gerald Graff suggests, pseudopolitics. In considering these matters, I focus first on recent commentaries about Renaissance drama, but only as examples; I quickly juxtapose the Renaissance critics with other sorts of writers—such as Althusser, Foucault, and Jameson—who can define new-historicist assumptions in the most general way and who can provide the clearest framework for the questions I want to ask: How do new-historicist critics characterize the text? What do they mean by history? How do they typically understand the relation between the two?

Claiming to describe a general or typical new historicism is presumptuous; simply to write about *the* new historicism is to construct a fiction, a critical fabrication, like the Elizabethan World Picture or the Medieval Mind. Many different and even contradictory critical practices are currently represented as new historicism. Nonetheless, as I understand the project, it is at its core—or, better, at its cutting edge—a kind of Marxist criticism. The label does not eliminate the problem of typicality or generality; it merely relocates it. By centering the new historicism in Marxist criticism, do I mean classical Marxism or some of the different, "softer" revisions prefaced by "neo-" or "post-"? The answer is that I mean all of them, to the extent that they all view history and contemporary political life as determined, wholly or in essence, by struggle, contestation, power relations, *libido dominandi*. This assumption, which I find the most problematic aspect of the new historicism, brings me to the last and by far the most important question I want to ask: Are there beliefs available to us—about the world, about texts, about the relations between them—more useful than those that typically generate new-historicist activity?

⚜

In his introduction to *The Forms of Power*, Stephen Greenblatt attempts to characterize a new critical mode "set apart from both the dominant historical scholarship of the past and the formalist criticism that partially displaced this scholarship in the decades after World War Two." Unlike the old historicism, which was "monological [and] concerned with discovering a single political vision," the new historicism recognizes a variety of competing centers of cultural power. This complex cultural environment, moreover, is itself constituted by interpretation. Here too there is a contrast with the old historicism, in which the cultural environment, having "the status of an historical fact [and] not thought to be the product of the historian's interpretation," could "serve as a stable point of reference, beyond contingency, to which literary interpretation can securely refer" (5). Greenblatt makes a similar point at the beginning of *Renaissance Self-Fashioning*. If we would not "drift back toward a conception of art as addressed to a timeless, cultureless, universal human essence," we must maintain the connection between literature and society. At the same time, he refuses to give presumed facts of culture priority over literary interpretation. "If . . . literature is viewed exclusively as the expression of social rules and instructions, it risks being absorbed

53

entirely into an ideological superstructure" (4). Greenblatt prefers to see literature and cultural knowledge as parts of the same interpretive enterprise, as interanimating each other. He therefore attempts to investigate "both the social presence to the world of the literary text and the social presence of the world in the literary text" (6).

Of the two claims here—one not to be monological, the other not to privilege the social order over the literary text—consider the second in conjunction with Greenblatt's brief essay "*King Lear* and Harsnett's 'Devil Fiction.'" The essay begins with a skeptical reference "to modern critics [who] tend to assume that Shakespearean self-consciousness and irony lead to a radical transcendence" of Renaissance culture (239) and then discusses Samuel Harsnett's *Declaration of Egregious Popish Impostures*. Observing that "where Harsnett had considered exorcism as a stage play, Shakespeare's play is itself a secular vision of the ritual of exorcism" (241), Greenblatt concludes:

> Hence the ideological and historical situation of *King Lear* produces the oscillation, the simultaneous affirmation and negation, the constant undermining of its own assertions and questioning of its own practices—in short, the supreme aesthetic self-consciousness—that leads us to celebrate its universality, its literariness, and its transcendence of all ideology. (242)

We have come a long way from the mutually generative interpretation of culture and text. Here the text is said to be produced by its ideological and historical situation; it is unambiguously dependent, while the culture is unambiguously determining. Gone as well is the acknowledgment that history is itself a text, constituted by interpretation; rather, Harsnett has assumed the objective status of a stable point of reference.

Elsewhere, too, Greenblatt's characteristic interpretive strategy is to begin from cultural history, typically with a colonialist episode, and then proceed to the literary text. Despite the reassuring disavowals of privilege, the cultural text tends to be the prior phenomenon, chronologically if not ontologically, at least for the reader who negotiates the course of Greenblatt's writing. Accordingly, after a dozen pages analyzing authority and subversion in Thomas Harriot's *Brief and True Report of the New Found Land of Virginia,* Greenblatt turns his attention to *Henry IV, Part I:*

> [T]he three modes that we have identified in Harriot's text—testing, recording, and explaining—all have their recurrent theatrical equivalent. . . . Thus, for example, the scheme of Hal's moral redemption is carefully laid out in his soliloquy at the close of the first tavern scene [I.2], but as in the act of *explaining* that we have examined in Harriot, Hal's justification of himself threatens to fall away at every moment into its antithesis. . . . I have spoken of such scenes in *1 Henry IV* as resembling what in Harriot's text I have called *recording.* ("Invisible Bullets," 53–55)

The flow here is markedly one way, from the cultural to the literary text, and the effect again is to privilege the cultural text as the stable and determining point of reference. Although the word "production" is not used, the implicit assumption is the same: as Harsnett (or the cultural matrix embodied in Harsnett) produced *Lear,* so Thomas Harriot produces *Henry IV, Part I.*

In the *Henry IV* essay Greenblatt avoids the triumphal rhetoric of his *Lear* piece and moves carefully to protect his assumptions against the kinds of evident vulnerabilities I remarked on earlier:

> There is, it may be objected, something slightly absurd in likening such moments to aspects of Harriot's text; *1 Henry IV* is a play, not a tract for potential investors in a colonial scheme, and the only values we may be sure that Shakespeare had in mind were theatrical values. The theatrical problems that beset such appeals to the self-referentiality of literature are beyond the scope of this paper. I would observe here only that *Henry IV* itself insists that it is quite impossible to keep the interests of the theater hermetically sealed off from the interests of power. (55–56)

Here Greenblatt implies that if we resist him we must be committed to a theory of the self-referentiality of texts; it is either Greenblatt or Brooks and Warren—or, rather, a parody of formalist autonomy. But this is a false choice, and it may serve to distract us from recognizing that Greenblatt's preferred alternative to a hermetically isolated text is equally extreme on the other side. Instead of insisting on the self-referentiality of theatrical artifice, he now says that *Henry IV, Part I* insists on being constituted by the forces of real political power. Is such a view any more tenable, any less restrictive? Some voices in the play, chiefly Hal's (on which Greenblatt focuses almost exclusively), support such a view. But other voices, chiefly Falstaff's (which Greenblatt almost completely ignores), are singing different songs altogether. Falstaff's voice is also part of the play's insistence. While *Henry IV, Part I* interests us in arranging its various insistences into a hierarchy, it also thwarts this effort, so that I am skeptical about characterizing the play itself as an insistence. "Like Harriot in the New World," Greenblatt says in the penultimate sentence of his essay, "*1 Henry IV* confirms the Machiavellian hypothesis of the origin of princely power in force and fraud" (57). But so many contradictory hypotheses are confirmed in the dramatic experience (and in the theatrical situation) of *Henry IV, Part I* that the play cannot be conceived of as an essentially hypothesis-confirming discourse.

In the introduction to *The Forms of Power*, Greenblatt dissociates himself from the old historicism, which he locates in Dover Wilson. When he comes to write about *Henry IV*, however, Greenblatt does just what Dover Wilson did in *The Fortunes of Falstaff*—privileges Hal's voice and narrative over the others in the play. Or consider that model old historicist Tillyard: "Shakespeare's Histories . . . cannot be understood without assuming a larger principle of order in the background" (360). Again my point is the continuity that exists despite (or perhaps because of?) all Greenblatt's energetically protesting disavowals. For Greenblatt too, the openness of *Henry IV*—by which I mean not so much its "undecidability" as its invitation to many contradictory interpretive decisions—represents a threat that must be controlled, and the way to acquire such control is to refer the play to its presumed social and political context, to gesture toward some vague tetralogical structure of containment in the background: "what lies ahead is the charismatic leader . . . in *Henry V*. . . . To understand this whole conception of Hal, from rakehell to monarch, we need in effect a poetics of Elizabethan power" (56–57). We may indeed need this, as we needed and still need the Elizabethan World Picture, but we need a lot more besides.[2]

"In Dramatic composition," according to Maurice Morgann's famous adage, "the *Impression* is the *Fact*" (4). In Greenblatt, however, dramatic impressions are subordinated to and controlled by facts of social history that seem to stand behind them. It would be easy to name other new-historicist critics who, like Greenblatt (though usually far less interestingly and sophisticatedly), fail to live up to their claims about not granting a determining priority and stability to social history. But at this point I think it is more useful to shift to a general discussion and ask why these claims are hard to achieve. Here once again Greenblatt can help us begin, because he fully understands the kind of problem he is dealing with and the critical history from which it develops. "Though Marx himself vigorously resisted [the] functional absorption of art," he writes at the beginning of *Renaissance Self-Fashioning*, "Marxist aesthetics . . . has never satisfactorily resolved the theoretical problems raised in the *Grundrisse* and elsewhere" (4). Nor do I find successful any of the solutions proposed in the current revitalization of Marxist criticism, of which the new historicism is a part.

It is tempting to construe the problem as inhering in the relation between theory and application, and in this context Fredric Jameson's work is exemplary. Jameson so interestingly and complexly nuances the relation between ideology and textuality that the distinction between them seems to disappear, as in his proposal for

the rewriting of the literary text in such a way that the latter may itself be seen as the rewriting or restructuration of a prior historical or ideological *subtext,* it being always understood that the "subtext" is not immediately present as such, not some common-sense external reality, nor even the conventional narratives of history manuals, but rather must itself always be (re)constructed after the fact. (81)

But despite this theoretical richness, Jameson's actual interpretations—of Milton and Conrad, for example—revive an old-left political allegorization that embarrasses even those critics who are most deeply committed to the historicization or politicization of the text (see Goldberg, "Politics," 515–22; Simpson, 74–75).

The problem in Marxist aesthetics, however, is not essentially in the relation between theory and application but in the theory itself. Take Althusser's attempt in *For Marx* to soften the rigid orthodox hierarchy of substructure and superstructure. The superstructures remain relatively autonomous in their "specific effectivity"; the substructure, the "economic mode of production," becomes determinant only "in the last instance" (111). But this last instance is apocalyptic. By contrast, "in History, these instances, the superstructures, etc.—are never seen to step respectfully aside when their work is done or, when the Time comes, as his pure phenomena, to scatter before his Majesty the Economy as he strides along the royal road of the Dialectic. From the first moment to the last, the lonely hour of the 'last instance' never comes" (113). While Althusser has come a long way from orthodox Marxism, the economic mode of production remains his conceptual point of reference, and thus the hierarchical idea persists, if in a less rigid form. In his "Letter on Art," Althusser attempts a similar strategic redeployment of the text (or "art") and ideology. Building on suggestions in Macherey's discussion of Lenin as critic of Tolstoy, Althusser develops the idea that art "presupposes a *retreat,* an internal *distantiation,* from the very ideology from which" it emerges (222–23).[3] Even in this formulation, however, ideology retains a privileged or substructural position, preceding and determining discourse.

The reason "the theoretical problems raised in the *Grundrisse*" have never been "satisfactorily resolved" is that they cannot be. This is elementary deconstruction: the moment we posit duality (inner–outer, center–margin, superstructure–substructure, female–male, etc.), we are inevitably involved in privileging and hierarchy. An absolute parity of literary and social texts is a will-o'-the-wisp. More important, even if such a parity were possible, it is not what the new historicists really want. Their whole endeavor is to situate the literary text in social history and thus to see it in a determined or secondary position. We might debate the extent and flexibility of this determination and withhold or accord value as we prefer. We might also debate the purpose or the intention of new historicists in claiming not to subordinate the text to social history. Are they trying to fool their readers, or have they succeeded in fooling themselves—and, in either case, why? There can be no debate, however, about the notion of dependency itself. If the new historicists abandoned the notion, they would forfeit altogether their claim on our attention.

Put another way, the theoretical problems raised in the *Grundrisse* are not just problems but solutions, the source of interpretive power for the new-historicist critics. To say that they see the text in a context does not imply a value judgment on their project, since contextualizing texts is something that everybody does perforce. It merely describes what happens in all interpretive activity. My complaint earlier about the way new historicists ignore theatrical impressions was itself based on contextualization, a theatrical one. I was marching under the banner of Morgann ("in Dramatic composition the *Impression* is the *Fact*"), but it is only when we agree that the theater *is* the right context (and, indeed, a particular notion of theater) that these impressions are there to become facts. Texts do not exist without contexts (or subtexts, or interpretations), and it is the context that allows us to determine the facts of the text. If I am skeptical, then, about the new historicists' project, the reason is not that it depends on contextualization but that I have doubts about the interest and usefulness of the particular forms their contextualization takes. And this brings us to what is really the main question or set of questions: What is the value of new-historicist contextualization? Are its versions of texts and of history useful and interesting? Why or why not? Who gains from them, and what is the gain?

❖

These questions about the value of new-historicist contextualizations have to wait, though, until we can determine just what that contextualization is. Before deciding whether it is good or bad to put the text back into society or recover its history, we ought to have a clear picture of the determining social history. Here we arrive at the second major claim made by the new historicists: whereas their predecessors were, in Greenblatt's words, "monological [and] concerned with discovering a single political vision," they recognize a variety of competing centers of cultural power. Their claim to be engaged in "thick" rather than thin interpretive description has become another conventional gesture among new historicists both in and out of Renaissance criticism.[4] And like the claim for a mutual constitution of the literary and social texts, it should be scrutinized with a healthy amount of skepticism.

For despite their protests about being open, new historicists tend persistently to fix and close their attention on the dominant institutions of Renaissance society, especially the monarchy. Jonathan Goldberg, for instance, in *James I and the Politics of Literature*, sees various Renaissance texts, both dramatic and nondramatic, as essentially feeding on and feeding a set of concerns about royal authority in James's own texts. Leonard Tennenhouse views *A Midsummer Night's Dream*, Petrarchan lyrics, and Shakespeare's histories (both middle and late) all as examples of a "literature [that] had to employ radically discontinuous political strategies for idealising political authority" according to the changes in James's court as compared with Elizabeth's (110). For Louis Adrian Montrose, too, *A Midsummer Night's Dream* is a monarchy-centered play: "whether or not Queen Elizabeth was physically present at the first performance," her "pervasive *cultural presence* was a condition of the play's imaginative possibility" (" 'Shaping Fantasies,' " 62).

Even when not directly concerned with royal power, new historicists still tend to locate the centers of plays by referring to the ideological interests of a dominant cultural force, such as the titled or moneyed classes, institutions of religious authority, or male power. The colonialist enterprise is frequently a base for their interpretations. Thus Paul Brown observes that *The Tempest* is "*obviously* . . . heavily invested in colonialist discourse" (66; my emphasis). According to Francis Barker and Peter Hulme, "the discourse of colonialism" is "the articulatory *principle* of *The Tempest's* diversity" (204). But the argument is not limited to *The Tempest* (to which, whether central or not, colonialism is *obviously* relevant). For Greenblatt, in *Renaissance Self-Fashioning*, colonialism provides the base from which to understand Spenser, Marlowe, and Shakespeare's *Othello*.

Seemingly important distinctions could be made among critics like these—between, for example, Tennenhouse's interpretation of *A Midsummer Night's Dream* as idealizing state authority and Montrose's contrary view that the play reflects Shakespeare's will to resist such authority, to create a space of his own that cannot be claimed by female-monarchial power. Such distinctions depend on whether the play is seen to ally itself with dominant cultural interests or with subordinate ones, but even these distinctions do not seem finally to matter very much. A case in point is Brown's discussion of "masterless men," a social phenomenon that embodies a countercultural threat to authority. "In *The Tempest*," Brown notes, Stephano and Trinculo "*obviously* represent such masterless men" (52–53; my emphasis), and thus the play serves as a kind of cautionary tale from the perspective of the ruling class: "the assembled aristocrats in the play, and perhaps in the original courtly audiences, come to recognize in these figures their own common identity—and the necessity for a solidarity among the ruling class in face of such a threat" (53). Brown recognizes an aspect of Stephano and Trinculo beyond the interests of ruling-class ideology, namely, our simple and raw pleasure in their appearance, but this pleasure turns out to be subordinated to the ends of magistracy after all, "a vital adjunct to power, a utilisation of the potentially disruptive to further the workings of power" (53). According to this argument, a favorite one of Greenblatt's, a dominant authority produces elements of apparent subversion or transgression as a means of maintaining its control.

The frequent recurrence of the words "power" and "discourse" in new-historicist criticism reflects the influence of Foucault, in whom Greenblatt may have discovered the idea that authority produces subversion. And yet, if we are to be precise, it is the early Foucault whom the new historicists follow. In his later work, he struck off self-consciously in a new direction, that of the *dispositif* rather than the *epistème*, and showed far more responsiveness to heterogeneity. In *The History of Sexuality* Foucault tells us that "we must not imagine a world of discourse divided between . . . the dominant discourse and the dominated one; but as a multiplicity of discursive elements that can come into play in various strategies" (100). He also redefines "power," vastly extending its reference. "We must," he says "conceive of . . . power without the king" (91):

> Power's condition of possibility . . . must not be sought in the primary existence of a central point, in a unique source of sovereignty from which secondary and descendent forms would emanate; it is the moving substrate of force relations which, by virtue of their inequality, constantly engender states of power, but the latter are always local and unstable. The omnipresence of power: not because it has the privilege of consolidating everything under its invincible unity, but because it is produced from one moment to the next, at every point, or rather in every relation from one point to another. Power is everywhere; not because it embraces everything, but because it comes from everywhere. (93)

Power is the whole thing, in other words—"thick description" indeed. In comparison with this passage, the work of even the most flexible and wide-ranging of the new historicists looks thin. For them, power is still reified in the monarch, or in a particular set of dominant institutions, and discourse is located in a starkly simple model of domination and subversion.

One measure of this thinness is the way new historicists ignore the contrasting rhetorical situations of the texts they discuss. Jonathan Goldberg, for instance, applies basically the same set of interpretive concerns to a Jonson masque, in which the king is at the center of the action and the audience, and to a Jonson play for the public stage, such as *Sejanus*, even though for Jonson himself the difference in audience and theatrical setting was of tremendous concern. Similarly, Tennenhouse can move from Petrarchan lyrics, with their more or less courtly audience, to a public theater play such as *A Midsummer Night's Dream* or *Henry IV* without feeling any pressure to modify his thematics. Or recall Brown's comment that Stephano and Trinculo strengthen the class solidarity of "the assembled aristocrats in the play, and perhaps in the original courtly audiences." The "perhaps" commendably disclaims certainty about the responses of Shakespeare's courtly audience, but an assumption remains that the audience *was* a courtly one and that the play must be understood with that specific reference in mind. That there were royal command performances we know, but we know also that *The Tempest* was performed at Blackfriars, and most people believe at the Globe as well, for economic reasons that new historicists especially ought to respect. It simply did not make sense to spend the time and the money to gear a play for a one-shot performance, or even for a very limited market run. And as Richard Levin points out (*New Readings*, 170, 240–41), no hard evidence indicates that any Renaissance play was written specifically and exclusively for any particular occasion.

In general, new historicists carefully avoid making any such claims (thus Montrose's indifference to the question whether Elizabeth was present for *A Midsummer Night's Dream*), but on what basis, then, do they persistently interpret these plays by citing the particular interests of cultural authority? Work by Ann Cook suggests that we might revise upward our notion of the popular audience's social status, but significant differences would remain among various audiences, and in any case the new historicists are not making use of either Cook's particular argument or arguments like it. They show no interest in the question, and this on the surface seems odd. If they conceive of the text as in essence socially and culturally instrumental, how can they be indifferent to the particular social and cultural setting for which the text is designed?

For an answer we can turn to Goldberg's explanation of how *Sejanus* can represent James's concerns about authority even though the play antedates James's accession or the availability of James's written representations of these concerns: "The play spoke to present concerns; . . . following Foucault, we can point to shared epistemic limits *conditioning* discourse and actions, onstage and off" (*James I*, 177; my emphasis). This argument is like Montrose calling Elizabeth "a pervasive *cultural presence*," a "condition" of "imaginative possibility"—not just for *A Midsummer Night's Dream* but for all imaginative possibility. The condition that Goldberg and Montrose claim to understand is really a precondition, in the sense that it stands above or exists before all the particular circumstances of the text. These circumstances—author, audience, chronology—can be ignored because they do not matter. What matters is "power relations," "authority and transgression," and the other recurring terms in new-historicist criticism; they constitute an "episteme," replacing what appeared in an older critical vocabulary as the zeitgeist or the "spirit of the age." The knowledge they furnish of "present concerns" in the Renaissance is a universal knowledge, good for all concrete situations.

According to Dollimore and Sinfield, "Historical context undermines the transcendent significance traditionally accorded to the literary text and allows us to recover its histories" (*Political Shakespeare*, vii). What I am claiming, however, is that the histories being recovered are themselves transcendental signifieds (or sometimes, perhaps, transcendental ways of signifying) in the sense that their capacity to explain seems independent of many particulars. In this sense there can be no question of "recovering history" (the rubric under which the first six essays in *Political Shakespeare* are grouped) in the way Dollimore and Sinfield mean, as though history were out there just waiting to be found. This is like Professor Welch answering the phone in *Lucky Jim*: "History speaking." But history speaks in our voice. History does not tell us what the text is, because we decide what history is, and then put history into the text, rather than the other way around. Or maybe it is better to say that we "recover" the text and history at the same time, but again in the sense not of finding what was lost out there but of adding our own needs and desires—coating anew, re-covering the text in a Barthesian manner with words of our own.

From this perspective, the new historicists' contextualization is just another form of interpretation, another way of deciding where and how to center the competing claims made on our attention by a variety of needs and desires. *The Tempest* can help make my point here. New historicists contend that colonialism is "the articulatory principle of *The Tempest*'s diversity," but colonialism can also be seen as only a marginal or allusive presence in a text with some other center. A metadramatic interpretation would put art at the center; an ethical one would put self-control or *virtus* or *sophrosyne* at the center; a textualist one would see the center as a supplement, arguing that the center is the margin or that there is no center. How do we choose among these *Tempests*? If we answer, "By determining which version is historical," we raise another question: "Which historical version?" History is something that we make or "do" (J. H. Hexter's word), and there are many ways of doing it: as the unfolding of God's providence; as bunk; as all the best that has been thought and said in the world; as a nightmare from which we are trying to escape; as the reenactment of past thought in one's mind; even as the doing of history. New historicists often privilege their criticism by assuming that their version of history is the thing itself, as if they were doing *history*, but if we understand that they are merely *doing* history, then that privilege disappears. To say that the colonialist *Tempest* is superior because "the Renaissance was an age characterized by the expansion of power" does not answer the question, it begs it. Deciding that some such statement is the right thing to say about the Renaissance is precisely the interpretive choice in question. As a version of the preferred view, it cannot be said to justify the preference. (In the same way, textualists cannot justify their version by declaring something like "recent criticism has demonstrated that words can connect only with other words." Whatever may be valuable in such a claim—probably as much or as little as saying that the Renaissance is an age of power expansion—derives from its interpretive power rather than from its descriptive accuracy.)

At the beginning of *Renaissance Self-Fashioning*, Greenblatt himself acknowledges, at least implicitly, almost everything I have said here. Though other new historicists usually do not make such acknowledgments (and though Greenblatt himself frequently writes as if he has forgotten them), we should recognize that nothing I have said undermines the new-historicist enterprise. In trying to divest these critics of their imperial new claims to privilege, I am leaving them naked only in the sense that all interpreters are naked. In arguing that they are not less "monological" than the old historicists, I do not dispute that they are monological in a different way. This difference is crucial, and it remains the basis for the value—real or imagined, great or small—of new-historicist criticism. We are back then to the main questions I raised earlier, but we can now phrase them a little more specifically. Earlier I asked: Why see texts as essentially determined by social history? Now the question is: Why see history as essentially determined by power relations? Who gain from such a view, and what do they gain from it?

❖

I can start to answer these questions by looking at what I take to be the most important characteristic of the new historicism: its detachment from the text. Sometimes this attitude is explicitly urged as a matter of principle. Dollimore, for instance, appropriates Brecht as an epigraph for *Radical Tragedy*: "Examine carefully

the behaviour of these people: . . . Consider even the most insignif-
icant, seemingly simple/ Action with distrust" (ii). And at the
beginning of *Political Shakespeare,* Dollimore and Sinfield make a
similar appeal for a "theoretical method [that] detaches the text
from immanent criticism which seeks only to reproduce it in its
own terms" (vii). Acknowledged or not, this detachment is an
inevitable consequence of the fundamental move of new-historicist
critics—trying to see the text as essentially generated from and
directed toward the politics of a historically remote period. What is
the effect when such writers as Goldberg and Tennenhouse see
plays as claims for absolute monarchial power? or when a writer
such as Montrose sees a play as resistant to royal female power? or
when Greenblatt, Brown, and Barker and Hulme see plays as implicated in colonialist domination? When addressed to the left-liberal
academic community, for whom the monarchy is an anachronism,
feminism an article of faith, and colonialism a source of embarrassed guilt, these critical versions cannot help draining the plays
of much of their potential to involve an audience.

One aspect of this draining strategy is the new historicists' tendency to deemphasize passages whose affective power seems
unusually great. In a fifteen-page discussion of *King Lear,* Dollimore finds no room even to consider the reconciliation between
Lear and Cordelia (*Radical Tragedy,* 189–203). Since Shakespeare
often gives us moving final scenes, the strategy of downplaying
such power may be a version of what Richard Levin has called
"refuting the ending" (*New Readings,* 102–25). Thus in Dollimore's consideration of *Antony and Cleopatra,* the last scene disappears, or virtually so; it is merely acknowledged by way of a
perfunctory contrast to Antony's speech in act I about Fulvia's
death: "True, the language of the final scenes is very different . . .
but there too we are never allowed to forget that the moments of
sublimity are conditional upon absence, nostalgic . . ." (207). So
much for Cleopatra's death scene. Dollimore's own last gesture is
a stern warning, under the rubric "Sexuality and Power," that
Cleopatra's kind of allure is dangerous and destructive in its

power to infatuate. This may be sound advice, as may have been, in their not so different ways, the lectures on moral duty and self-control that earlier critics delivered to Antony. But are there *no* moments at the end of *Antony and Cleopatra* "where we are allowed to forget," even encouraged to forget, such pragmatically self-protective prudence? The purest form of "refuting the ending" among new historicists is Goldberg's version of *Julius Caesar*. Commenting on the apparition of Caesar that comes to Brutus at the end of act IV, Goldberg says, "So, *finally*, Brutus sees 'that which is not in me.'. . . . *At last*, Brutus sees the very form of power before him. . . . Brutus, only *at the very end*, with the ghost, even sees what it was he wanted" (*James I*, 176, 185; my emphases). Here we are told, three times, that the play ends after the fourth act. Refuting the ending is one thing; erasing it, as Goldberg does, is another.

"In Marxist theory," Maureen Quilligan says, "as well as in all strong modern theories of interpretation, the assumption necessarily is that the text does not, at the surface level, want said what the critic finds in it to say" (29). From this perspective, we can see that the detachment of new-historicist criticism has the virtue of its defect: by reducing the power of the text, detachment increases the observer's power over the text—the power to see through the surface, penetrate its disguises. Hence for Catherine Belsey, detachment is a way of getting to the ideological forces behind the text, which are invisible to the culture in which the text was produced and accessible only from the privileged perspective of remoteness. What results then is "a scientific criticism":

> distancing itself from the imaginary coherence of the text, analysing the discourses which are its raw material and the process of production which makes it a text, [such scientific criticism] recognizes in the text not "knowledge" but ideology itself in all its inconsistency and partiality. (*Critical Practice*, 128)

For Frank Lentricchia, too, criticism is an antagonistic enterprise, though the struggle is not just with the text but with the conservative interpretive establishment. What we need, he tells us, is "a way of 'interrogating' the text so as to reproduce it as a social text in the teeth of the usual critical lyricism that would deny the social text power and social specificity in the name of 'literature.' The activist intellectual needs a theory of reading that will instigate a culturally suspicious, trouble-making readership" (*Criticism*, 11).

For many new historicists, the power over the text derived from this suspicion is instrumental to social change, part of the project of making the world a better place. Dollimore and Sinfield, for example, assert that "cultural materialism" (their phrase for the new historicism) "registers its commitment to the transformation of a social order which exploits people on the grounds of race, gender and class" (*Political Shakespeare*, viii). Frequently these political claims for interpretive styles are made tacitly, as in Edward Said's implication that a connection somehow exists between formalism and the bombing of Vietnam (2–3) or in Lentricchia's controlling suggestion throughout *Criticism and Social Change* that Kenneth Burke's version of reading leads to social justice and Paul de Man's to an acceptance of the absence of justice. Such connections seem too abstract and polemical to be convincing. It is impossible to serve Kant and Marx, say the new historicists, but the young Empson did just that. I am not denying that there are connections between interpretive and political actions; such a claim would be counterintuitive and intolerable. But the connections are tenuous and volatile, and they vary from reader to reader, text to text. Moreover, if transforming an exploitive social order should be the prime directive of one's activity, then there are simply more effective ways of proceeding. Sinfield admits as much in his wry and amusing concession that even the approved "cultural materialist" mode of "teaching Shakespeare's plays and writing books about them is unlikely to bring down capitalism, but it is a point of intervention" ("Give," 154). Maybe so, but not a very significant point, especially in the context of Eldridge Cleaver's remark that "if you're not part of the solution, you're part of the problem." "Marx and Engels were well informed of new and important literary developments," Pierre Macherey assures us, "but they never made anything of their knowledge because they never had the time" (105). When there is a world to change, even a thoroughly ideologized text may not seem important enough.

Despite the strong political advocacy of many new-historicist critics, it would be wrong, I think, to regard the new historicism itself as necessarily or essentially associated with political action, if for no other reason than that such a view would exclude the most powerful of all its practitioners, Stephen Greenblatt. His is not an activist criticism; in fact, the story that Greenblatt always tells is the reverse of a revolutionary one. "There is subversion, no end of subversion," says Kafka to Max Brod in a remark that Greenblatt quotes twice with approval in his *Henry IV* essay, "only not for us" ("Invisible Bullets," 53, 57). In the epilogue to *Renaissance Self-Fashioning* Greenblatt explains that this conclusion was forced on him:

> When I first conceived this book several years ago, I intended to explore the ways in which major English writers of the sixteenth century created their own performances. . . . But as my work progressed, I perceived that fashioning oneself and being fashioned by cultural institutions—family, religion, state—were inseparably intertwined. In all my texts and documents, there were, so far as I could tell, no moments of pure, unfettered subjectivity; indeed, the human subject itself began to seem remarkably unfree, the ideological product of the relations of power in a particular society. (256)

In this view, human power to shape the world, even to fashion that small part of the world called the self, turns out to be illusory. There is no free space in Greenblatt's functionalist conception of culture, not in the theater, not for the self. As sometimes in Foucault, or at least in the earlier Foucault, we are only what we are constituted to be by the power relations that govern, anonymously and without human face, even the governors.

New-historicist criticism then, though it can naturally take a politically activist form, need not be identified with that form, and its valuing of detachment cannot be hooked necessarily to the project of social change. Why then is detachment valued? Not because it is "scientific" to conceive it this way. This criticism is scientific only in the same way it is historical; that is, it is scientific in a particular way. By "scientific" Belsey means simply predictive; guaranteed procedures enable us to see the text as a move in a power game. But at issue here is precisely the assumption that the text *is* such a move—or the "proposition" that it is: "Althusser *proposes* that the task of ideology is to conceal its own role in reproducing the conditions of the capitalist mode of production" (*Critical Practice*, 128; my emphasis).

For an explanation of the new historicists' wish to conceive of the text as hostile and threatening, we can turn again to Lentricchia: "The activity of interpretation . . . does not passively 'see,' as Kenneth Burke puts it, but constructs a point of view in its engagement with textual events, and in so constructing produces an image of history as social struggle, of, say, class struggle" (*Criticism*, 11). In this view, the relation between the text and the audience replicates exactly the antagonistic power relations at the center of new-historicist thematics. According to Jameson, "History is . . . the experience of Necessity. . . . History is what hurts, it is what refuses desire and sets inexorable limits to individual as well as collective praxis" (102). The text, then, is part of history so conceived, and interpretive activity therefore acts out the deepest intuition of new-historicist critics, that of being surrounded by a hostile otherness, enmeshed in a complex matrix of forces all of which threaten their freedom.

⁜

I think we can now, finally, answer the question about the value of the new historicism. Whether the new historicism looks like a good or a bad kind of criticism will depend on whether or not we share its underlying intuition. Should we share it or not? Only a fool or a saint would not share it, at least in some measure. "It's a jungle out there" is a cliché, but the thing about clichés (or proverbs, or topoi) is that they express a common belief. But is this cliché the totality of legitimate belief, or even the dominant belief? Other beliefs and other intuitions—other clichés—are possible. They center on such concepts as kindness, or at least tolerance, and benevolence, or at least cooperation. Against "It's a jungle out there," they say "Love makes the world go round." This second kind of cliché has become a great embarrassment for us; it trails clouds of Wordsworthian diction, of something far more deeply interfused, or worse, of Tennysonian sentiment, of the hope that something good will be the final goal of ill. Such clichés are vulnerable to attack as screens masking a desire to dominate or as false consciousness, even in their weaker forms (those above prefaced by "at least"). Hence Lentricchia observes that "the mere pluralization of voices and traditions (a currently fashionable and sentimental gesture) is inadequate to the ultimate problem of linking repressed and master voices as the agon of history, their abiding relation of class conflict" (*Criticism*, 131).

Yet this sort of assertion is itself vulnerable, because it is not really an argument. Its persuasive capacity depends first of all on our believing the assumption that the will to power determines human activity and organization. It simply repeats this assumption as a way of responding to a contrary assumption, or a contrary intuition, about kindness and benevolence. This is like Ring Lardner: " 'Shut up!' he explained." Saying "It's a jungle out there" will not convince those who believe that "love makes the world go round." The reverse is true as well, of course. If then we choose between these competing intuitions, the choice cannot be determined by verification, for there is no way of deciding which intuition is right except from a position where the decision has in effect already been made. I am not arguing that choice is impossible, merely trying to relocate its basis, to make the primary consideration not correspondence to the way things really are but usefulness.

I myself do not find it useful to believe that human activity is essentially determined by the will to power, because it is hard to base much of a future on that belief. More to the point, Lentricchia finds himself in the same position, of having to imagine a future that somehow transcends antagonism: "a genuine community . . . the establishment of a consent, of a 'we' . . . Marx without Stalin" (*Criticism*, 13). Lentricchia nowhere gives us any substantial description of this goal or even the slightest idea of how to achieve it. He cannot, I think, because he has renounced not only notions of benevolence and bourgeois clichés about pluralism but even the Marxist version of such clichés, proletarian solidarity, to which his own training and theoretical commitment would naturally draw him. Indeed, some of the wittiest and strongest parts of *Criticism and Social Change* dismantle, or show how Kenneth Burke dismantled, those very clichés. But without these notions, or some version of them, or room among one's beliefs to include some version of them, how can we imagine a community of any kind, let alone "genuine" community? "It's a jungle out there" by itself leads only to more jungles, where the best we can hope for is to become King of the Forest. We do not therefore have to believe that love makes the world go round, but we should have room for this belief, next to the room for the jungle. It would be foolish indeed (or saintly) to hold that benevolence is *the* human essence, the force that through the green fuse drives our flower. But is it any less foolish to substitute the will to power? Getting beyond humanism is supposed to mean getting beyond such essences, not merely exchanging one for another, replacing the flattering with the cynical.

Anyone who, like me, is reluctant to accept the will to power as the defining human essence will probably have trouble with the critical procedures of the new historicists and with their interpretive conclusions. Acquiring power over the text will seem a costly achievement, since what it sacrifices is the potential power of the text—the power to open up new areas of experience, unfamiliar ways of being in the world. New-historicist procedures are designed to resist any such power, to work around or get beyond

73

immediate textual impressions to arrive at a predetermined point of theoretical understanding, which is the point from which one comes to the text in the first place. Lentricchia observes that critical activity "produces an image of history as social struggle, of, say, class struggle." The "say" is good, suggesting a coincidence, the possibility that any number of images might have emerged. Here we can also recall Belsey's remark that "scientific criticism . . . *recognises* in the text not 'knowledge' but ideology itself." New-historicist criticism is a criticism of recognition, of knowing again what one knew before. It is criticism that systematically deprives the text of its capacity to surprise, and who wants to go to a theater where there are no surprises?

To the extent that the new historicism takes the surprise out of theater, it seems to me a bad thing. Nonetheless, I want finally to acknowledge the enormous interest and energy this kind of criticism has generated. It has done so in part because, as I mentioned at the beginning, it is a more varied activity than my representation suggests. While the conception of the text as a hostile otherness is, I believe, the dominant or normal conception, new historicists sometimes work out of different and more useful assumptions.[5] Moreover, even their dominant assumption can sometimes generate engaging criticism, as it does for Greenblatt. Essentially a new historicist, he understands the antagonistic relation between text and audience and aims—no less than, say, Lentricchia does—to master the text before it masters him. But master the text he does. Like Dryden's Jonson, Greenblatt "invades authors like a monarch; and what would be theft in other[s] is only victory in him" (82). By organizing rich details from Renaissance literary and social texts into powerfully interesting narratives, he achieves a critical self-fashioning that is hard to resist. Whether or not Greenblatt delights in the sheer power of his critical performances, they are a pleasure for any audience. For this reason they frequently convey the impression not of a depressing impotence, the result one might expect from their recurring thematics, but of a great and highly individualized interpretive strength.

But the success of the new historicism should not be limited to local triumphs or particular criticism. The project answers a generally felt need within the profession. Most of us no longer find it helpful to isolate the literary text from other discursive practices and have moved toward a less specialized kind of critical activity, which might be called culture criticism or maybe, if we follow Richard Rorty, just criticism. I believe that this development is a good thing, despite my quarrel with particular new historicists. As Robert Scholes says, "one does not have to be a Marxist to endorse Fredric Jameson's battle cry, 'Always historicize!'" (qtd. by Graff, "Teaching Power," 180). Putting the text back into history (or better, histories: our histories, its histories) is clearly a valuable project. Maybe it is the only project. In any case, it is far too important to be left to the new historicists.

STEPHEN GREENBLATT'S EDIFYING NARRATIVES

I first wrote a draft of the preceding pages in 1986, for an M.A. course I was teaching called "New Approaches to Shakespeare and Renaissance Drama." I had asked students for papers about criticism, rather than about the applications of various critical practices to canonical texts: not what *Twelfth Night* looks like from different takes but what the takes themselves looked like—their assumptions, divergences, benefits, disadvantages, and so on. The students were confused, and "The New Historicism and Its Discontents" was supposed to give them an example of what I meant; but since "Approaches to" in the course title seemed to require precisely the exercise in application I was vetoing, I must have been confused myself. Or distracted: it was the "new" that seemed to me important then. In the mid-1980s, everything seemed new—not just historicism but approaches, accents, readings. The "re-" in the then-obligatory hyphenated constructs (re-reading, re-vision, re-writing, re-presenting, re-membering) was a bold assertion of freedom, not yet bogged down in historical constraint and determination—in repetition. The chief exceptions, the main old things on the critical horizon, were the canonical authors; they had become *past* masters.

Back then, I thought there was something called new historicism emerging into shape, and it seemed a good idea to try to define and evaluate it. But specters are notoriously transient ('tis here, 'tis here, 'tis gone) and indefinite (a camel, a weasel, a whale). Although I knew this at the time ("many different and even contradictory critical practices are currently represented as new historicism"), the knowledge obviously did not prevent me from trying to locate a stable center for this overdetermined collection of volatile and disparate phenomena. In the process, I exaggerated the shared qualities of some critical practices whose differences have become all too evident in time. If it ever made sense to call new historicism "a kind of 'Marxist criticism'" (and the inverted commas suggest my uncertainty even then), it makes no sense now in view of the substantial attacks on Greenblatt's work produced during the last few years by really rigorously hard-line materialists (Cohen, 33–38, Bristol, *Shakespeare's America*, 203–9). Still worse, I lumped together cultural materialism and new historicism—as if the very different academic environments of Britain and America would generate identical critical practices. I recognized that Jonathan Dollimore had already staked out a substantially different position from Greenblatt's as early as 1985 (n. 5), but once again the knowledge did not rein in my generalizing impulses, which issued in the insouciant statement that cultural materialism was Dollimore and Sinfield's "phrase for the new historicism"—a statement that was immediately spotted as a vulgar error (Werstine, 523; Porter, 745; Dollimore, "Introduction to the Second Edition," xxi).

Since this essay was written, defining new historicism has become a thriving enterprise in regions as diverse as the *Wall Street Journal* and *Diacritics*, but still without much success. (Post hoc isn't propter hoc; I take neither credit nor blame for this development.) There are some points of general agreement. Power—its establishment, stabilization, extension, and subversion—is a major theme. Juxtaposition is a recurring procedure. New historicists characteristically negotiate the distance we are used to seeing between different categories and domains: separate historical periods, high and low culture, different kinds of texts and professional disciplines. But these least common denominators do not solve the problems of lumping and difference. They fit a lot of critics who have neither enlisted in nor been conscripted to new historicism, and the putatively bona fide new historicists contained within these borders continue to stake out the special differences of their own territorial claims.

Greenblatt himself has not invested in this defining enterprise. On the contrary, he has deliberately distanced himself from the *Genre* piece, the closest thing to a theoretical manifesto he has ever produced (*Learning to Curse*, 146), and gone about his business apparently indifferent to the controversy surrounding the question just what his business is. A 1990 essay called "Resonance and Wonder" is something of an exception, but although he acknowledges some of the attacks, and in several instances claims that he has been misread, he continues to elude those of his critics who demand a strict theoretical accounting: "I am certainly not opposed to methodological self-consciousness, but I am less inclined to see overtness—an explicit articulation of one's values and methods—as inherently necessary or virtuous" (*Learning to Curse*, 167). Some people will find such a statement evasive and self-serving, but it may serve our interests as well as Greenblatt's. Attempts to determine what new historicism really is, *if* it really is, have not dispelled contradiction and confusion. My earlier suggestion that "the new historicism should not be limited to local triumphs or particular criticism" now seems to me the reverse of useful. Perhaps it is time to abandon the apparently vain quest for a theoretical mastery over the differences in contemporary criticism and transfer our attention to the practice of a particular critic, Greenblatt himself.[6]

During the last few years, evaluating Greenblatt has become as thriving an enterprise as defining new historicism (with which it is obviously connected), producing similarly inconclusive results. Critics regularly accuse Greenblatt of all kinds of appalling offenses. His work is said to be insufficiently theorized, or overly freighted with theoretical jargon. He is politically evasive, or obsessed with ideology. He concentrates too much on the same narrowly predictable range of themes, or dissipates his energy in a perverse fascination with the marginal and outré. His acknowledgment of textual play is inadequate, or excessive. His historical explanations are too grounded in positivism, or too unstably antifoundationalist, to possess authority. He is a pathetically residual humanist, still shamelessly committed to the experience of individual selfhood, or he has shamelessly abandoned individual responsibility for an agentless neo-Foucauldian functionalism.[7]

It would seem that Greenblatt can be guilty of at worst only half these charges. Although his reluctance to attach his work to a stable, fully developed conceptual model may have left him vulnerable to such a scatter-gun barrage, he cannot be held responsible for his critical reception. My own disagreements with Greenblatt in 1986—that he was arguing from a strict functionalist position; that he centered historical explanations in an arbitrarily narrow conception of exploitive power—seem relatively trivial now. This is partly because Greenblatt's positions have changed over the years, as no doubt my own have,[8] but even more because the question whether Greenblatt or his critics are right diverts us from more interesting and profitable matters. After all, what would it mean to be right about, say, the nature of historical authority in the context of antifoundationalist or poststructuralist assumptions? If we could get that one right, we would be living inside Monty Python's version of *Blue Peter.* "Boys and girls, today we'll learn how to build a tree house and then how to rid the world forever of racial prejudice." Historical authority is less an object to define than the problematic conditions within which we work, and clearly one of the main such problems.[9] This is equally true of functionalism, which is a version of Perry Anderson's "master-problem" discussed at the beginning of this chapter.

From this angle, the important thing about the attacks on Greenblatt is not whether they are justified or not but the imposing testimony they supply to the enormous influence of his work. His epigones are, of course, the more obvious measure of this influence (how many essays seem now to begin with an anecdote!); but detraction, no less than imitation, is a sincere form of flattery. You do not argue with critics whose work fails to impinge on and energize your own; you ignore them. Between Greenblatt-bashing and Greenblatt-cloning, then, we are dealing with a magnitude of critical power it would be hard to exaggerate.

In a piece written to introduce the publication in 1990 of a collection of his essays, Greenblatt himself provides, though indirectly, the best ways to account for this power: exemplarity and narrativity. Exemplarity is where he begins. After describing "the trajectory" of his professional career, from W. K. Wimsatt and formalism to Raymond Williams and cultural materialism, he comments that "I recount this personal history precisely because it is not entirely personal—I was participating in a more general tendency, a shift away from a criticism centered on 'verbal icons' toward a criticism centered on cultural artifacts" (*Learning to Curse*, 3). But Greenblatt's point is not to consign formalism to oblivion; on the contrary, historical continuity has always been a strong motivating factor in his criticism, as in the opening words of *Shakespearean Negotiations*: "I began with the desire to speak with the dead" (1). For all of his adventurous forays into the materialist domains of sociology and cultural anthropology, Greenblatt continues to devote himself with obvious delight to the leisurely exploration of verbal intricacy—"close reading," as it used to be called. This admixture of new and old critical practices, corresponding to the combination of "resonance" and "wonder" he writes about in the final chapter of *Learning to Curse*, is at the heart of Greenblatt's exemplarity. To be sure, plenty of contemporary critics think that Wimsatt (if they have read him) *should* be buried in the historical dustbin, and that the affectionate lavishing of hermeneutic energy on the pleasurable details of texts is a great leap backward. There are also plenty of critics around who continue to work out of Wimsatt (though they may not have read him either) as if nothing had changed since the New Criticism, or that the changes are all adulterations. But whatever the beliefs of particular critics, criticism is a social practice, and an individual's critical practice cannot be sustained apart from its context—the shared space that is at present a fiercely contested and fragmented space as well. Greenblatt's criticism can make us see in our own work contradictions that we may not have recognized—a capacity not just exemplary but uncanny. No wonder he provokes so much resistance.

But exemplarity does not by itself account for Greenblatt's importance. If we see his preeminence as exclusively historical or situational—if we claim, in the toughest-minded version, that his worth has been created by the market forces that confer value on academic commodities—then the question remains, Why Greenblatt? The short answer is that he is good, a brilliantly interesting and persuasive critic. Yet this kind of panegyric simply exalts Greenblatt to the level of inexplicable genius—exactly the kind of celebratory criticism he has resisted as a "secular theodicy" (*Learning to Curse*, 168). The further question is, What makes him so good, or why do so many critics find that Greenblatt represents (or does violence to) their own deepest concerns? It is here, I think, that narrativity comes in.

At the beginning of *Learning to Curse*, Greenblatt sketches an argument about "story-telling" (5–9) that helps to clarify his long-standing interest in the subject of "narrative self-fashioning."[10] The term "stories" obviously covers a multitude of phenomena. Stories differ in rhetorical situation (hearing and reading, telling and writing); serve different generic and social purposes, from the tales our parents tell us as children to the complex narratives of literary criticism and historical explanation; and are governed by a variety of evidentiary protocols (including, in the case of fairy tales, the apparent, but only apparent, absence of such protocols). Nonetheless, Greenblatt wants to show that these various kinds of narrative activity have a common objective: to enable us to understand ourselves and the world.

Greenblatt's ideas about narrative, though not astoundingly original, are nonetheless useful in suggesting the sources of his practical power as a critic. Loving to tell and hear stories is no doubt part of it, but so is Greenblatt's own magisterial narrative disposition. He is a masterful storyteller in two ways. Given the range of his knowledge, he has an abundantly rich repertoire on which to draw. Given his extraordinary intelligence, he is capable of organizing these diverse materials into explanatory structures of rare interest and power. Greenblatt in the magisterial mode is stunningly impressive. Maybe too impressive at times, the gist of my complaint in "The New Historicism and Its Discontents" about "mastering the text": the diverse components of his narratives seem occasionally to be the victims of a relentless will to explanatory power. I find it hard to recognize Spenser's Giant or Shakespeare's Jack Cade once Greenblatt has whipped them into shape behind other murdered peasants (*Learning to Curse*, 99–130), gathered together for a triumphantly conclusive examination rather like the suspects at the end of that most hermeneutically determined of narratives, the whodunit. Similarly in "Psychoanalysis and Renaissance Culture" (*Learning to Curse*, 131–45), the controlling structure of contrast (only inchoate notions of inner selves in the Renaissance versus fully developed ones in Freud) allows—perhaps even requires—Greenblatt to ignore not only the depth of commitment to authentic interior selfhood in so many Renaissance texts, but also the pragmatist construction of Freudian identity upon contingency.[11]

In his autobiographical narratives a similar desire for closure occasionally impels Greenblatt to theatrical revelations and transformations that strain credulity. A near nervous breakdown magically resolves itself: "When the voice left me, it did so suddenly, inexplicably, with the sound of something snapping" (8). A disgruntled student interrupts one of Greenblatt's regular courses in "Marxist Aesthetics" ("You're either a Bolshevik or a Menshevik—

make up your fucking mind"), and the teacher is reborn in Victor Turner: "After that I started to teach courses with names like 'Cultural Poetics'" (147). Such sudden conversions have been central to the way we experience and organize self-understanding since St. Paul on the road to Damascus and St. Augustine in the garden (*"tolle, lege"*), so this may be "what really happened"; but narratives have their own rhetorical constraints (the evidentiary protocols I mentioned earlier), and such stories in Greenblatt may be too true to be good.

If narrative is a means to understanding, then Greenblatt's achievement of mastery can hardly be a fault. Like most good writers, Greenblatt is more than half in love with monuments to his own intellect; like Iago (himself a great storyteller), Greenblatt "hates the slime / That sticks on filthy deeds" (*Othello*, V.ii.148–49). Moreover, it has become clear that Greenblatt has a contradictory narrative mode as well, one that chooses filth as a subject and tolerates, even celebrates, what he calls "the slime of history" ("Shakespeare and the Exorcists," 101), its unmasterable strangeness, a contingency that resists all of our best efforts to shape and understand.[12] The consequences for his explanatory disposition are unpredictable reversals and redirections in which the sheer recalcitrance of the historical and textual materials seems to defeat the attempt to impose meaningful sequence. The essay "Marlowe, Marx, and Anti-Semitism" (reprinted in *Learning to Curse*) is one example. Greenblatt is proceeding relentlessly in a demonstration of Barabas's perversity when the argument careens unexpectedly into a thrilled responsiveness to the sheer playfulness of Marlowe's protagonist. Frank Kermode points to another example, in the title essay of *Learning to Curse*, and remarks appreciatively about the way Greenblatt characteristically lets the reader "consider the evidence for a different view: he is unlikely ever to go in for simplicities that belie or distort the facts, for what he most enjoys is intellectual movement—negotiations, circulations and contradictions are proper to his kind of argument" ("Hail to the Chief"). Kermode is right to suggest that this collapse of argument is actually a "kind of argument"; Greenblatt's reversals may well be a conscious rhetorical strategy. Yet the effect of this strategy, far from celebrating the author's freedom and control, is quite the reverse: we are the products of history as well as its producers; our stories write us.

This is true of the personal as well as the historical anecdotes gathered together in *Learning to Curse*. The book opens with such an anecdote (of course): the young Greenblatt as a graduate student in the Elizabethan Club at Yale. The evident point of the story is Greenblatt's rejection of formalism, represented as a snobbish elitism. The Elizabethan Club is "all-male, a black servant in a starched white jacket, cucumber sandwiches and tea" (1). In view of Greenblatt's absorption in colonialism, we can detect in the conspicuous detail of the servant a resonance of Forster's memorable fan operator in the trial scene of *A Passage to India*: the cucumber sandwich wallah. But the elitism is conveyed first of all in religious rather than social or racial terms, Wimsatt as the high priest presiding over "the hierophantic service to the mystery cult" (1). The religious language may suggest a connection to Greenblatt's namesake in Joyce's *Portrait*, Stephen Dedalus, whose story, perhaps more than anyone else's, figures the shape of modern autobiography as apostasy. "Non serviam"; Greenblatt, too, will not serve. So off he goes cunningly into exile, where Raymond Williams converts him to materialism and he grows up to invent new historicism and live happily ever after.

But this saga of heroic freedom is not allowed to last long, if indeed it is allowed to exist in such a clear shape at all. For one thing, readers will come to it knowing how frequently Greenblatt's anecdotes, including the notable epilogue to *Renaissance Self-Fashioning*, describe and embody constraint rather than freedom. The character Greenblatt is more picaresque than epic: he doesn't make things happen; things happen to him. In this context, contradictory subtextual resonances emerge in the story of Stephen and the Elizabethan Club. It turns out that Greenblatt has already studied with Williams (so why has he gone backward?), and his freedom "to resist" the "mystery cult" of formalism is complicated by a counterwill that seems to make absolute freedom something of an illusion: "I briefly entertained a notion of going on to write a dissertation on uncertainty—to make a virtue of my own inner necessity" (1; this would be like Joyce's Stephen converting to Protestantism). And most important, this opening anecdote quickly bleeds into others. We regress with the child Stephen, his identity confirmed by maternal narratives, but also fragmented by a nasty doppelgänger, "Terrible Stanley, a child whom I superficially resembled but who made a series of disastrous life decisions" (6). This in turn regresses into a story about Stephen's father, Harry J. Greenblatt, and *his* secret sharer, an actual cousin called J. Harry Greenblatt, a crook with whom Harry J. becomes confused in the minds of friends as well as the public.

At this point we may well wonder what happened to the heroic freedom from which we seemed to start. As with his Joycean namesake, subsequent narratives seem to bring not freedom but an ambiguously fraudulent father, as well as anxiety and entrapment. "History," says Stephen in *Ulysses*, "is a nightmare from which I am trying to awake" (35). Stephen's declaration seems to echo, perhaps unconsciously (but it is the decisive relevance of conscious intentionality that is precisely up for grabs here), the statement of Marx's I cited at the end of the last chapter: "The tradition of all the dead generations weighs like a nightmare on the brain of the living" (*Eighteenth Brumaire*, 15). In this context the story of Stephen in the Elizabethan Club has begun to assume a very different meaning—not his heroic self-fashioning (like Coriolanus: "I banish you") but his exclusion as a fraud from the inner circle. Stephen does not have the right stuff for this elite.

And here again the religious connection comes in. The Jewish resonances in these anecdotes have been steadily accumulating in density—through the names and the social details (the near-collapse Stephen suffers in graduate school hinges on the decision whether to be a lawyer like his father)—and by the end of the "story-telling" section, the author himself (as it were) seems to have heard his own Jewish resonances and makes a passing remark about "the presence in my father's stories (and speech rhythms and perceptions of the world) of the Yiddish humor of the stetl" (8–9). Greenblatt confesses to an interest in the way this humor is "adapted to very different American circumstances, as . . . , say, in Woody Allen," but he declines to follow this line of thought because "it would be of interest principally to myself" (9). This is disingenuous, like telling us not to think about pink elephants. After all, whose voice are we hearing now, if not that of Harry J.'s son (like father, like son, even if Stephen J. did not choose to be a lawyer)? Or, "say, Woody Allen," who liked to repeat the typically Jewish joke associated with his spiritual (and fraudulent) father, Groucho Marx: "I wouldn't join any club that allowed me to become a member."

Is this now the meaning for the story of Stephen and the Elizabethan Club—not a saga of heroic freedom but an anecdote of ironically proud self-contempt? If so, it is not the final meaning; good stories do not have final meanings. (Neither does history, a point made by Greenblatt's mentor, Raymond Williams [*Marxism and Literature*, 128]). Like David Copperfield on the first page of the "personal history" that bears his name, Greenblatt cannot be sure whether he will "turn out to be the hero of my own life." Such determinations are always deferred to a future beyond any individual's capacity to control: "these pages must show." The Jewish question keeps returning in the pages of *Learning to Curse*, in the Marx-Marlowe essay, and at the end when, in an unassertive (and perhaps unintentional) da capo, Greenblatt tells of a visit to the State Jewish Museum in Prague (173–75; the Holocaust was of course a final solution for millions of Jews, but not for the Jewish Question). Here too, though within a very different tonal register, Greenblatt represents himself as both an insider and an outsider, chosen and excluded, masterful and perplexed.

This combination of lordship and bondage is wonderfully engaging. As the Hegel allusion may suggest, it can be called a dialectical style or a syncretic or sloppy one, depending on your point of view. My point is not (or not just) to celebrate the author's narrative genius, for as Foucault, another of Greenblatt's mentors, says, we are better off trading in the author question for an audience question: "What are the places in [this discourse] where there is room for possible subjects? Who can assume these various subject-functions" ("What Is an Author?" 160)?

There is a lot of room in Greenblatt's writing for different kinds of readers. Even those of us for whom the phrase "subject-function" is apt to induce something like Lucky Jim's "crazy-peasant face" can find a place to inhabit in this interesting, engaging, and irritating criticism. I have been emphasizing the unlordly Greenblatt—the voice of estranged admiration rather than of appropriation and possession. This is the voice that Greenblatt himself has been emphasizing in his most recent work: an "experience of wonder" that "seems to resist recuperation, containment, ideological incorporation," an experience both "strangely apart . . . and yet utterly compelling" (*Marvelous Possessions*, 17). But the magisterial Greenblatt is equally important; after all, despite its qualifications and contradictions, the opening anecdote turns out to celebrate just what it seemed to be at first glance: the freedom to fashion more interesting histories. Greenblatt did escape from the elegant but parochial and (by the time of his visit in the 1960s) exhausted culture of the Elizabethan Club; in his writing, and perhaps even more in his editorship of *Representations*, he has brought others out with him.

Greenblatt's critical narratives are "edifying" in Rorty's sense; they serve to build things, including the critical narratives of other people. The number of other works that Greenblatt's work has generated is prodigious. Much of this other work has been based on the rich variety of interesting material and powerful interpretation Greenblatt has given us; but even the negative responses, the arguments and the angry attacks, show Greenblatt to be not just witty in himself but, like Falstaff, the figure he so unaccountably elides in his discussion of Shakespeare's histories, the cause of wit in other people.

❖ 3 ❖

Of Ants and Grasshoppers:
Two Ways (or More)
to Link Texts and Power

*C**anada est omnis divisa in partes duo:* all Canada is divided into
two parts. We used to have Upper and Lower Canada but,
with the settling of the plains beyond Ontario, this division is now
expressed as East and West. There is also North and South and
lots of divisions not based on geography: a political division
between the provincial and federal governments; an economic
one between the have and have-not provinces; a sectorial one
between industrial regions and agricultural; a linguistic and cultural one between English and French. These divisions are divisive. Eastern and Western Canada don't like each other and so on
down the line to French and English Canada. Canadians like to
say that as a result of all their differences Canada is ungovernable,
but all nation-states are ungovernable—abstractions into which an
enormous variety of meaning is overloaded. These differences,

moreover, can be seen less as a resistance to government than as a form of government, since they give shape to something. After all, how can you divide something unless you can first of all conceive of the thing to be divided? These divisions, then, do not represent something that is already there; they constitute that something in the sense of packaging it in a way that allows us to see it; and what these divisions shape or package—namely, all of Canada—would be hard to see *except* for the packaging.

Maybe I can make this point clearer if I switch from Canadiana to Americana. At the end of his book, Huck Finn reckons he has "got to light out for the Territory." The Territory is empty space; it can be defined only negatively. It is the place where there is no Aunt Polly trying "to adopt me and sivilize me"—that is, no social constraints, no legal fictions; and no Tom Sawyer who had "his bullet around his neck on a watch-guard for a watch, and is always seeing what time it is"—that is, no history, no hypocrisy, no scars, no guilt. The freedom of this Territory is pure negativity; it is no place, Utopia. Gertrude Stein's phrase is truer about the Territory than it is about Oakland: "There's no there there."

If Huck heads due west in search of the Territory, we can place him in Oklahoma, Rodgers-and-Hammerstein style: "Territory folks should stick together, / Territory folks should all be pals / Cowboys dance with the farmers' daughters, / Farmers dance with the ranchers' gals." There is an appeal here to a transcendental ideal, shared existence in the Territory, but the Territory no longer exists. A new discursive Territory has been summoned into existence by virtue of the farmers and the ranchers. These two parts constitute the Territory, but since all the Territory is divided into two parts, they also threaten to break up the entity they have served to construct. The farmers want to build fences and grow cash crops, the ranchers want to keep the range open for cattle to graze so they can sell beef. The Territory has become land, property. Utopia has become filled with the topics of invention. Empty space has become a place and a place of contestation. However this dispute was settled, we may be sure it involved coercion. Moreover, any resolution between farmers and ranchers was bound to be only temporary, because it failed to resolve or even acknowledge another kind of difference. No one bothered to ask the ranchers' daughters and the farmers' gals how they felt about such arrangements. We never even asked them whether they wanted to dance.

Though it is hard to say what the Territory or Canada is as a God- or nature-given fact, it is easy to say that both are words. If I say *only* words, though, I am reproducing the metaphysical ideas I have been trying to dispute. The thing about words is that they have real power; they can be used to regulate human behavior; in fact, they are the best way to do so. The word "Canada" can be used to regulate quite a lot of behavior: more than "dog" or "Uruguay," less than "reason," "Lenin," or "the United States." People sometimes say dismissively that a particular dispute is "*only* semantic," but all disputes seem to go back to different claims about the meanings of words and seem to be resolved—at least temporarily—by means of the same kinds of claims.

According to Coleridge, "Every man is born an Aristotelian or a Platonist. I do not think it is possible that any one born an Aristotelian can become a Platonist; and I am sure no born Platonist can ever change into an Aristotelian. They are two classes of men, beside which it is next to impossible to conceive a third" (463). In other words, all critical activity is divided into two parts. In this context it should come as no surprise if I assert that the field of interpretation and power, as I see it, is both made up of and contested by two exemplary claims upon our belief. In one, interpretation is understood to be a tightly controlled activity, governed by the powerful institutions of collective life; and as serious, responsible critics we should be focusing on these institutions, seeing how they work, how they work on us, how we can change them. In the other view, interpretation is located in the power of the text or rather in a random responsiveness that allows texts to turn into experiences of energy, freedom, and pleasure. I will call the holders of these two exemplary positions the ants and the grasshoppers. I do not pretend to be describing ants and grasshoppers from a position above the battle. I am a grasshopper advocate because I think that grasshopper claims are good ones and deserve better representation than they tend to get these days. But beyond such advocacy, I want to consider at least a bit at the end whether this division is a good one, whether it enhances our projects more than it blocks them, whether other stories, potentially more useful, might be available.

⬧

First the ants. Consider the case of Lenny Bruce, a comic who made a career of transgression; he acknowledges as much in the title of his autobiography, *How to Talk Dirty and Influence People*. By talking dirty, Lenny Bruce not only influenced people, he got in trouble with the law. He was repeatedly charged with various legal offenses, all of which added up to talking dirty. As his law cases multiplied and dragged on, dirty Lenny, as he called himself, became obsessed with the law, and this obsession changed his act. In his last years his nightclub performances harped on his legal situation. He entertained audiences with the history of his arrests and court battles, sometimes reading from the legal transcripts: "On the aforementioned occasion, the said Mr. Bruce did twice use the word _____, and four times the word ____." The only time I saw Lenny Bruce, shortly before his death, he had already been obsessed with the law for years, and the performance of the history of his arrests had itself acquired a narrative history with meaning and consequences, which he described to us: after reading from the official transcripts in his act, he would be arrested and charged again for saying the same dirty words, even though these words were part of the transcript. How, dirty Lenny wondered, could it be illegal to read a legal document?

This question gets us to the center of interpretation and power. First of all, interpretation is contextualization. Texts look different, mean different things, in contexts. Lenny Bruce used this point repeatedly in his defenses. The dirty word that got him in trouble when he uttered it in a nightclub performance is clean in the mouth of a peace officer in a police station. But this is where power comes in. If the interpretive act of determining a context is what gives shape and meaning to the text, then who has the power to determine the context? By his statement that he was quoting a legal document as part of a legal argument, Dirty Lenny was claiming the right to establish a certain context for his speech. But his claim had no force in confrontation with the entrenched, institutionalized power of the police and their claim that he was trying to talk dirty and influence people.

We can expand on this point with reference to someone else who talked dirty and influenced people, Christopher Marlowe. In the Baines document, Marlowe skeptically analyzes religion as pie in the sky, a purely human institution invented as a means to social control: "Moyses made the Jewes to travell xl yeares in the wildernes, (*whi*ch Jorney might haue bin done in lesse then one yeare) . . . to thintent that those who were privy to most of his subtilties might perish and so an everlasting superstition Remain in the hartes of the people. . . . the first beginning of Religioun was only to keep men in awe" (MacLure, 37).[1] It is easy to connect this sort of thing with the plays. "I think hell's a fable," says Doctor Faustus, "trifles and mere old wives' tales." "But," says Mephistophilis, "I am an instance to prove the contrary, / For I tell thee I am damn'd, and now in hell" (scene v). But is he—*really*? Isn't he an actor, performing in a theatrical fable? Just how do we interpret this exchange; that is, what is the context?

If religion is the controlling context, then this exchange centers on a moral choice with real consequences—salvation or damnation. But then, maybe theater is the controlling context, religion a form of theater. This is just what the Baines document says: "That if there be any god or any good Religion, then it is in the papistes because the service of god is performed *wi*th more Cerimonies, as Elevation of the mass, organs, singing men, Shaven Crownes & cta" (MacLure, 37). From this perspective, the exchange between Faustus and Mephistophilis has no consequences. Plays are play, free play; the price of admission is the only one exacted. A lot of *Doctor*

Faustus can be seen in this context—the whole clown plot and much of the Faustus plot itself. Heads are cut off but they are only false heads; Faustus's leg is pulled off but it grows back. Faustus is only "slain-unslain," to use Kenneth Burke's phrase about Cinna the Poet in *Julius Caesar*, "like a clown hit by cannon balls" (*Philosophy of Literary Form*, 343). In the theater nobody dies.

This sort of argument—that theatrical performance has a special status outside the normalizing sanctions of cultural power—is one that occurred to Lenny Bruce, who noted that an amendment was added to the statute under which he was charged "which *excludes from arrest* stagehands, spectators, musicians and *actors*" (195). But dirty Lenny never got anywhere with this argument, and a seventeenth-century story about a production of *Doctor Faustus* suggests it won't work with Marlowe's play either:

> Certaine Players at Exeter, acting upon the stage the tragical storie of Dr. Faustus the Conjurer; as a certain number of Devels kept everie one his circle there, and as Faustus was busie in his magicall invocations, on a sudden they were all dasht, every one harkning other in the eare, for they were all perswaded, there was one devell too many amongst them; and so after a little pause desired the people to pardon them, they could go no further with this matter; the people also understanding the thing as it was, every man hastened to be first out of dores. The players (as I heard it) contrarye to their custome spending the night in reading and in prayer got them out of town the next morning. (Chambers, 424)

The "magicall invocations" must be Faustus's Latin speech in the third scene of the play, abjuring Jehovah and summoning Mephistophilis. These are perhaps the dirtiest words imaginable in Marlowe's culture, and though they are uttered in the play, they are not sanitized by that context, for the presumably free space of theatrical representation is seen to be occupied by a real devil—real in its power to effect belief, to suspend any temporary suspension of disbelief.

Like Lenny Bruce's bust for quoting a legal document, the extra devil at *Doctor Faustus* suggests the controlling power of cultural institutions in determining the context and therefore interpreting the text. The stories, though, are not the same. It would be easy to understand the Lenny Bruce story as a conflict between the heroically transgressive individual and the repressive forces of the state. But the *Faustus* story seems to be something less simple and less flattering since the extra devil is observed by the actors themselves. The devil invades their own consciousness and conscience, which turn out to be no more free than the physical space of theatrical representation. "The individual," Michel Foucault says, is "not the *vis-à-vis* of power; it is . . . one of its prime effects" (*Power/Knowledge*, 98). "The individual," Morse Peckham tells us, is "a mere cultural precipitate" (xviii). And so it seems with the individual actors at Exeter. They have internalized the official version of cultural authority. Convinced into feeling their own guilt, they cooperate in their own conviction.

But let us leave them for the moment and with them the interpretive ants, presumably hard at work contemplating those powerful institutions that shape and constrain all discursive possibility; let us consider instead how things might look from the grasshopper's point of view. Here is a grasshopper story about a man called Orazio Busino. Busino, who served as a chaplain to the Venetian ambassador in London in the early seventeenth century, kept a kind of diary, and in his entry for 7 February 1618 he refers to a theatrical performance apparently of Webster's *Duchess of Malfi*.[2] Although the entry is too confused to tell us much about the production practices of Jacobean public drama, it does tell us a good deal about the interpretive activity of Jacobean audiences—or at least about Busino's interpretive activity in a theater on 7 February 1618.

What it tells us seems at first perfectly consistent with the Bruce and Marlowe stories. Busino comes to the theater as a Catholic with connections to the Venetian ruling class. From this culturally derived perspective, the first thing Busino sees is that "the English scoff at our religion," and he experiences theater within this context: "They never put on any public show whatever, be it tragedy or satire or comedy, into which they do not insert some Catholic churchman's vices and wickednesses, making mock and scorn of him, according to their taste, but to the dismay of good men." This same position is reaffirmed at the end of the entry: "All this was acted in condemnation of the . . . church, which they despise . . . in this kingdom." Everything in the middle, then, is merely example and could have been drawn as well from other, nontheatrical sources—a royal decree, an anti-Spanish uprising of London apprentices, whatever. From this subjective space, plays are seen as political moves, strategic deployments in the power struggles of seventeenth-century Europe. Theater itself, as we might put it, doesn't seem to exist for Busino. Neither does genre as a purely formal category. Though Busino mentions genre right at the beginning, "be it tragedy or satire or comedy," his point is merely that antipapal feeling is all-pervasive and comes in plays of all kinds. He might as well have said: "be it at the Whitefriars or the Swan or the Red Bull." Genre as such isn't important to him. A literary or theatrical response as such, as we might put it, doesn't seem to exist for Busino any more than literature or theater itself.

According to Stephen Greenblatt, such responses *couldn't* have existed; they were historically impossible. For the early modern period, Greenblatt tells us, "art does not pretend to autonomy; the written word is self-consciously embedded in specific communities, life situations, structures of power" (*Renaissance Self-Fashioning*, 7). But in the long middle of Busino's diary entry things happen that should make us question such an assertion. We hear, for instance, about "a Franciscan friar [who] was seen by some of our countrymen introduced into a comedy as a wily character . . . , as given over to avarice as to lust. And the whole thing turned out to be a tragedy, for he had his head cut off on open stage." If Busino's point is merely that it is not nice to make fun of good men like Franciscan friars, then why the details about the decapitation that made the whole thing turn out to be a tragedy? He seems to have shifted ground. From saying it is not right to show nasty friars, he says it is not decorous to mix genres, to turn comedy into tragedy. For a moment Busino reveals a surprising formalist side. Not that this contradicts Busino's subject position with relation to the structures of power. Educated Italians read Scaliger and liked to keep their genres separate. Nonetheless, as the passage goes on, Busino floods us with theatrical impressions—of the cardinal, for instance, represented "in all his grandeur, . . . splendid and rich, . . . organizing a procession"—where the relation to genre or to religious and national allegiance is impossible to specify. Busino seems to have become absorbed in the spectacle of the performance in a way that is now independent of his original point of view. And finally this independence—this autonomy—seems absolute: "Moreover, [the cardinal] goes to war, first laying down his cardinal's habit on the altar, with the help of his chaplains, with great ceremoniousness; finally he has his sword bound on and dons the soldier's sash with so much panache you could not imagine it better done." Busino is not here objecting to the cardinal's transformation as a kind of anti-Catholic slur, nor is he approving of it as an embodiment of the Church Militant. Rather, the transformation— this quintessentially theatrical action: donning new garments and finding a new mode of being in the world—seems to have become the object of Busino's delighted attention for its own sake: "with so much panache you could not imagine it better done."

This delight lasts only a moment. In the last sentence Busino remembers his point or indeed remembers himself, an Italian Catholic chaplain in an English public theater, a stranger in a strange land. But for that moment, those features ceased to matter; he forgot them, just as Christopher Sly forgot about Burton-heath and Marian Hacket, the fat ale-wife of Wincot, all those papers and badges and labels of culturally derived identity, when he finally yielded to the power of theatrical illusion at the beginning of *The Taming of the Shrew*. In this moment, Busino becomes not only rapt in the pleasures of beholding transformation but absorbed in the experience of it. He becomes, in other words, a member of a the-

95

atrical audience. Invoking the power structures seems wrong-headed here. Peter Quince's astonished cry about Bottom serves as a better gloss for the condition of being a theatrical audience: Bless thee, Busino, bless thee! Thou art translated.

⚜

Now pretty clearly these stories seem to lead us to contradictory conclusions—or rather, I have led them there.[3] The Busino story suggests that the interpreting subject, far from being a precipitate of culture, can find space outside the ideological network, a position from which in this case the Catholic-Protestant division doesn't seem to exist. Further, the Busino story seems to offer a different direction for interpretive activity. Instead of fixing response onto the political institutions that are claimed to generate it, we are free to play with the text as a set of impressions that can lead anywhere. The interpreter is now a sovereign autonomous consumer in a free interpretive market, endowed with the inalienable right to pursue happiness, the pleasure of the text. It seems as if we have come upon mutually exclusive concepts of interpretation and power, between which we have to choose. What I wish to argue, however, is that they are not mutually exclusive and that the choice is unnecessary.

Consider first the question of sovereignty vs. cultural determination. Busino's response may seem culturally undetermined, but only because *we* have determined culture in an unnecessarily coherent way. I grew up with the idea of Renaissance culture as a monological structure called The Elizabethan World Picture. We have since moved to more complex, duological models that enable us to understand the Renaissance as more actively political, as including conflict and contestation. Hence the religious schism allows us to consider Catholic-vs.-Protestant as one possible candidate for a master theme of the early modern period. But the Busino story suggests ways in which Catholic-vs.-Protestant is not a master theme; lots of other Renaissance interpreters escaped from its domination as well, the most notable being Montaigne, and

some of these others into a theatrical or a quasi-theatrical space.[4]
We could then hunt out a new and improved master theme in
other divisions: power vs. transgression, authority vs. subordination—these are the leading candidates. They will work but only for
some of the people and only some of the time. Like "Canada," "culture" is a word, and the divisions that constitute this word, that
make it present to the understanding, are bound to be unstable,
and will always look arbitrary and incomplete from some positions.

One move here is to go beyond such divisions, from duology to
trilogy. Dividing into *three* parts is unconventional, potentially
even transgressive, crossing a conceptual Rubicon. It is a dirty
move that influences people's way of thinking, or it could; but in
the proposed trilogies I have seen, this innovative potential has
not been realized. Consider Raymond Williams's analysis of culture in terms of "residual, dominant, and emergent" elements
(*Marxism*, 121–27). These terms clearly correspond to past, present, and future. Expanded considerably by Fredric Jameson, this
correspondence is even clearer:

> Every social formation or historically existing society has in fact
> consisted in the overlay and structural coexistence of *several* modes
> of production all at once, including vestiges and survivals of older
> modes of production, now relegated to structurally dependent
> positions within the new, as well as anticipatory tendencies which
> are potentially inconsistent with the existing system but have not
> yet generated an autonomous space of their own. (95)

This is the Big Picture—"that large discourse," as Hamlet called it,
"looking before and after"; the historical narrative, whose three
parts are beginning, middle, and end. However, since it is the
interconnection among these three parts that gives the historical
narrative its explanatory power, they must be seen as parts of a
whole, a totality radiating from a center. You can call the center
"the godlike capability of reason," "the material mode of production," or whatever you want, but the thing about centers—as we've

learned these past twenty years—is that they can always be shown to be arbitrary, and the structures of thought built upon them can always be deconstructed.

This is not to say we should stop writing historical narratives, for what else is there? But the question is, how do we write them? For example: if we say that "art does not pretend to autonomy" in the Renaissance, we are saying something about Renaissance culture in the form of a narrative beginning. The middle of this narrative, Chapter 2, is Romanticism: imagination, stories floating randomly above power structures, responses generated out of a willing suspension of disbelief, the free play of the cognitive faculties for their own sake or for pleasure. It is no doubt fair to say that the Romantics invented Romanticism but only in the sense of combining a bunch of assumptions and beliefs in a way that made them into a newly visible subject. But if you say that the Busino story is impossible because it belongs in Chapter 1, then you are making a fetish out of your own narrative structure—blinding yourself not only to Busino's evidence but to other evidence of contemporary response to Webster, and to Renaissance theater in general, which suggests the same thing.

Consider first Samuel Sheppard, who, writing about *The White Devil* in a book published in 1651, goes on at length about the "prettiness" of Webster's lines and then the "liveliness" of his "persons":

> Brachiano's ill—
> Murdering his Duchess hath by thy rare skill
> Made him renowned, Flamineo such another—
> The Devil's darling, murderer of his brother.
> His part—most strange!—given him to act by thee
> Doth gain him credit and not calumny. (Hunter and Hunter, 36)

In other words, the aesthetic effect overpowers the ethical or ideological. This is very close to Keats's famous comment about the chameleon poet, delighting as much in creating Iago as Imogen.

Even Henry Fitzjeffrey's 1617 attack on "crabbed Websterio" (Hunter and Hunter, 30–31) is remarkable for the same aesthetic emphasis, the point being that Webster's difficult style called too much attention to its own labors to be successful. Nor should we consider these responses to Webster as unique or exceptional. As Paul Yachnin has argued, there is a lot of strong historical evidence for the claim that practitioners of Renaissance theater in general, far from being embedded in the structures of power, carefully negotiated a space for themselves that was "separate from the operations of power" (50). My point, again, is not to call a moratorium on the writing of history, or to deny the real differences between the Renaissance and ourselves, but to insist on the continuities that exist within the discontinuities. We should write our historical narratives with some measure of respect for Jean-Luc Godard's statement that, yes, of course he believed in beginnings and middles and ends—but not necessarily in that order (William Pechter, 246).

What about Chapter 3, though, the ending? In the ants' version of critical history, we awaken from the sleep of Romanticism, put away grasshopperish things, and return to a Renaissance sense of the embeddedness of texts in the specific power relations. There may be other versions of the Renaissance and Romanticism, but let's forget about the earlier chapters. The end crowns all. The end is a plan for the future, the expression of desire in the form of historical analysis. It answers the question, What is the function of criticism at the present time? And the answer according to ants is antism. If we interpret like ants, we have our best chance to live happily ever after.

Ant advocacy starts with the notion that all activity is purposive, with consequences in and for the world. Critical activity is therefore political activity and interpretation is power or a bid for power. From this position, ants argue against indulging in the pleasures of a text disembodied from its political matrix. In the name of free play, such grasshopper activity actually performs cultural work—namely, the diversion of energy from the political tasks at hand. In the name of an illusory free space outside the political, it disguises its own politics, which turn out to be conservative or reactionary.

Once again we are faced with an apparently absolute contradiction between the two exemplary positions I have been concerned with here. Once again I want to argue that they need not be seen as mutually exclusive, that you can start by accepting all antian assumptions about the political nature of interpretive activity (as I think we should) and nonetheless wind up at home among the grasshoppers.

Let us go back to Busino or to the play he apparently witnessed. *The Duchess of Malfi* is about male power and female transgression. By marrying her steward, Antonio, the Duchess violates the hierarchy of class, but gender difference seems to be the main code here. She disobeys the commands of her brothers not to remarry, and she initiates the wooing with Antonio—plays the man's part, as the play emphasizes. This wooing scene is full of great tenderness but also highly charged with an erotic and anxious sense of risk. "Wish me good speed," says the Duchess in the words that set up the scene, "For I am going into a wilderness / Where I shall find nor path, nor friendly clew / To be my guide" (I.1.358–61). We have to wait until the middle of the play to discover what it is the Duchess discovers on her dangerous journey, for it is not until then that the Duchess and Antonio are placed before us again in a domestic context. The scene (III.2) is one of quiet and relaxed intimacy. The Duchess brushes her hair, and they talk—or better, chat. In their casual and affectionate banter, the play systematically parades before us the topics of the wooing scene. All has changed; the anxiety is gone, any hint of the perverse; only the tenderness remains in the continued sexual delight the Duchess and Antonio take in each other, apparently unabated over the years. As a whole the scene is suffused with a sense of fulfilled desire. "I prithee," says the Duchess, "When were we so merry?—my hair tangles."

All that is left to complete what for us is a very familiar picture is the children. Children have been part of this picture since the wooing scene, in Antonio's answer to the Duchess's question how he feels about marriage:

> Say a man never marry, nor have children,
> What takes that from him? only the bare name
> Of being a father, or the weak delight
> To see the little wanton ride a-cock-horse
> Upon a painted stick, or hear him chatter
> Like a taught starling. (398–403)

This is a man who wants children and in a way that apparently has little to do with inheritance or property or power. The Duchess seems to hear in this speech an echo of her own desire for children and a confirmation of her desire for him: her response is to give him her ring, a gesture from which there is no turning back. The children are often on stage during the play, never far from their thoughts, and indeed they appear in this middle scene, at least verbally, in the Duchess's playful "I'll assure you / You shall get no more children" (66–67).

We can use Lawrence Stone's rubrics to describe this scene: The Closed Domesticated Nuclear Family, The Companionate Marriage, Child Rearing in the Affectionate Mode. The scene may appear not only familiar to us but too familiar, like Rodgers and Hammerstein again, this time *Carousel*: "When the children are asleep we'll sit and dream / The things that ev'ry other / Dad and mother / Dream." But to Webster's audience, as Frank Whigham (173) and Susan Wells (64) point out, the scene must have looked not old hat but newfangled. Stone applies those rubrics to the period 1640–1800. Obviously dates are not exact, but the example of Shakespeare leads to the same conclusion. There is nothing like this scene in Shakespeare. Marriage is an end in Shakespeare, a generic closure beyond which the plays do not really seem interested in looking. It is a social and economic arrangement, no more (and no less). Children sometimes appear in Shakespeare in a variety of contexts but hardly ever to arouse the strong delight of being a parent. (Maybe Kate and Hotspur are an exceptional couple, Leontes and Mamilius an exceptional parent and child, but the rarity of such exceptions is my point.) Sometimes this absence in Shakespeare is interpreted as evidence of abnormality of some kind, but "gentle" Shakespeare made a career out of seeming to be normal, giving his audiences what they would and giving it to them the way they liked it. It is Webster who shocks, perversely talking dirty.

For many of us, the Nuclear Family is a cultural investment that is no longer paying dividends; we look to divest. Gender politics is a large part of this disaffection, but so is the sense that a retreat from the material life of society is an illusion; we want to go public. Nonetheless, the invention of the Nuclear Family at the end of the seventeenth century looks like a step forward. It offered a mode of existence that was more productive than the residues of an exhausted postfeudalism. Webster's pre-invention of the Nuclear Family might have helped to realize this social change, at least for those who knew how to look for it: audiences willing to follow the performance's energies outside of their own consciously understood ideological agendas: grasshopper audiences.

There are, of course, different approaches to Webster's play. In the old historicism of Tillyard, the official view was that *The Duchess of Malfi* endorsed convention and ceremony, the sustainers of a fragile and valuable civility. By transgressing, the Duchess brought the house down. Lisa Jardine has argued that the cultural work in Webster's play was in the Duchess's torture and death, which served to reassure an anxious patriarchy that strong and independent women would be punished (68–93). Jardine reverses the old historicist polarity; from her point of view, the house should be brought down. This difference is real enough but it exists within a surprisingly shared ground, since in both versions the play is contained within the already understood structure of cultural authority.

If we approach the play this way, like the ants, in terms of specific power relations, a number of things might happen. Our anxieties might be assuaged or maybe intensified, our grievances confirmed or maybe relieved. But these are all the same in a way. Our ideological agendas may lead us to affirm or contest the structure of cultural authority, but so long as we restrict our understanding to the terms of these agendas, we are bound to reproduce the very structure we may wish to contest. Willy-nilly, ant critics replicate the situation; they tell the same old story. On the other hand, we can approach the play in a condition of random responsiveness to the incoherent variety of cultural phenomena that constitute us. This way, we might get anything out of *The Duchess of Malfi*; like its original audiences, if they knew how to look, we might even get a new story.[5]

According to Michael Ignatieff in *The Needs of Strangers*:

> The problem is that our language is not necessarily adequate to our needs. Language which has ceased to express felt needs is empty rhetoric. . . . Our task is to find a language for our need for belonging which is not just a way of expressing nostalgia, fear and estrangement from modernity . . . language adequate to the times we live in. We need to see how we live now and we can only see with words and images which leave us no escape into nostalgia for some other time and place. (137–38, 139, 141)

Ignatieff too wants to see new stories. "It is the painters and writers," he adds, "not the politicians or the social scientists, who have been able to find a language for the joy of modern life, its fleeting and transient solidarity" (141). Maybe, but this sort of argument can lead too easily to a fetishizing of art or the theater or the literary text. It is better to distinguish between categories of response than between categories of text. New stories can exist in any text, so long as we know how to look for them. This is the grasshoppers' way of interpreting, and it is the best source of power to enable social change. The moral is clear, and no socially responsible and serious critic can afford to ignore it: we should interpret like grasshoppers, because grasshoppers make the best ants.

❖

One thing that might happen here is that the ants among us, the scales having fallen from their eyes, will rush to join me on the grasshoppers' side. This will not happen. Though I have managed to contain the ants' arguments, they would now be able to contain mine. It is in the nature of ants to build well-articulated structures of containment. They see as far as the ultimate horizons into which we are all absorbed. They have purpose and seriousness on their side, and these motives have always controlled the language of controversy. As Muriel Bradbrook said about the Renaissance defenders of theater, "On the level of theoretical debate they stood no chance at all. The cards were in their opponent's hands" (*Rise of the Common Player,* 76). Maybe not. Such defenselessness can serve as a defense or even an attack. "We play for advantage, but we play for pleasure too," says Richard Lanham (4–5). Grasshoppers wink slyly at one another: they know the ants are fooling themselves, playing like us, only not having as much fun. Hence the moral at the end of Woody Allen's version of the fable: in winter the grasshopper went to Florida and the ant had chest pains. From here it is only an easy step to the rhetoric of antish high seriousness. We can claim priority—wasn't the rhetorical Gorgias there before the dialectical Plato, perhaps like the matriarchal societies overrun by the Hebrew patriarchs? With Huizinga, we can affirm that "play cannot be denied. You can deny, if you like, nearly all abstractions: justice, truth, goodness, mind, God. You can deny seriousness, but not play" (3).

In the capacity of each side to contain the other, maybe both win—but win what? Presumably the ability to keep the game going, which may be all we can reasonably expect. On the other hand, maybe we could expect more, if we could somehow get out of the structure of opposition that constitutes the game. "In all unimportant matters," according to Oscar Wilde, "style, not sincerity, is the essential. In all important matters," he adds, "style, not sincerity, is the essential" (296). If this were merely grasshopper advocacy, Wilde could have been clearer. He could have said that style, not sincerity, is the essential in both unimportant and important matters. What he does say, however, seems for a moment to collapse the structure of opposition—between style and sincerity, important and unimportant.

Barthes is engaged in a similar project in *The Pleasure of the Text*:

> An entire minor mythology would have us believe that pleasure . . . is a rightist notion. On the right . . . everything abstract, boring, political, is shoved over to the left and pleasure is kept for oneself. . . . And on the left, because of morality (forgetting Marx's and Brecht's cigars), one suspects and disdains any "residue of hedonism." On the right, pleasure is championed *against* intellectuality, the clerisy: the old reactionary myth of heart against head, sensation against reasoning, (warm) "life" against (cold) "abstraction" . . . On the left, knowledge, method, commitment, combat are drawn up against "mere delectation." (22–23)

Barthes proposes a tertium quid that has nothing to do with the oppositions of the first two, "a drift," he calls it, that "does not depend on a logic of understanding and on sensation," something "both revolutionary and asocial." One thing that might happen here is that all of us, grasshoppers *and* ants, might see the light, renounce our errors, and follow Barthes. This will not happen either; in fact it can't, because Barthes isn't going anywhere, he is just drifting. The space to which he points us is, in his word, "atopic"—that is, utopian, the Territory that is not divided into two parts. We cannot get there from here, and maybe we should not even try. For the time being, we have to make do with our "historical contradictions," as Barthes later calls this same mythology of difference (38–39). But as we go on trapped in the repetitions of the same old story, at least we can keep our eyes and our ears open. We will never see a place empty of contradictions but maybe we can see one where the contradictions are surprisingly new—a different mythology of difference. Maybe we can hear a new story.

✤ 4 ✤

Teaching Differences

W HERE I TEACH, the book order forms for fall courses arrive
in the second week of May, just a week after the grade-sub-
mission deadline for spring courses. The timing is particularly
cruel. A week's freedom to imagine projects independent of pedagogy: at last, some writing or esoteric research; putting a new toi-
let in the basement; rooting for the home team at the old ball
game. But all for nothing. The summer's free play is over before it
has begun. Next term's classes require hard decisions, immediate
closures. In this respect teaching is not unlike the situation as
Goneril understands it at the end of the first scene of *King Lear*. In
response to Regan's "we shall further think on't" ("it" being the
threat Lear represents to their new power), the firstborn offers
the harsh rebuke, "We must do something, and i' th' heat."

Of the many hard choices thrust upon us by the book order
form, I am concerned here with the question how we decide to
represent criticism to our students. To get a sense of the problem
we can return to Herbert Weil's statement for the 1990 Shakespeare Association meeting from which I began the first chapter of
this book. In contrast to the past when the one-volume anthology

seemed to fulfill our needs, at present "the abundance of criticism might make any selection inadequate." At first it is students who cannot be expected to manage: "Can we hope that most (or even many of [them]) will share any knowledge of influential critics and approaches?" But soon it is our own capacity as teachers to master the situation that is called into question: "Can many of *us* even agree on some critics and approaches for those . . . who want to know something of the best that we have done" as Shakespeareans? The problem is no longer just the amount of current criticism but its conflicting nature. So many seemingly contradictory activities are being performed these days under the name of Shakespeare criticism. Who could hope to represent all this disparate material in a complete and even-handed way? Which of us would ever presume to appropriate Kent's aggressive confidence, closing in upon Oswald: "I'll teach you differences" (*King Lear*, I.4.89)?

Of all the differences in front of us, I am arbitrarily limiting myself to one: namely, that between the sort of criticism that would have been recognized by most Shakespeareans as state of the art about twenty years ago and the sort of "alternative criticism" being produced at present. The old and new anthologies I listed in Chapter 1 can serve to embody the sort of contrast I am concerned with here. Even with this arbitrary limitation, however, I should say at the outset that I cannot solve the problem described in Weil's statement, and that I do not think anyone can. That is the bad news, and I will be spending most of this chapter trying to persuade readers that it is hopeless to try to master this problem of our differences. The good news, such as it is, will come at the end. I want to suggest finally that the resolution of difference, even if we could get it, is not what we need these days anyway. Our true need at present, or so I argue, is for a way of making do with our differences, not for a way of unifying or transcending them.

❖

Consider the case of *A Midsummer Night's Dream*, in particular the problem the artisans encounter as they engage in their theatrical endeavor. Bottom and the others worry first of all that the audience will not believe in their play. What about Moonshine and the lover-separating Wall? "A calendar, a calendar!" says Bottom. "Look in the almanac. Find out moonshine, find out moonshine" (III.1.53–54). The calendar is auspicious, but to be on the safe side an actor is assigned the role, and the same solution is found to the problem of Wall. But the artisans are anxious about another problem as well, the reverse of Wall and Moonshine—that the audience will believe their play only too well. This problem surfaces after Bottom's infectiously enthusiastic request to double Lion with Pyramus: "Let me play the lion too. I will roar, that I will do any man's heart good to hear me. I will roar, that I will make the Duke say 'Let him roar again; let him roar again.'" "And you should do it too terribly," says Quince, "you would fright the Duchess and the ladies, that they would shrike; and that were enough to hang us all." Quince's anxiety is shared by "*All.* That would hang us, every mother's son" (I.2.70–78); and the same "parlous fear" surfaces later about the violent and tragic catastrophe ("Pyramus must draw a sword to kill himself; which the ladies cannot abide" [III.1.10–12]) until Bottom comes up with the solution of writing prologues assuring the audience that the suffering Pyramus and roaring Lion are not really Pyramus and Lion, but Bottom the Weaver and Snug the Joiner.

These anxieties in both versions, too little or too much belief, are misbegotten from the same origin, an inability to distinguish between the belief we accord to works of fiction and the belief we grant to real life. We know better than to run up on stage and stop Othello from murdering Desdemona, because we know we are watching not a murder but the theatrical performance of a murder. At the same time, however, the knowledge that Desdemona's murder is not real does not prevent us from shedding real tears at the pity of it. This distinction between fiction and real life is, of course, easily deconstructable, and I offer it not as an immutable natural fact but as a culturally learned construction. Fiction and reality are not ontological categories that generate certain more or less appropriate responses. Rather, it is the other way round: the existence of certain expectations and responses and the institutional judgment of their appropriateness are what create the categories of discourse. Fiction is what we call fiction, however we define it, and there is no consensus at present on either the definition or the appropriate response—something that is painfully obvious in the case of *The Satanic Verses*.

A clear sense of the distinction between reality and fiction, arbitrary or socially constructed as it may sometimes seem, is just what makes *A Midsummer Night's Dream* work—at least in C. L. Barber's view of the play. According to Barber, the artisans' blunders function as a negative example; we are shown their beliefs about response as an encouragement to respond in just the reverse way:

> In dealing with dramatic illusion, he [Bottom] and the other mechanicals are invincibly literal-minded, carrying to absurdity the tendency to treat the imaginary as though it were real. They exhibit just the all-or-nothing attitude towards fancy which would be fatal to the play as a whole. . . . The confident assumption dominant in *A Midsummer Night's Dream*, that substance and shadow can be kept separate, determines the peculiarly unshadowed gaiety of the fun it makes with fancy. Its organization by polarities—everyday–holiday, town–grove, day–night, waking–dreaming—provides a remarkable resource for mastering passionate experience. (148–49, 161)

The assumptions generating Barber's commentary function powerfully among many recent critics (Frank Kermode and Michael Goldman, as examples),[1] and they have a deep history as well, extending back through the Renaissance to antiquity and Aristotle.[2] All this may help to account for the enormous influence and prestige Barber had for his contemporaries,[3] which in turn makes him a prime candidate to represent the older critical mode, against which we can now proceed to juxtapose some contemporary commentary.

If we begin with Terry Eagleton, it becomes immediately clear that Barber's "peculiarly unshadowed gaiety" has been replaced by something much more serious. Bottom's desire to play all the roles, which leads to the roaring problem we have seen, serves in Eagleton's version to figure forth the absolute indefinition and instability of human identity, and the consequence is anxiety for the author ("this is particularly *worrying* for Shakespeare"), the play ("to dismiss itself *nervously* as a dream is no defense"), and presumably for the audience as well (*William Shakespeare*, 23, 26, my emphases). According to Eagleton, the author's anxiety is rooted in the change from a late feudal to an early capitalist formation. Shakespeare is said to be committed to the "traditionalist belief that all identity is reciprocally constructed. . . . This doctrine is a powerful weapon in his critique of bourgeois individualism, [but] if the self lives only in social exchange, then Shakespeare's defence of the feudal doctrine of mutuality against bourgeois individualism begins to look particularly ironic" (23, 4).

In an essay called "Shakespeare in Ideology," James Kavanagh offers a similar argument. Like Eagleton, Kavanagh focuses on Bottom's promise to perform Lion's roar and the anxiety it evokes, claiming that

> this dialogue functions as a kind of internal commentary on Shakespearean ideological practice. The problematic of proto-professional ideological production denied autonomous political weight in a society struggling to preserve the hegemony of an aristocratic class-ideology is here displayed in order to be ridiculed. Shakespeare's artisans pose the issues quite clearly in their discussion: . . . for *us* to assert an effective ability to manipulate *their* sense of reality . . . would be an unacceptable usurpation of ideological power, possibly punishable by death. (154)

The polarities in Barber served to create a protected space, "master[ing] passionate experience" by excluding it. In Eagleton and Kavanagh, however, passionate experience will not respect such boundaries and the space of the play is overwhelmed by a threatening reality that cannot be kept at bay. They locate this threatening reality in political oppression and the class struggle. More generally it can be described as the "uncomic world of labor, fear, pain, and death" which "Puck begins to evoke" when the lovers go off to bed at the end of the play. I have been quoting Louis Adrian Montrose (" 'Shaping Fantasies,' " 74, 64), whose intention, though, is not to generalize the anxiety-producing reality that invades the play, but rather to give it a different name and local habitation—namely, sex and the marriage bed.[4]

Montrose's argument originates from the figure of Queen Elizabeth, the "one vital exception" to a social order in which "all forms of public and domestic authority . . . were vested in men" (64). The anxiety said to be generated by this exception is at the heart of the play's power. In Montrose's view, the play works primarily to reinforce patriarchal ideology, consigning Hippolyta's autonomous female power to a past irreversibly transformed by the beginning of the play, and representing Oberon's triumphant repossession of phallic power signified in the little changeling boy. But this restoration of patriarchy, Montrose tells us, "is not only undermined by dramatic ironies but also contaminated by a kind of intertextual irony," and the result is not only an appearance of the clouds whose absence accounted for Barber's unshadowed gaiety but of a vast black whirlwind of erotic fear and loathing:

instances of terror, lust, and jealousy which are prominently recounted and censured by Plutarch . . . Shakespeare uses Plutarch . . . highly selectively, excluding those events "not sorting with a nuptial ceremony" [but] the text of Shakespeare's play is permeated by echoes [and] traces of those forms of sexual and familial violence which the play would suppress: acts of bestiality and incest, of parricide, uxoricide, filicide, and suicide, sexual fears and urges erupting in cycles of violent desire . . . [Theseus'] habitual victimization of women, the chronicle of his rapes and disastrous marriages, is a discourse of anxious misogyny which persists as an echo within Shakespeare's text, no matter how much it has been muted or transformed. (74–75)

Faced with Barber's version of the play on the one side and Eagleton's, Kavanagh's, and Montrose's on the other, we can adopt Edmund's question, caught between Goneril and Regan: Which of them shall we take? Both? One? Or neither? beginning with "both," and with the fact that both of these different versions have been successfully represented in performance. *Dreams* of unshadowed gaiety are familiar to us all, and to judge from the notices of John Caird's 1989 RSC version, we may assume that nothing Eagleton and the others say is going to make them go away. But (predictably) anxious *Dreams* have themselves become a theatrical staple, at least since Peter Brook's in 1970. Liviu Ciulei's 1985 production for the Guthrie is a good example. The tone was established by a shiny red vinyl set ("reviewers referred to the set as 'blood red' and Ciulei was said to have thought of the color as signifying passion" [Clayton, 233]) and by a pretextual dumb show:

a black Hippolyta, as spiky as her insolent brush hair, [is] forcibly divested of black cotton battle fatigues, which are then incinerated on a brazier of coals. Her conqueror Theseus, wearing a long Victorian motoring coat, has not so much gained a bride as captured a sullen war prisoner, one who resists being assimilated in the white robes of the Athenian court. Power and subjugation are the major issues. (Brustein, 32)

This may be the most extraordinarily nightmarish *Dream* we have, but the contemporary theater is full of comparable interpretations, which, like Montrose's, think it's good to thrust patriarchal oppression and phallic aggression right up in front where we cannot help but see it.[5]

It is easy to see the power of this kind of production, as well as of the more traditional celebratory ones, but hard to see any way of accommodating both versions within the same performance.

The thing about "passionate experience" (that is, about political and sexual power relations, "the problematic of proto-professional ideological production" et seq, as well as about bestiality, incest, and the whole standing army of Montrose's -cide words) is that it is either in or out, and that once you let it in, you cannot get back to unshadowed gaiety. Roger Warren's discussion of the Brook production illustrates this point. After describing the raucous orgy orchestrated for the interval climax at the end of III.1— "the fairies hoisted Bottom on their shoulders; one of them thrust a muscular arm up between Bottom's legs like a grotesque phallus, [Titania] lay on her back and curled her legs around his, clawing at his thighs, gasping and gabbling in sexual frenzy"—Warren complains that in this production "the language which Shakespeare gives to Titania is of no account and can simply be disregarded. The text itself does not matter . . . only what Brook calls the 'hidden play *behind* the text'. . . . The lyrical beauty of Titania's speeches was completely thrown away in this performance's frenzied gabbling and gasping" (57–58). The kind of loss Warren describes here seems inevitable; reviewers of the Lepage production, both favorable and unfavorable, noted the same phenomenon.[6] If you want frenzy, you cannot have lyrical beauty at the same time. Hence "both," Edmund's first alternative, seems to turn out for us as for him to be a nonstarter.[7]

If we now consider "one" as the answer, this raises the further question, Which one? and why? By emphasizing the pleasures of formal beauty, the perception of which depends on the exclusion of passionate experience, Warren clearly points to Barber's version. For Warren the preference is based on "the text itself" as more authoritative than Brook's " 'hidden play *behind* the text,' " but this move simply reestablishes the good old-fashioned distinction between the text and the subtext, or between the text and an errant interpretation of the text, a distinction it has become very hard to maintain against recent arguments about interpretation. Once we have abandoned the concept of an autonomous text standing free and independent of interpretive activity, then instead of the text itself and the subtext, the relevant distinction seems to be rather between two different versions of a text, one you like because, corresponding to what is visible from your position, it appears as the text itself, and one you do not like because, illegible from your position, it looks like something that somebody else has read into "the text itself."

Maynard Mack's book on *King Lear* is a good example of this problem. "All of this is healthy, no doubt," he says of a range of diverse productions of *Lear* in mid-century, "but the question as to whether it is Shakespeare's play that is communicated by these means is not settled" (28). Before long, however, it becomes clear that Mack does not really think it is healthy after all, as upon reviewing a number of contemporary productions, including Peter Brook's, in which the focus is on the cutting of Cornwall's pitying servants at the end of the blinding scene, Mack complains: "After such knowledge, what forgiveness—for those who would be content to see *King Lear* as Shakespeare wrote it" (40)? Yet what exactly is the text itself here, "Shakespeare's play," "*King Lear* as Shakespeare wrote it"? Some time after his complaint about Brook's elimination of Gloucester's servants, Mack has praise for a Byam Shaw production in which, at the end of the same blinding scene, Regan ignores Cornwall's appeal for help, leaving him horrified and deserted. This is "a highly imaginative *exeunt*," we are informed, "which must have brought home to any audience the implications of a world in which language could be so perversely and solipsistically misused" (104). But it is difficult to see why Shaw is any closer to the play "as Shakespeare wrote it" than is Peter Brook. There is no more textual authority for Regan's desertion than for cutting the servants (probably less, in fact, given current arguments about the Folio as Shakespeare's own revision). Mack complains that "the newest and most unpromising form that efforts to rationalize *King Lear* have taken is that of playing what is called in today's theatrical jargon the 'subtext'" (32); but Regan's desertion is itself subtextual, surely. Your subtext is my "imaginative *exeunt*," Mack would have us believe, but the operative distinction here seems rather to be between two different subtexts—two interpretations of the text, that is—one valued, the other deplored. Predictably, anxious *Dreams* tend to be associated with textual theories different from those of the old formalism. In the most aggressively different version, the critic's job is to take advantage of a privileged historical or ideological position in order to make manifest the anxiety-producing contradictions that cannot be known to the author or the audience for whom the text was intended. This has become a relatively familiar position for critical activity these days.[8] It has been explicitly adopted elsewhere by Kavanagh,[9] and apparently by Montrose, who, in the passage I quoted earlier, requires us to behold sexual anxieties "which the play would suppress." At another place, however, commenting that "the play actually calls attention to the mechanism of mythological suppression by an ironically meta-dramatic gesture" in the entertainments Theseus rejects before agreeing to hear the artisans' play (V.1.44–60),[10] Montrose seems to retain the idea of the text itself, merely disagreeing with the Barber-Warren version of what it says. It is still a matter of creating a protected imaginative space, but now this project is assigned to characters within the play, in contrast to the play's own project, which is evidently to make us see through the characters' endeavor in order to acknowledge the power of an unmasterable experience. In yet a third place, Montrose seems to want to locate himself above or between these two positions: "At the same time that the play reaffirms essential elements of a patriarchal ideology, it also calls that reaffirmation in question; irrespective of authorial intention, the text intermittently undermines its own comic propositions" (74). This looks like waffling: just what is the distinction between textual and authorial intention (Knapp and Michaels)? But maybe waffling does not matter. After all, whether you work from a self-ignorant and contradictory text or an autonomous and unified one, such theories are not data but heuristic assumptions; they do not ground interpretive activity, they generate it. The anxious *Dream* can have authority either way.

But then just what is this authority, and where is it grounded? Eagleton and the others do not really address the question (as practical critics they do not have to do so), but if we look for a moment at a discussion by Jerome McGann, the silence in contemporary *Dream* commentary can be teased into speech. "The poem's special effect," McGann says (talking about Keats's "To Autumn," but in a way that is uncannily transferable to the Shakespeare play),

> is to remove the fearful aspects . . . , to make us receive what might otherwise be threatening ideas in the simpler truth of certain forms which the poet presents as images of The Beautiful. This effect is produced by so manipulating the mythological and artistic mediations that the reader agrees to look at autumn, and to contemplate change and death, under certain precise and explicitly fictional guises. (56)

This is pure Barber, but McGann is not finished: "From the vantage of an historical methodology the analysis has only just begun, for what we now have to develop is an explanatory context for the analysis" (56). This context turns out to be the political brutality and oppression of Keats's world in general ("the Terror, King Ludd, Peterloo, the Six Acts," etc. [61–62]), as well as Keats's illness, both of which are associated with the London environment from which Keats wishes to escape. In effect, McGann has shifted from Barber and is now doing with "To Autumn" what Eagleton and the others did with *Dream*: refusing to stop at the pleasures of self-contained formal beauty, carefully putting back into the text what the text or figures within the text have carefully tried to exclude. And finally McGann attempts to account for the value of this contextualization. The trouble with the original procedure, which appreciates the poem "without historical analysis," is that it "agrees to read the poem simply, that is wholly in terms of Keats's own artificially constructed fantasy. It takes the poem to be true, exclusively true, when in fact such a work—like all human works—is true only in the context of its field of social relations" (62).

In fact all human works are true only in the context of their social relations—what does this mean? McGann is not just making a claim for the context-specificity of all meaning; "social relations" signals an implicit commitment to politics as the master context. Like Plato (one of McGann's acknowledged models, who presides here as Aristotle does over Barber and Warren), McGann means to remind us that fictions are mimetic and morally purposive, that the world is full of injustice, and that making it a better place is the job of literature and criticism. In *The Symposium* Socrates grounds all desire in the will to transcend mortality, offering metaphorical procreation as one way of realizing this desire, the performance of civic virtue whose consequence is to send spiritual children out to an enriched political future. From this perspective making the world better is not just anybody's job but everybody's nature (hence the absoluteness of McGann's pronouncement, not just works but *all* works, indeed all *human* works, are not just *true* but true *only* and indeed are *in fact* true only). From the same perspective Barber's unshadowed gaiety will tend to look frivolous (as it did to Pepys: "the most insipid ridiculous play that ever I saw in my life"). McGann goes out of his way to acknowledge the consolations of formal beauty; they "promise a real human benefit," he tells us (56), but pretty clearly not enough to justify our investment.

It is Plato who provides a detailed cost accounting in his complaints that poetry and rhetoric satisfy us instead of making us experience our own alienation and thereby impelling us to an ideal (not these days the realm of spiritual forms, to be sure, but perhaps a closer approximation to a society where gender and social differences are more equitably disposed). McGann does not exactly spell this out himself, but he does not have to. Since making the world a better place has come to occupy a position near the motivational top of critical activity these days, McGann can assume that we know what he means. After all, if we inhabit the same discursive system as he does, enmeshed in the same institutional network, his pronouncement will be seen to embody its own validity: we see the truth of the claim that truth exists in the context of its social relations because we are positioned in the context of its social relations. We are a captive audience.

Or some of us are, some of the time. But if you are not a wholehearted Platonist, you are likely to see things differently, and you might want to echo Claude Rawson's objections to McGann's "portentous and oracular knowingness," his tendency in the form of "hectoring admonitions" to make claims that are either "impossibly literal" or "troublingly unspecific" (19). You can fill out this position (and empty out the one that has given us our nightmarish *Dream*s) in lots of ways. One is to deconstruct moral purpose and start it on its inevitably infinite regression. Making what part of the world better? you can ask, and for whom? and at what cost—indeed, what "real human" cost—to other inhabitants? Further, how and to whom is it an advantage to make sure that sexual anxiety and class oppression are put back into or kept securely at the center of the play? This question is almost always ducked, and prudently so, to judge from the nonconvincingness of the answers that seem to be available.[11] But even if we do not ask these questions, even if we accept social change as the only "right true end" of our actions, we can turn Adorno, another of McGann's models, back onto McGann himself, claiming (this is a version of the "new-stories" argument I sketched out at the end of Chapter 3) that it is the escapist rather than the anxious *Dream* that is really the more politically progressive, because "autonomous art" is a form of "non-identity thinking" that is more efficacious in promoting social change than ideologically engaged art, which simply reproduces the existing structure of authority. In short, from Barber's perspective the anxious or historicized *Dream* looks as much like a baseless fabric as does the unshadowedly gay *Dream* from the perspective of Eagleton and the others.

Where are we now? Starting from Edmund's question and having rejected "both" as impossible, we came to "one"; and having then tried to determine which one, we have rather discovered apparently that such a determination is impossible. Before giving up altogether, we can reopen the alternative of "both" on the very basis of our inability to determine which one. Indeterminacy in its positive form, the recognition of a multiplicity of contradictory meanings, has in one version or another long been a part of the Shakespearean scene.[12] These days, moreover, we are especially sensitive to the constructedness of meaning, to its historical specificity, and therefore to its inevitable multiplicity. The question, though, is whether this sensitivity helps gives us a perspective from which to represent *both* Barber and Eagleton and the conflict between them in a fair and disinterested way. My answer to this question is no.

To explain: First, consider that any theory of the indeterminacy of texts is independent of the textual determinations we continue to make. That is, recognizing the undecidable multiplicity of choices is one thing, choosing is something else; and choose we do, because knowing that knowledge is positional does not prevent us from being securely positioned in our knowledge.[13] Hence, those of us who delight in the unshadowed gaiety of Barber's play, or those of us who expose the disguised sociosexual conflicts of the current version, will continue to respond confidently as we do, even though we know that the other side can erode any grounds we might try to establish upon which either the delight or the exposure could be justified. Given this continuity, and our uninterrupted occupation of one or the other of the positions in conflict, it seems we must renounce any hope to represent the conflict itself from a neutral position *au dessus de la mêlée*. I am not saying that such fairness is meaningless or undesirable. What I am saying, though, is that the meaning of fairness is bound to shift according to one's perspective, and that an absolute fairness (that is, a fairness independent of context or perspective) can never be realized. To put this another way, our beliefs about the world and about what constitutes "fair play" or a legitimate entitlement to the advocacy of such beliefs are generated out of the same position. Hence Barberians will represent their differences from Eagletonians in one way, Eagletonians will represent their differences from Barberians in another, and in each case the representation of difference will be an interested reenactment rather than fair play.

There is one last move to consider. If we cannot transcend our beliefs, can we shed them? Can we shift our focus away from the particular interpretations of *A Midsummer Night's Dream* and over to the origins and history of the conflicts that have brought us to our arguments about Shakespeare's play (and all other texts)? This is what Gerald Graff wants us to do in his attractive program of "foregrounding conflicts";[14] but whether we choose to follow Graff's program (as I am inclined to do) or not, we should resist getting our hopes up too high, because like all the moves I have described or can imagine describing, this one is horizontal rather than vertical. The kinds of theory courses Graff's conflict model envisages simply reproduce the same problem, for theories themselves differ, and their differences have to be represented, and the representation of theoretical differences, no less than the representation of differences among practical critics, will be an interested reenactment rather than fair play. Indeed, the problem may exist at an earlier stage, before that of representation—for consider, how can we even get to offer (and therefore represent) these desired theory courses to begin with? Although in a given year my chairman may excuse me from my Shakespeare course so I can teach a course in theory, the particular situation will quickly be perceived to be a matter of principle—namely, whether the limited faculty personnel and curricular space ought to be devoted to Shakespeare or to theory—and the resulting situation will almost certainly issue in an all-out war in the department. Although this war is not likely to develop in a scientifically predictable fashion—Shakespeareans with three-piece suits and horn-rimmed glasses and crew cuts on one side, theorists in denim skirts and work shirts and steel-rimmed glasses and crew cuts on the other—it will nonetheless be organized in some recognizable version of the conflict lines I have been describing.

In short, Graff's move is not a way out of our situation. There is no way out. If (as I said at the beginning) we cannot master the conflicts of our situation, it is because being in a situation means not being on top of it. The only thing on top of our situation is another situation. Graff's proposal is like Edmund's *tertium quid*: "neither." Instead of both Goneril and Regan (impossible) or one of them (also impossible), "neither" appears to offer the prospect of something *completely* different—a way out of the game. Should Edmund have explored this alternative more fully? Perhaps he could have founded a pre-Christian order of mendicant ascetics. It would not have worked. There is no way out of the game except to a different game, but a different game is still a game and therefore not completely different. Like Edmund's "both" and "one," "neither" turns out to be a nonstarter, which makes us o for 3, and as the grand old song has it about the grand old game, "it's one, two, three strikes you're out at the old ballgame."

⬧

To summarize by way of a return to the Shakespeare Assocation statement from which I began: there is no way "many of us can agree on some critics and approaches" as constituting "the best that we have done." To be able to do so, we would have first of all to establish Shakespeare criticism as a unified totality, but what I have tried to argue here is that the fundamental conflicts within Shakespeare criticism cannot be resolved into such a coherent subject. What follows then from this position if not despair? One possibility is to limit the nature of the subject to an artificially and arbitrarily manageable homogeneity. We could close ranks around a beseiged formalist humanism or an insurgent materialist feminism, and simply not expose our students to the contaminants of difference. Some people do this, teaching as if Shakespeare criticism began with Louis Montrose, or ended with G. Wilson Knight; but though few of us can muster the confidence (if that is the right word) to effect such violent foreclosures, this move is one that we should all be able to understand. After all, in any time of teaching differences such as ours, violence seems possible, maybe even necessary. In the stress of conflict, as Lear says, "the art of our necessities is strange."

Nonetheless, I do not recommend this kind of resolution. I recommend, pusillanimously, that we do not even try to solve the problem, but ignore it. This is, in effect, Edmund's advice. When his analysis reveals to him that all his alternatives are impossible, he concludes that "my state / Stands on me to defend, not to debate." Edmund cannot master the contradictions of his situation (his "state" in one sense of the word). No logical conclusion is possible except to conclude the logical analysis and get on with it. Like Goneril rebuking Regan's proposal for further thought, Edmund has to do something, and in the heat.

Adopting Goneril and Edmund as pedagogical authorities will not seem self-evidently good to everybody. There are other kinds of stories about teaching available to us. Paul de Man tells one in *The Resistance to Theory*:

> Overfacile opinion notwithstanding, teaching is not primarily an intersubjective relationship between people but a cognitive process in which self and other are only tangentially and contiguously involved. The only teaching worthy of the name is scholarly, not personal; analogies between teaching and various aspects of show business or guidance counseling are more often than not excuses for having abdicated the task. (4)

There are only two characters in de Man's story, one called Mind, the other called Text. Like Beckett, de Man reduces his narrative materials to a bare minimum, and the result is an austere beauty that helps to account for the story's appeal.[15]

The story I want to tell, however, is more scandalous, more carnivalesque; it includes episodes like the following: (1) For no clear reason, a bunch of noisy sociology majors have taken your

Shakespeare course, so though you were planning in effect to teach the anxious Eagletonian *Dream*, you find yourself driven to the refuge of Barberian gaiety. (2) Same premise as above, except that this time you were planning to do Barber and wind up doing Eagleton. (3) In the middle of the year an eastern potentate offers a reward to anybody who will kill a writer who has offended his religion. You and your students become obsessed with issues of state power and censorship, and so you want to do *Measure for Measure*, which you had not planned on doing, and in order to make room for it you drop *A Midsummer Night's Dream* altogether. (4) It's a Monday morning in October, you burn the eggs again, your Significant Other complains, a really good domestic argument ensues, and you go into the class in a state of confusion and dismay. The students do not or cannot help you out, and a residual sense of embarrassment hangs over the course, never wholly to disperse until it is too late. (5) Same premise as the preceding, but this time you roar into the class in a state of high dudgeon that somehow translates itself into your own and the students' elation, and the momentum, now positive, results in one of the best courses you have ever taught. (6) A hot Monday in October. The stunning redhead in the front with the porcelain skin is wearing jeans that look as though they have been sprayed on. Despite the distraction, your teaching seems unaffected. You and the redhead bump into each other exiting from the class and you talk for a minute, but he is meeting his girl friend and you have got to pick up the kid from day care because your husband is out of town on business, or at least you think it's business, so there are no apparent consequences for either the short or the long run in either the pedagogical or the erotic domains.

A story made up of episodes like these does not mean that teaching is a chaotic or anarchic activity. There are many factors at work in the teaching situation that guarantee continuity and coherence: the same time slot, the same room, the same students and teacher (subjective continuity may be an illusion, but it is usually a powerful one), gravitating as though by natural law to the same positions in the same room, the structure of the curriculum, the reward-and-punishment mechanisms within the academic institution and the larger world. As a result of all this, anarchy is the last thing we need to worry about. But if teaching is not anarchic, neither is it governed by a sovereign rationality. It is one thing to decide in May what you should be doing in the eighth week of your Shakespeare course next November; but when November comes, what you should be doing may look different altogether, and what you wind up actually doing yet something else again.

The problem, if it is a problem, can be expressed in terms of two variables. One of them is you (no matter how effective it usually is, subjective continuity does remain an illusion), and the other is time. The two come together in Edmund's words to the Captain at the end of the play. "Men are as the time is," he says, and this is a true and nourishing doctrine, I believe, for all teachers, men and women. For the Captain Edmund's proposition becomes the basis for murdering Cordelia ("if it be man's work, I'll do it"), but this is not a necessary consequence. There are plenty of pragmatist relativists around who do not murder innocent women, and history is full of innocent women who have been murdered by positivist essentialists.

For those of us trying to figure out what to teach as Shakespeare criticism and how to teach it, the consequences of Edmund's doctrine are uneven. Different people will have different choices, but all choices will have to be specific to a particular context and subject to change. I for one believe that an anthology conveniently juxtaposing recent and contemporary critical activity along the lines I have illustrated for *A Midsummer Night's Dream* would be a useful pedagogical tool. It would not provide a way out of the game, of course, but it would furnish the occasion for an interesting and potentially productive way to play, and for a variety of players who find themselves located in fundamentally different teaching positions. Even if such an anthology were available, however, it too would have to be supplemented by the reserve shelf and dittoed handouts that become relevant according to the variables of the teacher and the time (not to mention the students and the Ayatollah's successor).

One final bit of reassurance: these days even a small fry trying to stay afloat in an academic backwater is likely to have, as I do, an IBM clone and Word Perfect and access to a laser printer, so handouts on the spur of the moment are much easier to manage. Easier, but not easy; I grant that; but in graduate school they never told us it was going to be easy. (The truth is, in graduate school they never mentioned teaching at all.) Stephen Greenblatt talks about the "slime of history" ("Shakespeare and the Exorcists," 101), its resistance to all our efforts to shape it into clarity and coherence. I have been talking about the slime of teaching. What with all our differences, it's a dirty job teaching Shakespeare. But somebody's got to do it.

❖ 5 ❖

In Defense of Jargon:
Criticism as a Social Practice

ACCORDING TO *The American Heritage Dictionary of the English Language*, jargon is "nonsensical, incoherent, . . . meaningless utterance," or the "specialized or technical language of a trade, profession, class or fellowship." Neither definition gets us very far. They allow us to groan at terms like "phallogocentrism," and "the hegemonic," and "beauty"; but like all lexical discourse—dictionary jargon, as it might be called—these normative definitions leave the big questions unasked, let alone answered. The big questions include: How can we explain the dramatic increase in the number of people who seem to be using jargon these days? And why do these same people persist in the belief that they are not the ones using jargon, *we* are?

I propose to argue first of all that jargon is not (as the dictionary suggests) a linguistic quality embedded in words but an interpretive category generated out of conflict. Jargon is the kind of language used by people who believe differently from us. And finally I will claim that jargon so conceived is not just a necessary evil but a positive benefit.

In a book called *The Pleasures of Reading in an Ideological Age*, Robert Alter argues that in "looking at literature with the apparatus of different systems of abstract thought" (10) we have lost touch with a "passionate engagement in literary works [and the] deep pleasure in the experience of reading . . . literature itself. One can read article after article . . . in which no literary work is ever quoted, and no real reading experience is registered" (11). Alter's lament is based on a sharp distinction. On the one side is something called the "real reading experience" of something called "literature itself"; on the other, those nastily "abstract systems of thought" whose effect, Alter informs us, has been to divide us into "competing sectarian groups" (14). The first procedure produces the "pleasures" of Alter's title, but the second, since each sectarian group has "its own dogmas and its own arcane language" (14), produces nothing but "this jargon of the new literary technocrats" (17). Alter predictably parades a series of examples for our horrified amusement: "sectarian cant . . . close to nonsense," he tells us after quoting one passage (18). And after another: "It goes without saying that the proverbial common reader would be able to make little of this" (16).

The examples of jargon to which Alter's argument leads may be quite as amusingly horrible as he says, but his argument itself remains a perplexing one, generated out of distinctions that seem to disappear the moment you look at them. One such distinction is between bad and good critics. It is only the bad ones who, by offering us "discussion to the second degree," are the jargon purveyors; the good ones, so he tells us, produce "the discussion of literature itself" (11). But since Alter's definition of good criticism is that it "requires . . . a *special* liking for literature [and] an ability to discriminate between derivative and original, second-rate and first-rate writers" (13, my emphasis), this good criticism turns out to be no closer to passionate experience and natural instincts, as technocratic and as abstract (though in different ways) as the "jargon of the new literary technocrats" to which it is supposed to be contrasted. Good criticism, in other words, is revealed as merely the jargon of the *old* literary technocrats, and it is hard therefore to see how Alter's "proverbial common reader" is going to make any more out of it than out of the current stuff he finds so repellent.

Once the distinction between good and bad criticism disintegrates, we are left with the basic distinction between criticism—all of which, good, bad, or indifferent, is jargon—and some immediate affective apprehension of "literature itself." But the moment Alter says anything about "literature itself," even this distinction collapses. "Literature speaks through its own complex and distinctive language" (14), he tells us; and again, "the language of literature is distinct from the use of language elsewhere in its resources and in its possibilities of expression" (19). In a word, the same word for both bad and good criticism, "literature itself" is jargon.

If Alter's distinctions turn out to be all untenable, it is because everything on the other side from jargon and its purveyors is Alter's own invention. His common reader is not only "proverbial" but mythical. By the time you have gotten rid of the cultural baggage that makes a reader uncommon, all those unpleasantly "sectarian dogmas" that make us Marxists or heterosexuals or baseball fans or right-to-lifers or formalists or ballet dancers, it is hard to see anything left. Culture, as Rorty says, "goes all the way down" (*Contingency*, xiii). The same point can be made about Alter's conception of a language that is totally unspecialized and unmotivated and unrelated to any particular set of concerns, beliefs, and interests. Such language is impossible to find. It is always somewhere else—"language elsewhere," as Alter himself is constrained to call it when he gets down at last to acknowledging the specialness of literature itself.

Despite what he thinks, the distinction Alter makes between jargon and accessible common language is not between specialized and unspecialized language. Rather, it is between two kinds of specialized language, one kind that Alter likes and is used to, one that he doesn't and isn't. Jargon is the language specific to the beliefs and interests we find inimical to our own; it is the hellish language of other people.

If jargon is a function of difference, we can say that it has always been with us. The Tower of Babel story may be the primary myth to explain the origin of jargon, but it just emphasizes the linguistic consequences that are part of the general inauguration of difference in the story of the Fall. In naming the animals, Adam did not use jargon. His names corresponded to their true general nature; he was seeing the animals as in themselves they really were, independent of any designs he might have upon them—to tame, hunt, or preserve for future generations. All such designs are postlapsarian. They separate us from Adam's "speech degree zero"—he is speaking "language elsewhere."

If jargon has always been with us, why then do we seem to have so much of it these days? There is an easy and logical answer. Since jargon is a function of difference, we have so much jargon now because we have so much difference. It might be argued that new historicism is dominant at present, but the various theories and critical approaches it has displaced—old historicism, new criticism, deconstruction—remain a presence. Besides, new historicism has itself become fragmented—new historicism vs. cultural materialism or cultural poetics, say—and, as Louis Montrose argues, what we have at present is not so much new historicism as "new historicism*s*." Such fragmentation is particularly striking in the case of feminism, where an earlier consensus has collapsed into an astounding multiplicity of competing points of view—and languages. It is of this collapse that Catherine Stimpson is thinking when she tells us that "the differences are spreading" ("Nancy Reagan" and "Are the Differences Spreading?").

My guess is that everybody feels that the differences are indeed spreading, and any proposition supported by such different critics as Robert Alter and Catherine Stimpson must command substantial authority. Still, we should reserve an element of skepticism about this explanation. How can we be sure we are more divided than we were a generation ago? Institutional historians such as

Gerald Graff (*Professing Literature*) and Jonathan Culler (*Framing the Sign*, 3–40) have the irritating habit of quoting eloquent testimony about the erosion of an earlier academic consensus and then identifying the author as belonging to the very period in which we locate the consensus we have presumably lost. Those of us old enough to remember what professional life was like in the happy (or unhappy) age before the flood of theory might wish to confirm the idea, but we cannot really be trusted, for memory is notoriously fallible.

Whether or not our differences are spreading, it is more useful to attribute the current ubiquity of jargon to our increased *consciousness* of difference. I am referring here to our differences not just from one another but from ourselves. Writing in 1976 in a seminal book called *The Motives of Eloquence*, Richard Lanham said he knew a big shift was occurring when the greeting "Hello" began to be replaced by "What's happening?" (219). Lanham developed the shift in terms of a distinction between the serious and philosophical on the one hand and the playful and rhetorical on the other. These days we are more likely to express the distinction in such terms as essentialism, as opposed to constructivism. Instead of conceiving identity as a hard gemlike flame, some stable individual essence, we reckon ourselves to change as our situations change, to be different people in different circumstances. As "cultural artifacts" or the "intersections of a variety of discourses," we are characterized by "discontinuous subjectivities."

To someone like Alter, such phrases probably sound like the voguish jargon of the new literary technocrats, but the concepts seem to have been around for a long time. Lanham claims that they were effectively there at the beginning, in the sophists whom Socrates wished to displace. They were certainly around in the Renaissance—as witness *Hamlet*:

> Was't Hamlet wrong'd Laertes? Never Hamlet:
> If Hamlet from himself be ta'en away,
> And when he's not himself does wrong Laertes,

Then Hamlet does it not, Hamlet denies it.
Who does it, then? His madness. (V.2.233–37)

So says the Prince in Act V, assuring us that he is no longer the
same person who murdered Polonius in Act III. The play not only
describes such transformations, it acts them out. Thus in the
"rogue and peasant slave" soliloquy, after five lines of violent rage
against Claudius, Hamlet's tone precipitously and inexplicably
shifts:

> Why, what an ass am I! This is most brave,
> That I, the son of a dear [father] murthered,
> Prompted to my revenge by heaven and hell,
> Must, like a whore, unpack my heart with words,
> And fall a-cursing, like a very drab,
> A stallion. (II.2.582–87)

From this new discursive position, the words Hamlet has just
uttered sound to him like somebody else's words—a male whore's,
not those of a king's son. An exchange between the mighty oppo-
sites in the play scene can serve as a comment on this transforma-
tive process: "I have nothing with this answer," Claudius says,
feigning ignorance or innocence, after one of Hamlet's veiled
threats. "These words are not mine." Hamlet responds, "No, nor
mine now" (III.2.96–98), as if he had become alienated from his
own words merely in consequence of the time it took to utter them.

In this context Olivier's famous voice-over is misleading. Hamlet has no problem making up his mind; his mind is made up all
the time—just made up differently from moment to moment. It is
better to say that this is the tragedy of a man who is suffering from
discontinuous subjectivity.[1] But don't we all so suffer, these
days?—which brings me back to jargon. Why are there so many
inverted commas in the critical prose we currently read? And why,
occasionally, those queer lines scored through words? To say we
use words under erasure does not seem to me quite right. We use

words, and then we move to erase them, or enclose them within quotation marks, because they *have become* alien to us, or we to them, as we have shifted to a new position. If like Hamlet we have learned to do without a framing totality such as essential human nature, we will have to put up with a constant sound of jargon in our ears, including not least the echo of our own.

❖

I come now to the biggest of those big questions, the value question: Is jargon a good or bad thing? If jargon is an interpretive category determined by difference, then it seems the only way to answer the value question is to find a position above the differences. If you have been convinced by the antifoundationalist argument, which holds that the claim to transcend belief is itself a belief, then this presumed position above difference is nowhere, or is itself just another different position. This idea makes people very nervous. They think that such "framework relativism" means that critical activity is therefore without direction and value. I argue at length in the following chapter that such anxieties are unfounded—whether from the right, left, or center. Here it should be enough simply to say that in abandoning definitive judgment, we have abandoned nothing but definitive judgment. There is a great deal left, namely, all of Barbara Herrnstein Smith's contingencies rather than definitions of value. In a word, rhetoric. Instead of asking whether jargon is good or bad, we should ask: Who is speaking here? To whom? For what purpose? Given the answers, we will be in a position to say this is good or bad language. Since these topics of author, audience, and purpose all require lots of interpretive assumptions, the final answer to the value question will not prove to be final. Somebody else will come along with a different set of assumptions to provide a different answer. But the antifoundationalists are not to blame for the way interpretive debates fail to achieve definitive closure. Since this was the case even when the positivists or realists seemed to be in charge, the real villain here (as always) is history.

In the space remaining I want to ask the value question about a single passage—one I quoted at greater length and in a different and more fully developed theatrical context in Chapter 4. This is James Kavanagh's discussion of *A Midsummer Night's Dream,* more particularly of the artisans' anxieties about the reception of their play. After quoting an exchange between Bottom and Quince, Kavanagh comments that "this dialogue functions as a kind of internal commentary on Shakespearean ideological practice. The problematic of proto-professional ideological production denied autonomous political weight in a society struggling to preserve the hegemony of an aristocratic class-ideology is here displayed in order to be ridiculed" (154). Some people might say that if this isn't jargon, nothing is. My point, though, has been that nothing *is* jargon but that position makes it so. To a confirmed Althusserian, Kavanagh's discussion will sound like the voice of unadorned truth. The more useful question is whether, given our understanding of author, audience, and purpose, this is good writing, to which I propose three answers: no, yes, and yes.

To begin with no, consider Kavanagh's context. Kavanagh's essay appeared in John Drakakis's anthology, *Alternative Shakespeares,* where (to recall the discussion in the first chapter of this book) it was offered as one of several alternatives to the humanist paradigm said to have dominated Shakespeare studies from Rymer's time to the present. Now whether or not we agree with this argument in all or any of its parts, what do we think of Kavanagh's writing within such a context? Very little, I suggest. If Kavanagh wants to waken Shakespeareans from their centuries-long humanist sleep, he must persuade them to break habits—not least linguistic habits—that are very deep. Kavanagh should be more accommodating, more respectful, as Aristotle advises in the *Rhetoric* (3.1.1404^a), of "the defects of our hearers" (165). There must be some non-Althusserian Shakespeareans around who are not totally locked into humanism, and some of them might be interested in trying something new, if Kavanagh could somehow cajole them into believing that it would be worth the risk. Instead, by intransigently piling up only the terminology specific to his own contestatory belief, Kavanagh effectively scares away the very constituency he should be courting.

In answer two, "Yes, this is good writing," we start from the same context but make a different judgment about Kavanagh's target audience. In this view, Kavanagh does not want to cajole people into sharing his views, because all you get by following the accommodating route is soft support that disappears when the going gets tough; or worse, co-optation, where the purity of your critique loses its integrity and is absorbed into the corruption it is working to replace. Kavanagh has traded in Aristotle as his model now for Jesus (or at least the Jesus who came to bring not peace but a sword). There is no point wasting Althusserian pearls on humanist swine. Kavanagh is interested only in the audience willing to take him on his own intransigent terms, and his writing is brilliantly crafted to achieve its purpose.

At this point I want to decide the issue with a final yes, but a yes of a different kind from both the answers I have already furnished. Despite their differences, both earlier answers can be understood in terms of the same cliché: preaching to the converted. In saying that Kavanagh was writing badly, I claimed he was preaching to the converted, that is, limiting his audience to those who shared his belief instead of reaching out for converts. But the yes answer too was based on the assumption that preaching to the converted is a bad thing. It simply offered a different judgment about the qualities desired in potential converts, and therefore the stylistic qualities needed to reach them. My final yes, though, is based on the belief that preaching to the converted is itself a good thing.

Most preaching, of course, *is* to the converted. We do not go to the preacher's house to hear something new; we go to confirm what we already know in solidarity with a community of fellow believers. Anyone who has gotten lost in the chorus of a really rousing Anglican hymn—like "O God, Our Help in Ages Past" or "This Is My Father's World"—knows what I mean. You may think

God's past help has not been all it might have been, you may believe it is time to talk about our *mother's* world, but this does not matter. Jews will recognize the same process in the *Sh'ma*, the most important prayer in the Hebrew service. It translates as "Hear, O Israel, the Lord our God, the Lord is one," but when you hear a really strong cantor belting out the *Sh'ma*, you do not turn to your neighbor and say, "What, we're monotheists here?" You probably know you're monotheists, but this knowledge has much less to do with it than does the pleasure of the shared experience. It does your heart good to hear the *Sh'ma*: let him roar again, let him roar again.

According to Frank Kermode, "We always underestimate the power of rhetorical and narrative gestures in familiar modes of discourse. If the priest said his *Ite, missa est,* or whatever it is they say nowadays, before the Benediction, a lot of people would get up and go" ("Sensing Endings," 146). Kermode's point not only reinforces the argument I have been making about theatrical and religious experience, which I take to be a commonplace; it allows us to add a third analogue: academic criticism. Academic criticism is also a "familiar mode of discourse," at least to those of us who are academic critics, and a highly conventionalized one as well. Unlike theater and religion, however, criticism seems to perform more strictly cognitive functions. "To engage in the study of literature," Jonathan Culler has said, is "to advance one's understanding of the conventions and operations of an institution, a mode of discourse" (*Pursuit of Signs*, 5). I think that most of us are committed to this idea that criticism serves primarily to advance cognitive frontiers, and I will come to acknowledge agreement with it myself by the end. But for now, note the situations for which Culler's definition is evidently inadequate.

Consider first our behavior with regard to publishers' displays and exhibits at academic conferences. Why do some of us rush straight to Routledge, while others make a beeline for Oxford? Compare what might have occurred on any given Sunday in Britain a century ago, one line to chapel, another to church. Both groups knew what awaited them—moral fervor for one, high ritual for another. Like the Holiday Inn, church and chapel promise no surprises. How different is it for us and Routledge and Oxford?

It may look as though I am stacking the cards. What we do as part of a crowd at academic conferences cannot be considered typical of "the study of literature." As Erving Goffman points out in a lecture called "The Lecture," there is a big difference between listening to a public lecture and reading a text in the privacy of one's own study. As readers we are not subject to the influences of the crowd (160–96). Alone and undistracted, we can control the flow of information and ideas to allow for reflection, reconsideration, scrupulous analytical examination. Here at least we are in a position to advance cognitive frontiers.

But are we? Is this what typically happens when we read? Consider the experience of a subscriber sitting down with the latest issue of a journal—let us say *Social Text*. To see why this experience is not Culler's "advancement of one's understanding," we must recognize first of all that there is such a thing as a *Social Text* essay, and it is different from a *Review of English Studies* essay, for example. Now suppose some night-tripping fairy diverted an *RES* essay into the pages of *Social Text* so that the *Social Text* subscriber, expecting to read about the use of Dickens by the educational state apparatus in the hegemonic project of constructing the bourgeois subject, finds herself instead stumbling into some blathering humanist jargon about Dickens's rounded characters or beautiful image patterns. In theory—the theory behind criticism as advancing understanding—the subscriber's cognitive dissonance is just the right precondition for learning something new. But I think what is likely to happen here is nothing of the kind. Rather, the subscriber will simply skip over the imported *RES* essay and move on to the familiar territory of the next one. She might even think of canceling her subscription, since the reason she subscribed to *Social Text* in the first place was that it confirmed her already in-place beliefs, and reassured her about her participation in a community of fellow believers; it spoke her language.

It might be said that, even if criticism does work in some ways like theater and religion, it shouldn't. But religion and theater have been shaped through their long histories to serve a variety of deep cultural needs, and it would be impoverishing to define our professional lives in a way divorced from these needs. The deepest of these needs, I take it, is the need to feel we are participating in some project larger than our own particular interests—the need not to feel alone. In the current academic scene this need is particularly difficult to satisfy; with our spreading differences and an increased consciousness of them, it is very hard to know to whom we are writing, and why; sometimes it is even hard to know for whom—for which of our different voices—we speak.

The president has pointed to the problem in a piece on educational goals. "In a divisive world no good growth goes unpinched. [This] profusion of . . . theories and facts . . . threaten[s,] exhausts and bothers some of us." Since the president I am quoting is writing not from the White House but from the "President's Column" of an *MLA Newsletter* (Stimpson, 2), you will see that it is not just the right for whom fragmentation is painful. The left feels the pain too, maybe more acutely. For someone like James Kavanagh, who knows that the bad guys own not only the means of production but the Ideological State Apparatuses as well because these are always determined "in the last instance" by the means of production, the burden of isolation and alienation has assumed extraterrestrial proportions.

Like all extraterrestrials, James Kavanagh wants to go home. *Home.* This is not to be confused with the house where we grew up, still less the house where we grow old. Home is what Joe Cocker and Jennifer Warnes croon about at the end of the treacly movie a few years back: it is the place "where we belong," where everybody is an officer and a gentleman (even the ladies, maybe especially the ladies). Home is where you never have to say you're sorry, because there is no one to say it to. The other people there are not other people; their being is continuous with your own. "Part of my Soul I seek thee, and thee claim / My other half," as

Adam says when he discovers Eve, who, because she feels just the same way, knows how he feels before he says so (4.487–88). Home is where you don't have to say anything at all.

The passage I quoted from James Kavanagh is rich in analytic and explanatory power, but its main power has nothing to do with either analysis or explanation. This is language as pure gesture. Partly it is a gesture of exclusion. By restricting himself to the special language of poststructuralist Marxism, Kavanagh says, "Abandon all humanist hope, ye who enter here." But it is an inclusive gesture as well. The prose interpellates us as Althusserian subjects. Those of us who wish to respond positively to the invitation can join him in feeling at home in this discursive space, a little place where we belong. Even those of us who don't, however, should be able to recognize that the needs satisfied by Kavanagh's jargon are needs that we all share.

❖

I want to end with two points of clarification, the first about change, the second about criticism as advancing knowledge.

I may have seemed to suggest that we are all locked into our own jargon-constituted systems of belief with no way to get out even if we wanted to, and therefore to deny the possibility of change. Such a claim would be foolish. The study of literature has clearly changed profoundly in many ways during the last twenty years or so, and all of us have perforce participated in these changes with varying degrees of delight, resistance, confusion, excitement, and so on.

What I have denied is the proposition that criticism serves *primarily* to advance cognitive frontiers. The story I told about the *Social Text* subscriber and the *RES* essay seems to me a fair representation of what reading criticism is like for most of us most of the time, in the sense that its final effect is to confirm beliefs already in place. But this is not what happens for all of us all the time. Frequently enough to be significant, we encounter different ideas that cause us to change our minds. (Whether this constitutes "cognitive *advance*" is another question—advance toward what?—but it is certainly change.) It did not happen for the *Social Text* subscriber I made up for a variety of reasons: she was a materialist without any residual humanist traces, and the essay she encountered was a humanist piece utterly devoid of materialist contaminants. In other words, the difference was too great for any contact. In practice things rarely work out this way. First of all, most readers are of more than one mind; this goes back to my point about the discontinuous subjectivity we share with Hamlet. To be sure, we cannot match Hamlet's heroism or madness in the range of differences to which his mind is open, and in his refusal or inability to order these differences into some hierarchy. No! We are not Prince Hamlet, nor were meant to be; but we *are* like him. Second, criticism rarely achieves the univocality of the *Social Text* and *RES* essays I invented. Since the conventions of critical prose tend to place a high value on consistency, the essay examples are probably closer to reality than the reader example; closer, but still exaggerations.

For these reasons, change is possible. What is not possible is radical change—a qualitative shift to something totally new. Total novelty would be invisible; the new is always significantly continuous with what it replaces. I take it this was Marx's point in the passage I keep coming back to from the beginning of *The Eighteenth Brumaire*: we are free to create our own history, but not totally free, only within the predetermined circumstances over which we have no control. Within this constraint, as a wide variety of recent commentators have argued, including Thomas Kuhn, Jonathan Dollimore ("Subjectivity"), Stanley Fish (*Doing*, 141–60), and Barbara Herrnstein Smith ("Belief"), change is not only possible but inevitable.

This clarification may seem like a qualification so substantial as to deny the claims I have been making in defense of jargon, so let me return finally to the strongest version of my argument, that jargon is not just a necessary evil but a positive benefit. Eric Bentley, commenting on a statement of Brecht's to the effect that you don't paint a still life when the ship is going down, remarked that "you don't paint at all when the ship is going down," simply hang on for dear life to anything that might keep you afloat (127). Certain minimal conditions of social stability are required for art or for criticism or indeed for any kind of action (including mental action) that has designs beyond the immediate moment. In the felt absence of such conditions, no agenda for social change (or for conserving traditional values, for that matter) has any chance of being articulated, let alone endorsed. If you believe that the felt presence of such a minimal stability within the profession of academic criticism is very low at present, then jargon, as something that keeps it from getting dangerously lower, can be seen as a good thing.

I can justify this conclusion one last time by way of a return to Culler's claim for criticism as advancing knowledge. Of course Culler is right: what could be the purpose of academic literary criticism if not the advancement of our understanding? My disagreement is meant to say not that Culler is wrong so much as incomplete. Culler defines criticism as a scientific discipline, but it is also a social practice. Since everything is a social practice, it makes sense to distinguish criticism from, say, Scottish country dancing or major-league baseball, not to mention the Shakespeare Festival in Stratford, Ontario, and the United Church of Canada. My point, though, is that such distinctions, though useful and necessary, are also secondary and potentially misleading.

When you describe criticism as a scientific discipline, you distinguish it from other social practices in a way that can obscure the fact that it *is* a social practice. The idea of scientific advance is still likely to conjure up images of heroic individuals, voyaging in strange seas of thought alone, like Abdiel or Coriolanus transplanted from the domain of war to that of theoretical speculation. If there is a single direction to criticism recently, it has been to show that such images of isolated individual behavior are misleading.[2] I am not trying to resummon the conference crowds in their browsing frenzy at the publishers' exhibit. Even the solitary reader in the study is now perceived as part of a crowdscape, for the book she is reading is made available to her only by virtue of a publishing industry, and her interest in the book is part of a research agenda determined by the collective influence of her history and training. Academic critics are pack animals. The paths we travel have been marked out for us by predecessors of whom we may know nothing at all. If we find something new (and Marx in the same passage I remembered a moment ago from *The Eighteenth Brumaire* has some skeptical comments about this possibility), we will be able to disseminate it only through the existing modes, basically publishing and teaching, over which we have very limited control.

I do not mean to be discouraging; I mean only to insist on the ontological priority of criticism as a social practice. If we fail to function effectively as a social practice, we cannot succeed as a scientific discipline or anything else. We have to take care of ourselves first as a social practice, though this may mean ignoring or even hindering our activity in advancing knowledge. If you assume, as I have done throughout this book, that the equilibrium of our practice is dangerously fragile at present, then jargon may be defended with the simple claim that its way of helping is more important than its way of hurting.

❖ 6 ❖

Against "Ideology"

THROUGHOUT THIS BOOK I have assumed and sometimes argued explicitly that all criticism is occasional in nature, responding to and directed toward some specific situation. There are degrees of specificity, however, and this chapter, beginning in the middle of things with memories of a session at the 1989 MLA Conference in Washington, wears its occasional nature on its sleeve. For those who were not there, a word of explanation is in order.

The story begins (or can be said to begin) a year earlier when the *PMLA* published an essay called "Feminist Thematics and Shakespearean Tragedy." The author, Richard Levin, enjoyed a richly deserved and entirely honorable reputation for stirring up trouble, but the consequences must have surprised even him. Twenty-four academic critics, most of them either Shakespeareans or feminists or both, some of whom had seen their work criticized in Levin's piece, joined to sign a letter of protest. As the pamphlet war followed in the pages of the *PMLA* Forum, Ivo Kamps, at that time completing his doctorate on Renaissance history plays, hit upon the idea of organizing a special MLA session devoted to the affair. The session was called "The Place of Ideology in the Criticism and Metacriticism of Shakespeare," and it included presentations by Levin, Gayle Greene, and Michael Bristol (the last representing a materialist approach, attacked in other recent Levin pieces), as well as a comment by Victoria Kahn. All of these papers formed the basis for an anthology Kamps edited called *Shakespeare Left and Right*, to which this chapter was a contribution.

⚜

One of the most powerful moments in Ivo Kamps's MLA session on ideology in Shakespeare criticism occurred near the end of Gayle Greene's paper. In response to Richard Levin's remark about the success of feminist criticism, Greene said, "From where I sit as a feminist it does not look to me as if I control *PMLA* or much of anything else in the profession" (27). Greene recounted the familiar but no less depressing statistics of women's position and pay in the academic workforce, the rage of the patriarchal right against her work, and the contemptuous dismissal of the same work by the neomaterialist feminist left. Since Greene writes in a beautifully direct way, readers can pick up from the printed text how frustrated she feels at the increasing marginalization of her work by both left and right.

A similarly moving moment came a few minutes later when Richard Levin rose to respond to the criticism lavished upon his work by the other panelists. He had a lot to choose from, but oddly enough he focused on an apparently incidental remark of Michael Bristol's, that Levin's writings sometimes "sound . . . like those of a lapsed or fallen liberal" ("Where," 34). Not so, Levin assured us; his liberal faith he kept. He was still "that L word," proud of being, even in those days of the Bush presidency, a card-carrying member of the ACLU. Unlike Greene's, Levin's frustration never found its way into the printed record; you had to be there to feel it. This is one among many differences between them, yet what struck me then, and lives in my memory still, is their similarity. For Levin too sees himself pincered between a neoconservative right and a neomaterialist left. "If you really want to know, I feel beset from all sides." It was Greene who said this (28), but it might as well have been Levin.

This similarity does not bear much scrutiny. Since the positions of Greene and Levin are supposed to constitute the field, they cannot both represent themselves as the besieged victims of a dominant majority. One of them must be wrong, one of them must *be* the dominant. In retrospect it would be easy enough to decide who was right (though we would not all come to the same conclusion), or even to analyze why the sense that they are both right was an illusion of the moment. Conference papers always include a theatrical element that tends to blunt analytical response, and all elements of the theatrical last only a moment, dying in the cradle where they lie. But the flip side of this transience is the particular immediacy of the moment: "In Dramatic composition, the *Impression* is the *Fact*" (Morgann, 4). I want to stick to the impression. Let us say that Gayle Greene and Richard Levin are, with all their differences, both right, and further that they speak for all of us, with all our differences, Shakespeareans or otherwise, left, right, or wherever. This starting point leaves me with two questions to consider here. How can it be that we all feel beset from all sides? And what should we be doing about it, or, in the famous Lenin version, what is to be done?

My subject here—the topic from which I want to construct answers to these questions—is ideology; or rather, "ideology," the term as it is used in current critical practice. The distinction is important because, for reasons I hope to make clear, ideology is something you can be neither for nor against, since you are in it and it is in you. "Ideology," though, the term as variously deployed in current critical arguments, is a different matter, and it is this "ideology" I am against. In announcing my opposition, though, I have to acknowledge at the outset that the term has a wide and bewildering range of often contradictory meanings. I will be talking about this problem, but for the moment it should be enough

to stand proudly with Groucho Marx as Professor Wagstaff, break-
ing into song in *Horse Feathers* upon his inauguration as president
of Huxley College: "Whatever it is, I'm against it."

I

The argument I wish to make about ideology is in many respects
similar to the one I made in Chapter 5 about jargon, and once
again Robert Alter's book, *The Pleasures of Reading in an Ideological
Age*, can serve to set it in motion. Alter, it will be remembered,
complains that in "looking at literature with the apparatus of different systems of abstract thought" (10), we have lost touch with a
"passionate engagement in literary works" and the "deep pleasure
in the experience of reading." This situation "is distressing"
because such abstract "discussion in the second degree" has
"come to displace the discussion of literature itself." Hence, "one
can read article after article, hear lecture after lecture, in which
no literary work is ever quoted, and no real reading experience is
registered" (11). The practitioners of this abstract criticism are so
given to "ideological tendentiousness," Alter says, that they "might
be better off teaching sociology or history, psychology or political
science" (13).

Alter's argument is based on several unexamined and (as I
think) indefensible assumptions. One is in the phrase "literature
itself," which Alter seems to take as a natural phenomenon of the
real world. He nowhere confronts the various current arguments
about literature as historically determined and socially constructed. He merely asserts its existence as a stable and self-sustaining category of being, and thus winds up assuming what he is
obliged to demonstrate. The "deep pleasure" of "real reading
experience" rests upon similarly problematic assumptions. If
reading were truly such an innocent and instinctive activity with
pleasures so immediately accessible, why do we have literature
professors or literary critics? Alter never answers this question; he

never even asks it, though it hangs like a cloud over the discussion right through to the very end of his book.[1] Maybe he does not really believe his own claims about the immediately pleasant accessibility of literature. If so, why remind us that the critical practice of those tendentious ideologues currently invading literature departments "requires neither a special liking for literature nor an ability to discriminate between derivative and original, second-rate and first-rate writers" (13)? When did the natural instinct for reading professionalize itself into "a *special* liking?" When did passionate experience turn into the abstract business of discriminating between the great and the near-great?

Alter's argument is based on a set of distinctions that do not stand up to analysis. For instance, he complains about the "ideological coerciveness" of a "neo-Marxist" critic such as Terry Eagleton "in proposing that a curricular move be made from literature to 'discourse studies,'" but what is Alter himself if not ideologically coercive in proposing that we decontaminate literature departments of neo-Marxists by banishing them into the sociological wilderness? Alter claims to speak for real pleasure against ideological abstraction, but as Barthes points out (22), the distinction between textual pleasure and political tendentiousness is itself a familiar, conventional, public construct, appropriable according to one's interests; in other words, an ideological distinction. Alter lines up behind common sense against special interests, but as Catherine Belsey points out (1–36), common sense, like literature itself, seems to be a floating category of various meanings (that is, a category capable of serving different special interests), whose least and perhaps only common denominator is the claim to be a transcendent signified, to mean the same uncontestable and non-ideological thing no matter who is using it.

In short, although Alter believes he is distinguishing between ideology and something ontologically prior, some instinct inherent in nature and common sense, he is distinguishing rather between two kinds of ideology, one he likes and is used to, one he doesn't and isn't. Moreover, this claim to be above ideology has the effect, whether intentional or not, of disguising ideological interest (from the author maybe even more than from his audience); and as any neo-Marxist (and many of us who are not) will tell you, disguised ideology is one good working definition of ideology at its best.

The points I have made about Alter can be applied to Richard Levin's critical arguments as well, which seem to depend on similarly unsustainable assumptions. In "Ideological Criticism and Pluralism," for instance, Levin excludes ideological critics because their presence seems to disallow the possibility of negotiated settlement. But why is it that the only "real discussion" (like Alter's *"real* reading experience," the adjective has a strong evaluative implication) is one that "tries to reach some kind of agreement" (15)? The same question can be asked of another essay of Levin's, "The Problem of 'Context' in Interpretation." After granting that interpretation requires the establishment of a context, Levin tries to solve the problem of determining which context is appropriate by limiting the differences to those critics who share an intentionalist assumption. His reason is that "the nonintentionalist critic is completely free to choose any context he pleases" (89). Even if this contention were right, Levin's argument is nonetheless going in circles around the same unacknowledged and apparently unacknowledgeable central assumption—namely, that agreement is self-evidently the goal of critical activity. For a lot of nonintentionalists, those who see a repressive censorship and exclusion at work in both psychological and political domains, agreement is not a good thing. Since it is the opening of critical activity to such nonintentionalist assumptions that has effectively created the problem, Levin's exclusion of the nonintentionalists does not solve the problem so much as beg the question. If we could limit the discussion to people who agree with us, we would eliminate disagreement: if we had some bacon, we'd have bacon and eggs—if we had some eggs. But suppose, instead of bacon and eggs, that we want *cervelles au beurre noir* or *matzoh brei*. Suppose we are not even hungry. If (but only if) agreement is an absolute value, then

147

exclusion is necessary; but if the inclusion of new and different voices is the goal, then disagreement may be necessary. Levin seems unable to stand outside the belief that agreement is a good thing; he assumes what is at issue. And this is where coercion comes in, another similarity with Alter. Levin complains about the coerciveness of ideological critics, but for those who do stand outside the belief that agreement is a good thing, it is Levin, with his inaugurating gesture of exclusion, whose intention looks coercive, like "enforced submission—poetics from the barrel of a gun" ("Ideological Criticism," 19).

The chief similarity between Levin and Alter is in their desire to contrast themselves to ideological critics; like Alter, Levin distinguishes rather between the ideology he likes and the ideology he doesn't. In the move to exclude, in tolerating a restricted difference, the kind that can be articulated, negotiated, and resolved, Levin is following the familiar lines of pluralism. Pluralism allows for a limited and gradual change; it therefore serves the interests of those who want both to contain and to enlarge the area of legitimate exchange, to distribute the limited goods available more widely yet within definite boundaries. Pluralism will seem good or bad depending on where you stand. To some, it is bad for its containment and restriction; to others, good for its distributive largesse; to yet others, it may seem like a good trade-off between contradictory goods. But whether you like it or not, it is hard to see how it can be characterized in contrast to an ideological position.

So much for the right and the unattainable desire for the transcendence of ideology. If we waffle now to the left, what we find is the unattainable desire for the critique of ideology, which turns out to be pretty much the same thing.

Consider Francis Barker and Peter Hulme's argument about "alternative criticism" (192–94) in their essay on *The Tempest*. Starting from the position that all texts are "installed in a field of struggle," Barker and Hulme try to determine the best way of "combating the dominant orthodoxies" in order "to displace" them. With combat, struggle, and displacement, we have been moved to a position diametrically opposed to Levin's negotiation and reconciliation. Such language makes it clear that negotiation is not (*pace* Levin) a universally shared or self-evident good. But it works the other way around as well; someone inhabiting Levin's position would wonder why struggle is installed as a desideratum, a question for which Barker and Hulme either do not or cannot provide a direct answer.

Perhaps, though, they provide an implicit answer in the main argument they make about alternative criticism, that it should not invest too heavily in original meaning. The trouble with original meaning, they tell us, is that it is irretrievable with any certainty. As a consequence, any argument about it is likely to be "wholly dissolved into an indeterminate miscellany [and] the only option becomes the voluntaristic ascription to the text of meanings and articulations derived simply from one's own ideological preferences . . . a procedure only too vulnerable to pluralistic incorporation, a recipe for peaceful coexistence with the dominant readings, not for a contestation." Such contestation "can only occur if two positions attempt to occupy the same space," so Barker and Hulme exhort us to shift attention away from indeterminate historical questions and over to the "critique of the dominant readings of a text" as they exist in the present. The dominant contemporary orthodoxy can be seen and challenged for what it is; it thus provides a purchase for authentic critique, or what Barker and Hulme call "a *properly* political" criticism, in which the "different readings struggle with each other on the site of the text, and all that can count, however provisionally, as knowledge of a text, is achieved through this discursive conflict."

But why assume that the contemporary dominant is any easier to determine than original meaning or critical history? What allows Barker and Hulme to believe they have direct access to it—the contemporary dominant *as in itself it really is*, unmediated by their own interpretive interests? Such questions arise when you consider that the text they chose to illustrate contemporary orthodoxy, Kermode's New Arden "Introduction" to *The Tempest*, was thirty-four years old at the time Barker and Hulme's piece was published, and written by a critic who, it may sometimes seem, has done nothing *but* change during the course of his career.[2] Even more problematic is their definition of the critical views that they say constitute the dominant orthodoxy. Though "no adequate reading" of *The Tempest* "could afford not to comprehend *both* the anxiety [of irresolution] and the drive to closure it necessitates," it is just "these aspects of the play's 'rich complexity,'" Barker and Hulme tell us, that "have been signally ignored by European and North American critics, who have tended to listen exclusively to Prospero's voice: after all, he speaks their language. It has been left to those who have suffered colonial usurpation to discover and map the traces of that complexity by reading in full measure Caliban's refractory place in both Prospero's play and *The Tempest*" (204). But despite this claim, there were plenty of humanist critics around before Barker and Hulme who were able to recognize and respond to just such subversive energies in the play. In the New Penguin "Introduction" (published almost exactly halfway between Kermode and Barker and Hulme), Anne Barton emphasizes at length how the play works against the resolving gestures of conventional closure (40–44). And the claim that the dominant version of the play is uttered by or within Prospero's voice simply ignores the very substantial body of nonalternative interpretation that has made a nasty Prospero into such a regular feature of Shakespearean interpretation both academic and theatrical— arguably even the *dominant* feature.[3]

To reverse a memorably tendentious phrase from Stephen Greenblatt's High Functionalist period, Barker and Hulme can be described as transgression producing authority (the dominant orthodoxy) as a way of extending its own (counterhegemonic) legitimacy. From this perspective, Barker and Hulme's entire rationale for concentrating the struggle in contemporary criticism disappears. Stick to the current stuff, they tell us, and the argument will not be "wholly dissolved into an indeterminate miscellany"; but this move merely displaces the problem of indeterminacy onto the very question (what *is* the current stuff?) that was supposed to eliminate it—and thus turns out to be a horizontal rather than vertical move. Let's get beyond "simply . . . one's own ideological preferences," they urge us, to provide a ground from which to critique ideology; but what I am suggesting is that, since Barker and Hulme's understanding of the dominant orthodoxy is perforce derived in fundamental ways from the interests they bring to the question, it cannot satisfy their desire to ground the critique of ideology because it is itself ideologically constituted.

In *Criticism and Ideology*, Terry Eagleton provides a clear statement of the strong claim for left critique: "Historical materialism stands or falls by the claim that it is not only not an ideology, but that it contains a scientific theory of the genesis, structure and decline of ideologies. It situates itself, in short, outside the terrain of competing 'long perspectives,' in order to theorise the conditions of their very possibility" (16–17). There are many similarities here to the claims on the right for the transcendence of ideology. In both a category of genuine being (*real* reading experience, literature *itself*, conditions of *very* possibility) can be discerned objectively (that is, either *rationally* or *scientifically*) from a disinterested position (either above *political interests* or outside the *terrain of competing long perspectives*). Both positions rest in self-validating assumptions vulnerable to attack from anyone inhabiting a different set of assumptions. At this point, though, a difference emerges. For while right transcendence is more or less internally consistent, left critique seems to stand in a contradictory relation to its own instituting assumption, that of materialism. Once you invert Hegel and thereby arrive at the belief that ideas in consciousness are derived from the particular social relations in a given situation, then the ideological nature of all knowledge—its specificity, that is, to a particular position or set of interests—seems to follow as the night the day. How can Eagleton claim to situate historical materialism outside of history when it is precisely the situatedness in history that historical materialism is all about?

The answer is in Althusser's maxim that "the accusation of being in ideology only applies to others, never to oneself" (*Lenin*, 175). Althusser thought this was "well known," and the point has indeed become something of a commonplace these days,[4] but it is not a new discovery. The extraordinary inconsistency was already old when Karl Mannheim noted it in the 1930s. "It might have been expected," he wrote in *Ideology and Utopia*, "that long ago Marxism would have formulated in a more theoretical way the fundamental findings . . . concerning the relationship between human thought and the conditions of existence *in general*," adding that the situatedness of thought "was perceived only in the thought of the opponent" (277). Again the same conclusion: Once you accept the materialist argument about determination, you cannot make any claim for "universal validity." Since (I'm now quoting Kenneth Burke's commentary on Mannheim) any " 'unmasking' of an ideology's limitations is itself made from a limited point of view" (*Rhetoric of Motives*, 198), "the edges are so knocked off the Marxist definition of ideology that Marxism too becomes analyzable as an ideology" (199).

The remarkable thing is that, despite its relative familiarity and long pedigree, this same inconsistency continues to underwrite (and undermine) the project of left critique. Catherine Belsey is a case in point. *Critical Practice* begins with the claim "that ideology is not an optional extra, adopted by self-conscious individuals . . . , but the very condition of our experience of the world, *un*conscious precisely in that it is unquestioned, taken for granted" (5). By the last chapter, however, Belsey wants us to engage in "a scientific criticism [that] recognises in the text not 'knowledge' but ideology itself in all its inconsistency and partiality" (128).[5] But how can we achieve a scientific mastery of the "conditions of our experience"? Since these conditions are the ones within which we live and move and have our being, they are identical to what in a different system of thought, Augustinian Christianity, is called God—the object, so to speak, of ultimate ideological concern. Renaissance Neoplatonists were well aware of this problem, frequently pointing out that you cannot know God, at least not in the sense of specular ("scientific") knowledge; any such knowledge would require us to get outside of that which we are inside of, or indeed, that which is inside of us. Donne plays with the problem in "Negative Love," making a commonplace connection between the impossibility of knowing God and the impossibility of knowing the self. The point is particularly relevant to Belsey and other cultural materialists in the sense that any such commitment to "the scientific knowledge of ideology itself" serves willy-nilly to reinstall the sovereign subject of humanism (self-sustaining, self-knowing), which it has been the virtue of so much materialist work to call into question.

Eagleton's *Criticism and Ideology* is the text that most richly develops the analogy between ideological and theological analysis—and most clearly embodies the problem I am trying to get at here. Ideology, he tells us, "cannot survive the traumatic recognition of its own repressed parentage—the truth that it is not after all self-reproductive but was historically brought to birth, the scandal that before it ever was, history existed" (96). In this metaphoric narrative, ideology plays the role assigned to Satan, who labors mightily to assert his being as self-begotten (*Paradise Lost*, 5.853ff.) only to wind up with the evidently idiotic assertion that he must have created himself because he does not remember being created. The metaphor, thus, equates ideology with sin. What then is God? History, of course: "ideological space is curved like space itself, and history lies beyond it as only God could lie beyond the universe" (95). Or again: "Ideology seems to determine the historically real rather than *vice versa* [but it] is itself naturally determined in the last instance by history itself . . . the *ultimate* signifier of literature, as it is the ultimate signified. What else in the end could be the source and object of any signifying practice but the real social formation which provides its material matrix?" (72). I do not understand why we need recourse to an ultimate signifier or signified, to last-instance sources and objects, or to anything at all beyond the ample curves of our expanding universe. But even granting the existence of history in Eagleton's sense, we should ask what you can say about it. How, to adapt Milton's words in "Of Education," do we succeed in "regaining to know history aright" (631)? We all know about the problem attached to specificity about God in *Paradise Lost* (the problem of divine attributes in Chapter II of *The Christian Doctrine* [904–11] is equally interesting though less familiar). Eagleton has the same problem with history. As the "untranscendable horizon, ground, and absent cause" (Jameson, who also has a theological side), history is that whose nature cannot be known and whose true name can never be uttered. Say it and you lose it.[6]

Between Belsey's two statements—first that ideology is inside us and second that we should achieve a scientific knowledge of ideology—a whole book intervenes, and while nothing in the middle solves the problem of inconsistency, the sheer distance tends to make it less conspicuous. But critique does not shy away from conspicuous inconsistency. In Barker and Hulme, less than a page intervenes between an assertion about "the rootedness of texts in the contingency of history" and the authors' claim that they can themselves attain to a critical position beyond that of "ideological preference"—in other words, produce a text not rooted in the contingency of history. Sometimes these inconsistencies exist within a single paragraph, as in Michael Bristol's *Shakespeare's America*. Bristol starts from the materialist premise that "neither Shakespeare nor institutional practice stands outside historical and social determination" (4), which in turn constitutes an "acknowledgment" that any "researcher" is necessarily "position[ed] within a culture already constituted by Shakespeare." Nonetheless, Bristol proposes to undertake "a critique," that is, "an attempt at emigration from that cultural ground." But this leads back to the Belsey question, how can you get out of where you are, except to yet another "position within a culture already constituted by Shakespeare"? Unlike Eagleton, Bristol does not solve the problem by fiat. "It is clear," he admits, "that such emigration can scarcely expect to locate a frontier, let alone cross it," but if that is so, then emigration is what it cannot be. The emigration from history is an impossible voyage; the "critique of ideology" (the word falls predictably into place in a moment—see p. 8) is a self-contradictory concept.

Nonetheless, this is not the conclusion Bristol reaches. Instead, he exits from the same brief paragraph that initiated and sustained a convincing argument against the possibility of critique by concluding that he intends to do just what he has shown that neither he nor anybody else is capable of doing: "In undertaking a critique of Shakespeare then, I necessarily proceed on the understanding that I am implicated in and defined by the very institutional reality I propose to analyze" (4). Bristol is, of course, aware of the contradiction. In fact, the awareness is his main point, the subject of the independent clause, and his strong implication is that the awareness is somehow empowering, as though understanding the impossibility of the undertaking makes the undertaking possible. But such "antifoundationalist theory hope," to use Stanley Fish's term,[7] remains an empty gesture; it can never be translated into productive action, for any first step that might be imagined up and out of the institutionally and historically determined space (emigration as elevation) turns out to be, like Barker and Hulme's definition of dominant orthodoxy, just another horizontal move. And this brings us back finally to the basic similarity between left critique and right transcendence: they are doomed to fail by virtue of the same constraint—namely (to sum up the argument that I have been making here), that horizontal moves are the only kind we can make.

II

At this point we can return to the questions I asked at the beginning. The first of these, How can it be that we all feel beset from all sides? may seem now like the wrong question. Better to ask, How can we not? To be sure, there was a time when we didn't, a real historical time within memory when academic criticism, and not just about Shakespeare, seemed to proceed out of a consensus. Whether this consensus was good or bad, real or illusory, is subject to debate; in fact, it *is* the debate, or at least one version of the debate that led to (and leads from) the MLA session on ideology in Shakespeare from which this chapter began. My point is that the "ideological preferences" that now divide us also serve to define the space that is divided. If you are committed to reconciliation and negotiation, the current scene may well look as though it has been taken over by tendentious ideologues; if you are committed to radical change, then it will look as though the neocons are blooming, in control at the helms, or at best that the forces for change are being co-opted into meaningless tokenism. In this context it is not only possible but perfectly reasonable that all players feel like underdogs, and every position like a minority beset from all sides.

This leads to the second question, What is to be done? Bristol and Greene suggest that the first thing to do is define "ideology" properly, but even in the unlikely event they could resolve their own differences, this would not constitute an argument to change Levin's mind. After all, Daniel Bell, *fons et origo* of Levin's definition, has reissued *The End of Ideology* with a new Afterword saying that he had the term right in the first place. In the absence of a consensus around a lexical norm, the assertion of such a norm will seem just that, an assertion, with no authority beyond those who share the asserters' beliefs. The proper meaning of ideology cannot decide the conflict since it is itself the subject of the conflict—a "keyword" (Williams), an "essentially contested concept" (Gallie).

Another option apparently is open to us here: jettisoning the term altogether. I think this is a good idea. In arguing that everything is ideology (i.e., that all knowledge is bound to be historically situated, positioned in a particular set of social interests, and therefore contestable from a different position and set of interests), I have also been arguing that nothing is ideology. The term has too many meanings, because it has no meaning. Any and everything that might serve to give it meaning, all those contrasting binary captives (ideology vs. true consciousness, science, the Godlike capability of reason, real social relations [ummisrecognized], what really happens [undistorted], etc.)— these contrasting categories are all nowhere to be found. (Or rather, we find them in too many places, all depending on the position from which we see them, which adds up to the same thing.) To turn Saussure around: ideology is a positive term without a difference.

Some years ago Raymond Williams suggested we would be better off dropping "ideology" from the critical lexicon (*Marxism and Literature*, 55–71); but people did not listen to him, and they are certainly not going to listen to me. Some will simply refuse, preferring to unmask the ideology hidden behind the suggestion we stop using "ideology." But even those who may wish to buy into my argument will not be able to do so, unless they simply abandon any ambition to engage with those critical practices (and they are among the strongest and most influential ones on the current scene) that do make use of the concept. The inevitability of "ideology" in our critical lexicon these days is part of a historical weight from which there is no escape.

It is a weight that would be hard to overestimate. The standard histories of the term usually start with Destutt de Tracy around the French Revolution, but the assumptions that generate the controversial appropriations of the term on the contemporary scene have a much deeper past. Plato invented the concept of ideology, though his term for it was ("untethered") opinion, to which he contrasted ("stable") knowledge.[8] Most of the arguments on the right for the transcendence of ideology can be traced back more or less directly to this dualism in Plato. But the critique of ideology on the left has a long pedigree as well, even the particular strain identified earlier. Antifoundationalist theory hope is not a postmodern discovery. The idea is central to the Frankfurt critical theorists, for whom the knowledge of cultural determination is frequently represented as the basis for critical detachment. Even

Mannheim, with his insistence on the specificity of all knowledge to a contingent context of interests, could not resist the same temptation. He backed away from the resolute relativism of his argument and rechristened it "relationism." In relationism, relativism has become conscious of itself, and this self-consciousness somehow allows for a move in the direction of a substantial scientific foundation, called the sociology of knowledge, on which a progressive hope could be built. But high modernism, in either the Mannheim or Frankfurt version, is still too recent to serve as a *terminus ab quo* for antifoundationalist theory hope. We have to go back to early modernism, for as Victoria Kahn has shown in a brilliant essay, the idea that the self-conscious acknowledgment of ideological interest somehow empowers the critique of ideology reenacts a central argument of Renaissance humanism. And we can go back further still, once again to Plato, where the admission of ignorance serves as the base from which genuine critical knowledge is possible.

What can account for the perennial hardiness of ideology, and of those more or less interchangeable dualisms—being/seeming, nature/culture, essence/accident—on which the concept depends? It is sometimes argued that the endurance of these dualisms proves they are right, or satisfy some essential human need. The counterargument is that their installation at the time of Plato was a matter of contingent choice (Rorty, *Philosophy*, 155–64); that they have survived, as lots of cultural values do, largely because of inertia (we are used to them; they are famous on account of being well known [Barbara Herrnstein Smith, *Contingencies*, 47–53]); and finally that the same history that has entrenched the concept of ideology also includes, as a kind of poor brother or (better) weak sister, a long tradition of antifoundationalist thought, going back to the sophists who antedated Plato, and Ovid (in contrast to Vergil), and rhetoric (in contrast to dialectic or logic).[9] However we understand the history sustaining the term, it is the commitment now to the concept of ideology that chiefly interests me here, both from the right and from the left, each of which claims that its abandonment would have terribly disabling consequences.

On the right the consequences take the form of chaos come again. Unless we have some nonideological grounds to regulate critical activity—authorial intention, the text itself, *consensus gentium*, tradition defined as a more or less consistent body of thought—then it is anything goes, a situation without any sense of purpose or direction. But this fear is groundless. The abandonment of, say, the text itself does not mean that we have no way to direct critical activity, only that the way associated with the text itself (with this presumed alternative to ideology which is itself an ideology) no longer carries authority. If anything is clear about criticism during the last twenty years or so, it is that there *has* been purpose and direction to, among other things: the introduction of gender and social position and political power as relevant considerations in the production and reception of texts, the opening up of disciplinary boundaries; and the move away from literature itself to discourse studies. This transformation has been the result not of a free-for-all but rather of a widespread effort to transfer attention to a new and different set of concerns. Such transfers are always problematic even when they do not constitute an actual paradigm shift in Kuhn's sense. But they do not leave us with no rules to decide matters, they simply leave us with a new set of rules, or caught between contradictory sets of rules. Hence Gayle Greene can assure Levin and the rest of us that "I believe in supporting assertions by reference to the text" (25). She does not of course mean the same thing by the text as Levin does, but the point is that she is not at a loss for evidence, or for ways of presenting evidence. All she has lost (she may well think it good riddance) is the particular set of beliefs and assumptions underlying Levin's sense of what constitutes real evidence and the proper way to present it.[10]

The left, too, is anxious about the disappearance of ideology from critical analysis. Again the problem is deregulation, for if ideology disappears, then the category of the nonideological goes as well. But where the right sees a threat to stable order, the left sees a threat to meaningful change. "If 'all is permitted,'" Michael Bristol warns (sounding uncannily like Levin's "free to choose any context he pleases"), "then there are no grounds for maintaining that the overthrow of the humanistic dispensation constitutes any kind of progress, social, intellectual, or otherwise" (*Shakespeare's America*, 117). But again this anxiety is unnecessary. The absence of nonideological grounds from which to argue for social change does not mean that such arguments cannot be made. To say critique is impossible does not mean criticism is impossible. Critique (emigration) is impossible because there is nowhere to go that is not inside of history and society, but since the social history within which we are situated is itself full of variety, not to say contradiction, there are lots of importantly different positions to be occupied. Bristol therefore can (and does) rise from the pathos of his emigration paragraph to write a brilliantly interesting book of just the kind he wants, one highly critical of "more affirmative types of scholarship" (4), though the book itself remains sociohistorically determined and ideologically constituted—and eminently contestable.

Part of the anxiety on the left seems to be rhetorical and strategic: it is a worry that antifoundationalists lack authority. Who is going to believe a constructivist? In some situations, to be sure, essentialism may be persuasive, but the reason lies not in essentialism but in the situation. For instance, a strategic essentialism might be persuasive if you are talking to an essentialist (it would constitute an effective ethos, in the old terminology). But there are other situations in which a constructivist argument would look better—maybe, say, if you are appealing to a pragmatist to cut her fee for a lecture. There are also some situations in which neither constructivism nor essentialism will work. Rorty says that "irrationalists who tell us to think with our blood cannot be rebutted by better arguments about the nature of thought, or knowledge, or logic" (*Consequences*, 172), but neither will they be persuaded (Rorty would acknowledge as much) by claims for the value of keeping the conversation going.[11] Lots of things help make an argument persuasive: who's talking, how, and to whom (a mere three categories but they admit of a virtually unlimited number of variables); and the incalculable and unpredictable category of luck as well (un coup de dés jamais n'abolira le hasard). But all such determining factors work because of their specific fit to a varied and variable situation, and not because of the arguer's general theory of knowledge.

Perhaps the worry here is less about convincing others than about sustaining our own convictions. In the absence of a nonideological category of truth, how can we even believe ourselves? And how, without such belief, can we avoid a paralysis of the will? Shakespeareans will recognize this as the *Hamlet* (or maybe *Troilus*) problem, and like *Hamlet*, it has been appropriated all across the political spectrum. On the right, the putative abandonment of purpose and value dooms the young to wander aimlessly through the streets, souls without longing, listening to Guns n' Roses on their Walkmans.[12] The center can be represented by Paisley Livingston, who argues that "framework relativism" means we are condemned to a mushy formalism. As an antidote Livingston proposes scientific realism, which, he claims, will permit us to anchor critical activity in a sociohistorical context. But in fact the move to historicization can be (and often has been) made independently of a realist epistemology, and this move has not in any case solved the problem of indeterminacy, simply situated it in a different position.

The fullest discussion is on the left, where the problem is usually defined as functionalism and the erosion of authentic resistance and oppositional agency. For a brilliant representation of the way things look from this perspective, consider Paul Smith's book, *Discerning the Subject*. Smith begins with a vigorous rebuttal of Althusserian functionalism, locating the weak spot not in constructivism but in totalization: it is one thing for Althusser to say that we are all interpellated as subjects, another for him to claim that the interpellation is performed under the direction of a unified cultural mechanism. Having emphasized the variety and contraditions within our situation, Smith is in a position to concede that all action is ideologically constituted without conceding anything at all. But Smith argues against such a conclusion, affirming instead that we can allow for "the possibility (indeed, the actuality) of resistance to ideological pressure" (xxxv). How? By "positing a constitutive non-unity in the subject," Smith claims he can "point toward a category of agency" (22–23), adding that "the place of that resistance has, then, to be glimpsed somewhere in the interstices of the subject-positions which are offered in any social formation" (25). All this leads to the triumphant conclusion "that ideological interpellations may *fail* to produce 'a subject' or even a firm subject-position. Rather, what is produced by ideological interpellation is contradiction, and through a recognition of the contradictory and dialectical elements of subjectivity it may be possible to think a concept of the agent" (37).

But how do we recognize subjective contradictions except through the knowledge and understanding derived from our various histories? What then enables us to claim that such recognition *is not itself ideologically determined?* Or that the spaces between ideological apparatuses in disunified formations and the spaces between ideological interpellations in the divided subject *are not themselves ideologically filled?* Smith is willing to concede that we can play only the hand we have been dealt, but he refuses to concede that even knowing when to hold and when to fold 'em and knowing when to fight and when to run belong to us only as derivatives from the same cultural dispensation that dealt us the hand in the first place. As Rorty says, "socialization, and thus historical circumstance, goes all the way down— . . . there is nothing 'beneath' socialization or prior to history which is definatory of the human" (*Contingency*, xiii). And if it is culture all the way down, then it is ideology all the way up and all across the board, including those gaps and interstices that Smith has invested with such hope for authentic oppositional agency.

Again, though, this investment is not necessary. Once you can establish the variety and contradictions in culture, you have taken

care of functionalism anyway, and you do not need to fall back to
any interstitial subject position to be able to claim what you want:
namely, that change is possible (indeed, inevitable), and that our
actions contribute to such change (though not in masterfully predictable ways).[13] In short, anxieties about antifoundationalism on
the left, though different from those on the right or at the center,
are equally misplaced, and for the same reason as earlier: beliefs
are not logically dependent on or necessarily produced by epistemological theories. To quote Rorty again: "A belief can still regulate action, can still be thought worth dying for, among people
who are quite aware that this belief is caused by nothing deeper
than contingent historical circumstances" (*Contingency*, 189).[14]

To see how this works, we can juxtapose two passages, one from
M. H. Abrams explaining why he will not accept Jonathan Culler's
suggestion to retitle his book *The Mire and the Swamp*, the other
from Raymond Williams explaining why he is a socialist:

> What I have said does not constitute a knockout argument, far less
> the demonstration of an absolute foundation, for my standpoint. I
> believe, in fact, that this matter of the choice of the primitives for
> intellectual discourse is beyond all demonstrative argument
> except—and the exception is of high consequence—the prag-
> matic argument of the profitability for our understanding in
> choosing one set of intellectual premises over another. What I
> have said, then, is really an announcement of where I take my
> stand—a stand on certain primitives to be used in our explanative
> discourse about human talking, doing, and making. Which
> amounts to the confession that, despite immersion in the decon-
> structive element of our time, I remain an unreconstructed
> humanist. (M. H. Abrams, 174)

> There is of course the difficulty that domination and subordina-
> tion, as effective descriptions of cultural formation, will, by many,
> be refused; that the alternative language of co-operative shaping,
> of common contribution, which the traditional concept of 'cul-
> ture' so notably expressed, will be found preferable. In this funda-

mental choice there is no alternative, from any socialist position, to recognition and emphasis of the massive historical and immediate experience of class domination and subordination, in all their different forms. This becomes, very quickly, a matter of specific experience and argument. (Williams, *Marxism*, 112)

There is a world of difference between Abrams's unreconstructed humanism and Williams's cultural materialism. They disagree, for instance, about whether social conflict or cooperative shaping constitutes the better position from which to analyze and evaluate the world—a disagreement that corresponds quite closely to Levin's negotiation and to Barker and Hulme's contestation, from which we began. In addition, the differences between them would include a wide variety of beliefs ("opinions" might be used here, or "ideological preferences"): maybe what we teach, and how, and abortion law, and the designated hitter rule, and who knows what (for these beliefs are not specified or predictable). But in one area, causally unrelated to these various beliefs, Abrams and Williams are saying the same thing—that the beliefs themselves do not rest on any more secure (read "nonideological") basis than that of an assumed position. Do not rest, *and do not have to.*

Thus Abrams acknowledges he cannot disprove Culler's retitling argument. Williams knows there is no logical way to persuade humanists to become socialists, since what is involved in such "preferences" is not "choice" in the Miltonic sense ("reason also is choice") but the contingencies of history ("immediate" and "specific experience")—not refutation but "refusal." Both Abrams and Williams know as well that their own positions are no more securely grounded in principle than those of their antagonists, but this knowledge does not prevent them from continuing to believe what they believe. They stick to their guns and go on advocating their positions. Williams's word at the end is "argument," and in this context he can hardly mean logical demonstration. He means rhetoric, with its inevitably agonistic and contestatory ambience, the same ambience as Abrams's "knockout argument."

Winning isn't the main thing, it's the only thing. Winning, though, is impossible. In giving up foundations in favor of pragmatic profitability, Abrams has not exchanged closure at one end (origin) for closure at the other (consequences). According to Rorty (whose terms Abrams must expect us to recognize here), the pragmatist argument ends up by not ending up; it just keeps the conversation going. The same is true of Williams's history. "In most description and analysis," Williams tells us, "culture and society are expressed in an habitual past tense. The strongest barrier to the recognition of human cultural activity is this immediate and regular conversion of experience into finished products" (*Marxism*, 128). *It's not over till it's over*, what Abrams and Williams both add is that it's never over. The game goes on, and there is no way out of the game, but this does not prevent you from continuing to play and playing to win.

Abrams and Williams enable us to answer the second of the two questions I raised at the beginning of this chapter—the question, in fact, that has been hovering over the discussion from the beginning of this book: What is to be done? The answer is, Nothing is to be done; or at least nothing special. There are two reasons: (1) nothing can be done (there is nothing outside of ideology), and (2) nothing special needs to be done (accepting reason 1 does not inhibit our ability to believe what we believe and to advocate the actions that we understand to follow from these beliefs).

Is there a down side to this situation? Maybe. It creates some messy pedagogical inconveniences (the sort of thing I described in Chapter 4), and it means that we can look forward to further bellicose exchanges in the journals we read and the conferences we attend, such as the one I described at the beginning of this chapter, or the running debate on feminism vs. new historicism, which I discussed in Chapter 1. This is a bad thing if you believe it would be better to return to something like the consensus that existed in Shakespeare criticism and in academic criticism generally twenty years ago. Anyone who feels this way may be comforted with the plausibility of assuming that something like a consensus will emerge eventually from the situation we have at present. It is impossible to predict the nature of this more harmonious future, though we can be reasonably sure it will not be a simple return to the status quo ante. The impossibility of predicting also adds up to definite limits on our ability to bring such a future about (*The Eighteenth Brumaire* again). Yet it will come; the readiness is all.

There are others—including me, "if" (to recall Gayle Greene's words) "you really want to know"—who derive no particular comfort from the prospect of a restoration of consensus. The question, anyway, is what we do in the meantime, whichever side we are on, however positioned we are to "feel beset from all sides." Apart from watching and waiting, St. Mark's always useful advice for difficult times, reading and teaching and writing should be kept on the agenda. Business as usual, in other words; nothing special. We may think that the institutional and disciplinary arrangements that underwrite business as usual do not serve our interests very well, but along with the fundamental and irresolvable disagreements I have been concerned with throughout this book, they are what we have to work with and within in the unsure and uncertain hope of resurrecting better ones. As a result of this situation, our "conversation" may sometimes seem like a dialogue of the deaf, but keeping it going had better be enough because, like ideology, it is all we have got.

Notes

✤

Introduction

1. There have been many good histories of these changes, going back to Frank Lentricchia's *After the New Criticism*. Hugh Grady's *Modernist Shakespeare* is of particular interest to Shakespeareans.

2. The scientific model may underlie even Rorty's metaphor of conversation as well. Since in Rorty's description conversation cannot trace its way back to a point of origin and cannot even imagine a point of closure, it might as well be called *argument* in the nontechnical sense. "Conversation" tends to conjure up an image of gown-clad, sherry-sipping Oxbridge dons all talking like a C. P. Snow novel—an implication for which Rorty has often been criticized (e.g., West, 211–12). It may be that Rorty was trying to counteract the influence of the scientific model—trying to redeem dispute by giving it a polite name and sneaking it through the back door. It is not just scientific protocol that resists Rorty's program but social norms as well: "It's rude to argue." (Someone ought to undertake a study of the hegemonic connections between science and bourgeois politesse; maybe someone already has.) Then again, Rorty probably was not fully aware of what he was doing when he hit on "conversation" as his key metaphor, or was still subject to the influence of the model he was trying to replace.

1. What Was Shakespeare?

1. Evans's lament that "nine out of ten pieces of Shakespeare criticism will as ever remain unreadable and unread" (94) at the least strongly implies in its con-

text the suggestion not only that we should do Shakespeare criticism differently, but that we should transfer our energies to different texts. Cary Nelson is more explicit in his rhetorical question: "When a curriculum requires a course in Shakespeare but not a course in black literature, what message does it give students about black or Hispanic people, what message about the cultural traditions that are valuable and those that are expendable?" (49–50).

Such complaints seem new to criticism, but they have been a staple of theater for some time. Think of Brecht, Shaw, or, for that matter, Dryden, whose example suggests that these complaints go back to the very beginnings, as though the establishment of Shakespeare's power and the resistance to it are part of the same felt belief.

2. The new, postformalist modes of criticism have augmented our interest in Shakespeare, not displaced it. As for new areas of writing, Shakespeare has for some time been branching out from the canonical center of Eng. Lit. into the non-European margins: of Japanese culture (a point apparently emphasized at the International Shakespeare Conference at Tokyo in 1991); of South African and Indian culture (witness Orkin and *Hamlet Studies*); of the Middle East (where, according to Mahmoud F. al-Shetawi, a "steady growth in the interest in Shakespeare" during the early twentieth century has "fostered Arab writing in emulation of Shakespeare"). See also Marder, "Shakespeare Heard 'Round the World,'" for lots more such material.

3. According to information and explanation generously furnished me by James Harner of the World Shakespeare Bibliography project at Texas A & M, the *SQ* bibliography moved in 1989 and again in 1991 to new policies of conflation and of cutting back on the cross-referenced items, especially reviews of productions; as a result, the total number of works listed would have been down from previous years. With allowances made for this shift, the new record for 1990 is indeed impressive, and even more impressive the 1992 figure (the latest available to me as I write), which would have been even higher except for a printing schedule that reduced the period covered by as much as four months. The *SQ* numbers are generally consistent with the totals from the *MLA Bibliography*: 1989 saw a significant downturn in Eng. Lit. production generally, but there was basically no change from 1989 to 1990 (Franklin, 5). Here too the matter may be complicated by a change in the reporting procedures—in this case again, an earlier cutoff date.

4. Its antecedent, the 1971 Muir-Schoenbaum edition, reprinted six times by 1984, had only a single chapter devoted to "Shakespeare Criticism since Bradley," written by Wells himself. In the new edition, "Twentieth-Century Shakespeare Criticism" is divided (generically) into three essays by different authors and a separate essay on "Shakespeare and New Critical Approaches"—a compressed and lucid performance by Terence Hawkes that takes off from the idea that Bradley's premises no longer seem tenable.

5. Kernan includes a section called "Intellectual and Theatrical Setting," but it consists of only two essays: a Foakes piece, "The Profession of Playwright," and a substantial excerpt from Patrick Cruttwell's *Shakespearean Moment*, a book about lyric in which history is primarily intellectual history and its importance is limited primarily to its influence on the individual psyche. A similar sort of reduction is evi-

dent in Kernan's title for the excerpt, "The Age and Its Effect on Literary Style."
Though from the current perspective all the old anthologies look inadequate in
their representation of the historical, Kernan's is unique in its virtual elimination.

6. The existence of such conflicts has been a staple of feminist commentary at
least since Domna Stanton's "Language and Revolution: The Franco-American
Disconnection," and more recently Catherine Stimpson has declared that "the
feminist cultural consensus, that contract about opinions," not only has been
eroded but "is beyond restoration" ("Nancy Reagan," 237). For Graff, see *Professing Literature*, "What Should We Be Teaching?" and "Teach the Conflicts." As for
recent Shakespeare anthologies: *The Woman's Part* (Lenz et al.) begins by declaring
that "it is as difficult to define feminist criticism as it is to define feminism itself" (3;
see Kolodny for a well-known justification of this position). At the beginning of
Political Shakespeare, Dollimore and Sinfield point to a shift from a unitary subject
to the multiple perspectives of interdisciplinarity: "One of the most important
achievements of 'theory' in English studies has been the making possible of a truly
interdisciplinary approach to—some might say exit from—the subject" (2). The
very use of the word "question" conjoined to "theory" in Parker and Hartman's
title moves in the same direction.

7. See Alcoff, Rabine, Poovey, and Hirsch and Keller. In recent versions the
lines tend to be drawn between politics and theory (see Carol Cook's dispute
about Shakespeare with Jonathan Goldberg [68–74]; and McDowell's discussion
of different modes of accounting for the writing of women of color). The surprising (or maybe predictable) resurgence of "essentialism" is worth noting in this
context. See Paul Smith, de Lauretis, Fuss, Dollimore (*Sexual Dissidence*, 39–78),
Bredbeck, and Miller (*Getting Personal*).

8. I am not fabricating these examples—see Carton, and Graff's response to
him ("The Nonpolitics of PC"), as well as Taylor, and my response.

2. The Rise and Fall of the New Historicism

1. *Critical Inquiry* 9.1 (1982): 1–280 and *Diacritics* 14.2 (1984): 1–81.

2. Both the Harriot–*Henry IV* and the Harsnett-*Lear* essays were later expanded
from the original publications I have been quoting, the first under the same title
and the second as "Shakespeare and the Exorcists." The later versions are included
in the Works Cited. Since Greenblatt's capacity to interest depends on the inclusion and orchestration of circumstance and detail, expansion is nearly always
improvement: more is more—but, in regard to the critical procedures and
assumptions I have been examining, more of the same.

3. Greenblatt refers to this essay in a somewhat different context (*Renaissance
Self-Fashioning*, 153). Terry Eagleton discusses Althusser's position, which he con-
siders "suggestive" though "radically unsatisfactory" (*Criticism and Ideology*, 82–84).

4. "Thick description" is Gilbert Ryle's phrase, appropriated by Clifford Geertz
(a major influence acknowledged by Greenblatt) as an interpretive method at the
beginning of *The Interpretation of Cultures*. Similar claims for social analysis that

acknowledges a variety of cultural forces are made by Sinfield, *Literature*, 3; Dollimore, *Radical Tragedy*, 7 (borrowing from Raymond Williams); and Jameson, 95.

5. Both Foucault in "What Is an Author?" and Belsey in "Disrupting Sexual Difference" allow for the possibility that texts may destabilize the normalizing force of cultural authority. Disagreeing with Greenblatt's contention that subversion is produced by authority, Dollimore argues that Renaissance theatrical texts can be appropriated in different ways ("Introduction: Shakespeare," 12); and Dollimore and Sinfield point out that the interpretive decision on how to appropriate a play depends on assumptions about the play's "diverse conditions of reception" ("History," 225).

6. In effect, this is what Terry Eagleton and Frank Kermode advise in their reviews of *Learning to Curse*. Eagleton declares that "the new historicism, so the transatlantic medical bulletins inform us, is pretty well dead on its feet, but its prime begetter, Stephen Greenblatt, refuses to lie down" ("Historian as Body-Snatcher"). In the *LRB* for the same month, Kermode declares that Greenblatt "is bringing about a transformation in the way people think" about the Renaissance, and that "one can describe the way he goes about this work without elaborate recourse to the growing and rather rickety structure of theory it is attracting" ("Hail to the Chief"). The disagreement whether new historicism is flourishing or "dead on its feet" is precisely the sort of confusion we will have to endure in the absence of a consensus around a definition. But both Kermode and Eagleton, for all their evidently different understandings of new historicism (as well as lots of other things), share the belief I am advocating here about the importance of Greenblatt's own work.

7. Apart from items mentioned elsewhere in this section, see Barton ("Perils of Historicism"), Boose, Dawson ("*Measure*"), Holstun, Horwitz, Lentricchia (*Ariel*, 86–102), Lerner, Liu, Pease, Rosenberg, Thomas (esp. 179–218), Waller, and Wayne. There is other useful material in a special issue of *ELR* (Winter 1986), expanded and published as a book (see Kinney and Collins), and in three anthologies, two edited by Veeser and one by Richard Wilson and Dutton.

8. On the issue of functionalism, Greenblatt claims he was misread (*Learning to Curse*, 164–66). Maybe; but why was he misread by so many people in the same way? And why, once it should have been obvious that "Invisible Bullets" was at the heart of the problem, did he keep reprinting the essay without clarification? It looks as if Greenblatt is following a path similar to Foucault's. In his later work, Foucault abandoned an earlier functionalism for pragmatism, and then read the pragmatism back into his earlier work as a way of denying that the functionalism was there. See Foucault's Afterword, "The Subject and Power" and "Questions of Method." For an interestingly different recent formulation on this question, see Greenblatt's discussion of "the forces of domination," *Marvelous Possessions*, 120–21.

On the question of an arbitrary and totalized view of history and culture, Greenblatt has changed his mind. The change is evident in the first chapter of *Shakespearean Negotiations* and acknowledged by Greenblatt himself in "Culture" and even more strikingly in his recent *New Yorker* piece, "Kindly Visions." (For citations and discussion see Felperin [*The Uses of the Canon*, 142–56], Appiah, and Hunt.) The subject of European expansion into the New World is a good index to Greenblatt's changing position. In the wonderfully engaging *Marvelous Possessions*, the purpose is considerably expanded from the relentless critique of Eurocentrism I was describing in "The New Historicism and Its Discontents." In "Improvisation and Power," for instance, Greenblatt had focused exclusively on appropriation and manipulation, but in *Marvelous Possessions* he is eager to include a different kind of response to difference, articulating "the hidden links between . . . radically opposed ways of being and hence to some form of acceptance of the other in the self and the self in the other" (135). Greenblatt discusses Herodotus and Mandeville as examples of such nonappropriative responses. If the focus were on *Othello*, as it was in "Improvisation and Power," then Greenblatt would in effect be adding Desdemona's voice to the discussion, a voice ignored earlier in favor of Iago's, just as Falstaff's was ignored in favor of Hal's.

9. See Attridge et al., Cressy, and Hunt.

10. See "The Improvisation of Power," Greenblatt's revision of his "Improvisation and Power," in his *Renaissance Self-Fashioning*, 222–54.

11. See Joseph Smith and Kerrigan, and also Rorty's discussion of Freud in *Contingency*.

12. See Horwitz for a particularly generous and interesting discussion both of the phrase and of Greenblatt's work in general.

3. Of Ants and Grasshoppers: Two Ways (or More) to Link Texts and Power

1. I am rather blandly assuming that the Baines document represents Marlowe's statements, but work by John Manningham and Constance Kuriyama have inclined people to be less skeptical about Baines. See Kuriyama's summary.

2. The entry, in the same unattributed English translation, is conveniently available in the collections of Webster criticism edited by the Hunters (31–32) and by Moore (34). The original Italian is in Chambers (511) and Stoll (29).

3. I have called them ant and grasshopper stories, as though their meaning were textually embedded, but, like all stories, they can be appropriated in different ways. Busino, for instance, could be turned into an ant story if, armed (say) with Virginia Woolf's discussion near the end of the first chapter of *Three Guineas*, you understand his diary entry in terms of gender politics and phallic aggression: men always like to dress up and play soldier. So we would find ourselves not floating freely above power but embedded in the *real* power relations screened by Catholic-and-Protestant—namely, male and female. (As always, I mean "real" in a positional rather than a metaphysical sense.) This might work the other way round for the Marlowe story; though I have given it an antish interpretation, grasshoppers could use it for their purposes. The move here would be to look a little more closely at all the versions in Chambers. Quite possibly, they all derive from Middleton's "Hee had a head of hayre like one of my Diuells in Dr. Faustus when the old Theater crackt and frightened the audience" (Chambers, 423), in which the actors

are themselves unafraid. If this is true, then the original story is generated from within the theater and testifies to the power of theatrical illusion, and subsequent antitheatrical revisions (the next version is Prynne's in *Histriomastix*), including the one I quoted, place the fear in the actors rather than in the audience as a way of containing any such theatrical claims—thereby of course providing additional testimony to the power of such claims.

4. We have already seen Marlowe's suggestion that religion is just a kind of theater. Sir Thomas Browne said, without any evident irony, "I could never hear the *Ave Marie* Bell without an elevation. . . . At a solemne [Catholic] Procession I have wept abundantly, while my [Protestant] consorts, blinde with opposition and prejudice, have fallen into an accesse of scorne and laughter" (9). Donne's theatricality at the end of the sonnet on the church and throughout the third satire might, with some hard arguing, be brought in here as well.

5. We can never see *The Duchess* as its original audience might have seen it; the play is always bound to seem different, historically strange. I have not tried to account for the special problems of historicization in interpretive activity, but I would (of course) base any such attempt on the proposition that all historical activity is divided into two parts, and then proceed to claim that grasshopper historicists are more useful than ant historicists because they allow for the possibility of a historical understanding that can displace us from our familiar subject positions. In short, I would want to argue that there are ways in which old stories can be appropriated as new stories.

4. *Teaching Differences*

1. When Kermode tells us in *The Sense of an Ending* that "we have to distinguish between myths and fictions," he describes different modes of belief that correspond exactly to Barber's: an "absolute" assent that "presupposes total and adequate explanations of things as they are and were" and a "conditional" assent that changes "as the needs of sense-making change." It is in the nature of Kermode's fictional belief to understand its own difference from myth: fictions are "consciously held to be fictive," and "we are never in danger of thinking that the death of King Lear, which explains so much, is *true*" (39, 40). Michael Goldman, working out of Piaget and analogies between children's play and theatrical experience, comes to a similar position. In his description of "the flow of unbroken ego-satisfaction" in both kinds of experience, Goldman too emphasizes exclusion and separation: the " 'refusal to allow the world of . . . ordinary reality to interfere with play' " and "keeping the outside world under control." Hence, "though we are aware . . . that the symbols of art are not real for us, it is still true that as we watch the play, to the extent that it is successful, *we do not consider whether the symbols are real.* We do not judge them by standards that refer directly to the outside world, but by standards established within the work itself" (82, 3).

2. Although the coalescence of Barber's assumptions into a normative theory may be associated with Romanticism, it would be simple-minded to believe that

they were invented out of nothing in the late eighteenth century. Sidney is one figure who ought to be invoked here, with his famous description of the poet who "nothing affirms, and therefore never lieth"—that is, who never "affirm[s] that to be true which is false"—because he "never maketh any circles about your imagination, to conjure you to believe for true what he writes" (123–24). In a wonderful passage in the *Confessions* which may have been echoing in Sidney's mind, Augustine distinguishes the usefulness of poetic fables from the soul-destroying consequences of false philosophy. "These things," he says, speaking of the Manichean cosmogonic allegories, "simply do not exist and they are death to those who believe in them. Verses and poems can provide real food for thought, but although I used to recite verses . . . , I never maintained that they were true; and I never believed the poems which I heard others recite. But I did believe the tales which these men [the Manichees] told" (III.6.62). I assume finally that Aristotelian connections are obvious, most notably the distinction between probable impossibilities and improbable possibilities at *Poetics* 1460ᵃ.

3. No fewer than four of the six older anthologies I discussed in Chapter 1 include Barber, a distinction shared only with G. Wilson Knight. Northrop Frye, Maynard Mack, Cleanth Brooks, and J. F. Danby are represented in three of the six. (Barber is still, of course, widely respected and influential.)

4. Montrose's " 'Shaping Fantasies' " has been twice reprinted, by Greenblatt (*Representing*, 31–64) and, in an abridged version, by Ferguson et al. (65–87). My quotations are from the original publication.

5. Two Canadian versions can serve as illustrations. In Guy Sprung's 1987 Vancouver production, according to Malcolm Page's description, "the curtain rises . . . to reveal an officer pointing a revolver at the head of a blindfolded, kneeling woman in khaki uniform. Behind are four more blindfolded prisoners (the program refers to them as guerrillas) guarded by soldiers. . . . Then the officer fires in the air, removes the blindfold, embraces the woman and starts the play." It is conceivable that Ciulei was behind this opening, but if not Ciulei it might have been Elijah Moshinsky or John Hirsch, since as Page points out, "as in the BBC television version and at Stratford [Ontario] in 1984, we have been vividly reminded that Theseus 'wooed thee with my sword'" (24).

The other Canadian version, though performed in London, was directed by Robert Lepage and designed by Michael Levine for the Olivier Theatre at the National in 1992. This production begins (where *Othello* ends) with a bed, on which Theseus and Hippolyta stand over the four entwined lovers. Beds (there were four of them) appear throughout the production, one of them serving Bottom and Titania in IV.1 as the place for what the promptbook describes as a "simulated copulation," apparently performed with some intensity: "their coupling is bestial and noisily orgasmic," according to the *Telegraph* (Spencer); a "disturbing . . . rape fantasy," according to the *Observor* (Coveney). But the chief feature of this production was a shallow pool surrounded by mud ("the wet Dream," as Timothy Spall, who played Bottom, called it), through which the actors "run, crawl and splash [spectators in the two front rows were provided with plastic overcoats], swapping sexual partners." For Benedict Nightingale, whose *Times* review I have been quoting, the filth suggested "primordial slime": "the aim here is to find darkness . . . particularly sexual darkness."

6. According to Michael Billington in the *Guardian*: "Clearly Lepage sees Angela Laurier's Puck as the key to the play. Laurier is a formidable contortionist and a remarkable physical presence. But it is typical of the production's upside-down values that the one gift nature denied Laurier was the ability to speak the verse with comprehensible clarity." Unlike Billington, who hated the show ("the most perverse, leaden, humourless and vilely spoken production of this magical play I have ever seen"), Robert Hewison in the Sunday *Times* liked it a lot, but as it were for the same reason, viewing the loss of detached elegance as part of a trade-off constituting a net gain: "There is a price to pay for Lepage's brilliance. The verse has too stately a pace, and Laurier's French-Canadian accent loses words. But when they are being spoken by someone doing a forearm stand, gesticulating with articulate feet, the loss is small. The gain is a gallery of visual images, the watery reflections cast by light on to the back walls, or the joyful sight of the lovers at last showered in clean water. . . . The mud makes everything, not just the groundlings, funnier."

7. A good illustration of the problem in literary as distinct from theatrical terms occurs in Gail Kern Paster's discussion of the play (125–43). Like most recent versions, Paster's starts with an emphasis on the "profound anxiety" generated by the play (138), especially in the erotic resonances of the Bottom-Titania material: Bottom as a male, passively (anally) purged by an overpowering maternal presence; Titania as a female shamefully betrayed by infantile and bestial dotage. But then, in a heroic responsiveness to contradictory evidence, Paster acknowledges that "what is missing from these scenes is precisely the experience of shame in them" (140). Paster's attempt to get out of this problem seems to me less interesting than her willingness to recognize its existence.

8. See Catherine Belsey on "the object of the critic" (*Critical Practice*, 109), and Maureen Quilligan on "all strong modern theories of interpretation" (29).

9. At least if you can trust Frederick Crews's description: "The orthodox Althusserian J. H. Kavanagh . . . defiantly states that his reading of 'Benito Cereno' will not be constrained by Melville or the text but only by his own wish to 'challenge a dominant ideology'—that is, to make the story 'available for a certain form of [Marxist] teaching practice'" (77).

10. You can argue that all the play's exclusions are made in an overt way. Consider, for example, the conspicuous "he-who"-ing in the questions the Fairy asks Puck in II.1, where the play both takes care of exposition (we have to know right away whether Puck is in the benevolent or malevolent tradition of little people) and calls attention to the fact that it is taking care of exposition. Any realism-seeking director is bound to be embarrassed by such creaking machinery, and the passage Montrose hits on may be particularly embarrassing. Perhaps this is why, according to the promptbooks housed at the Shakespeare Birthplace Trust and at the National Theatre, the Peter Hall, Ron Daniels, and Robert Lepage productions divide the speech between Theseus and either Philostrate or Lysander.

11. For one such answer, see Belsey (*Subject of Tragedy*, 222–24); for a skeptical response to Belsey, see Levin ("Bashing," 85–86).

12. In Harry Berger's more recent version, worked out in essays published over a dozen years or so and now conveniently available (with some modifications) in *Imaginary Audition*, textual indeterminacy (perceived by the "slit-eyed reader") is set up in contrast to the theater, where, it is claimed, a single overt surface meaning is inevitably privileged (by the "wide-eyed spectator"; on this distinction see Worthen and Dawson ["Impasse"]). For me the problem resides in the fact that Berger's story can be told equally well the other way round, as we have seen in Roger Warren and Maynard Mack, both of whom locate (and value) coherent meaning in textual experience as governed by an integrated authorial intelligence, and find incoherence in the theater where meaning is unstable from moment to moment and uncontrollably the product of too many inputs (author, director, actors, designer, physical stage). You can not only reverse the polarities; you can multiply versions of this kind of distinction pretty much indefinitely: texts that are classical vs. modern, writerly vs. readerly, metaphoric vs. metonymic, literary vs. nonliterary. The resulting taxonomies will always work, although, since work implies resistance, it would be better to say that they will always play.

13. I will develop this "no consequences" position at greater length in the last chapter. Its most influential advocates are Richard Rorty (passim, but most recently in *Contingency*, 44–54) and Stanley Fish (*Doing*, 315–41, and "Commentary"). For other strong advocacies of this position, see Kenshur, "Demystifying" and "(Avoidable) Snares"; and Horwitz.

14. See Graff, *Professing Literature*, "What Should We Be Teaching?" and "Teach the Conflicts" (in Craige). Perhaps I am attributing to Graff's program ambitions that are not really there for rising above conflict. Or maybe they were there and have been shed in such more recent work as "Teach the Conflicts" (*SAQ*) and "Other Voices."

15. This kind of story is by no means limited, of course, to de Man. For another version, see Shklar (151–52).

5. In Defense of Jargon: Criticism as a Social Practice

1. See Barker and Belsey (*Subject of Tragedy*) for other versions of this view.

2. I am thinking of Fish's emphasis on communities, or Samuel Weber's on institutions, or the institutional histories by Graff and Culler mentioned earlier. (Culler has again been in the vanguard of critical change here: his remark about criticism as advancing knowledge [*Pursuit of Signs*] was made in 1981.) In more general terms, I am thinking of the widespread shift away from the sovereign subject of humanism and over to various forms of historicism and materialism.

6. Against "Ideology"

1. In his last paragraph, Alter once again asserts that "reading is a privileged pleasure," and that literary criticism (by which he means not the discussion in the

second degree but discussion in the first degree, the putatively nonideological sort of criticism he approves of) "is one of the most gratifying responses to literary creation, second only to reading itself" (238). One remove from reality may be better than two, but why bother with either when you can have reality itself?

2. Kermode of course went on to write, among other things, *The Sense of an Ending* (1967), and subsequently to write that during the half a dozen years after its publication, "I remember feeling rather dismally that quite a lot of work had gone into a book which became antediluvian almost on publication" (*Art of Telling*, 3).

3. For the theater I am thinking of Derek Jacobi's recent RSC performance, as described in various reviews and by Jacobi himself in a recent *Shakespeare Quarterly* interview. For academic criticism see Cutts; Berger, "Miraculous Harp"; Pearson; and Richard Abrams. (My thanks to Richard Levin for calling my attention to the Cutts and Pearson items.) Curt Breight can mention "the fact that the audience is *outside* Prospero's play and can therefore view it with critical detachment" as though this were self-evident—that is, the dominant contemporary view (9). Of course Breight is publishing five years after Barker and Hulme, but the change he serves to illustrate was hardly limited to those five years. For a brilliantly interesting discussion of the general pattern represented by Barker and Hulme, see Howard Felperin's argument about *The Tempest* in *Uses of the Canon*, chaps. 2 and 9. Felperin's basic point is that *The Tempest*'s romance qualities are always already demystified, and that claiming to have progressed to the point of seeing the romance ironically "is to reveal . . . the mythic status of modernism itself" (33).

4. Paul Smith quotes Stuart Hall's question "why some people—those living their relation to their conditions of existence through the categories of a distorted ideology—cannot recognize that it is distorted, while we [Marxists], with our superior wisdom, or armed with properly formed concepts, can" (11).

5. In both passages Belsey tells us she is following Althusser, who is also self-contradictory on the issue of ideology, conceiving of it as on the one hand the precondition of our thought, that which subtends our subjectivity, and on the other, a scientifically knowable object of thought, that which unifies all the ISAs in "the last instance," which, even if the last instance does not come, remains available as the understanding that frames knowledge as a totality. For interesting different versions of this kind of problem in Althusser, see Jay (385–422) and Paul Smith (14–21, discussed below). On the other hand, see Kavanagh ("Ideology") for an interesting and accessible replication of Althusserian inconsistency.

6. Jonathan Goldberg has remarked ("Politics," 515–22) that Jameson tended toward the banal once he descended from theory to practical criticism. This is equally true of Eagleton, who, after breathtaking theoretical arabesques, stoops (102–61) to a set of comments about a grab bag of "major authors" that reads like a high-class *Cole's Notes*.

7. Fish, whose arguments stand behind a lot of the claims I am making here, discusses antifoundationalist theory hope throughout *Doing What Comes Naturally* as well as in his essay on new historicism, "Commentary: The Young and the Restless."

8. The distinction is of course formative and made frequently. One good example, from which I have quoted those epithets, comes near the end of the *Meno* (97ᶜ–98ᵃ; 381–82).

9. Lanham's *Motives of Eloquence* is the great account of this countertradition. The gist of Lanham is conveniently available in two Fish versions (*Doing*, 471–502, and "Rhetoric").

10. Levin himself seems to have come closer to this position in his 1990 *PMLA* piece. Though he again focuses his attack on the contemporary abandonment of authorial intention, the problem is now not anarchy but repressiveness: "The rejection of The Author Function . . . creates a hermeneutic vacuum that must be filled . . . what fills the vacuum is a universal law—the Law of Concealed-but-Revealed Ideological Contradiction. . . . The Death of the Author, then, has left these critics not more but less free—certainly less free than a comparable group of formalist-humanists trying to interpret Shakespeare's intended meaning" ("Poetics," 502). Levin seems more convincing here than earlier, though of course there is plenty of room to disagree with his understanding of how current criticism determines meaning, as well as with his implied definition of freedom and the value he places on it (*"certainly* less free"?).

Miltonists are experiencing similar difficulties about changing evidentiary protocols. I refer to the kerfuffle surrounding Leah Marcus's attempt to interpret *Comus* with reference to the judicial process, presided over by the Earl of Bridgewater, involved in a rape case dating from around the time Milton composed the poem. Since no good evidence exists, even inferentially, to believe Milton knew about the case, Marcus's argument entirely abandons authorial intention, but this does not leave her without evidence to marshal for her conclusions. On the contrary, her essay is (characteristically) filled with the meticulous accumulation of detail derived from laborious research into primary documents. It is just that the evidence and the evidentiary rules are determined by a different set of assumptions, unspecified but probably along the lines of those I suggested earlier, that issues of gender and power are the most important ones to keep in mind in determining interpretive conclusions.

11. Jonathan Dollimore, who has written with characteristic astuteness about this problem, remarks that a homophobic response to a constructivist argument might be aversion therapy, and to an essentialist argument enforced sterilization or worse ("Shakespeare," 478–79, and "Culture," 94–96).

12. I am alluding to Allan Bloom's jeremiad about the dire consequences for the young of relativist philosophy and rock music (68–81).

13. Why, then, does Smith cling against his own better knowledge to concepts, however chastened and reduced, of subjective sovereignty and nonideological truth? My guess is that he cannot finally escape from the historical nightmare I mentioned earlier, and its apparent demands precisely to transcend ideology by pulling ourselves up by our own bootstraps.

14. Cf. *Contingency,* 44–54 and 182–83: "one would have to be odd to change one's politics because one had become convinced, for example, that a coherence theory of truth was preferable to a correspondence theory."

Works Cited

❖

Abrams, M. H. "A Reply." In *High Romantic Argument: Essays for M. H. Abrams*, ed. Lawrence Lipking, 164–75. Ithaca: Cornell University Press, 1981.

Abrams, Richard. "*The Tempest* and the Concept of the Machiavellian Playwright." *English Literary Renaissance* 8 (1978): 43–66.

Adorno, Theodor W. *Aesthetic Theory*. Trans. C. Lenhart. Ed. Gretel Adorno and Rolf Tiedemann. London and Boston: Routledge & Kegan Paul, 1984.

———. *Negative Dialectics*. Trans. E. B. Ashton. New York: Seabury, 1973.

Alcoff, Linda. "Cultural Feminism versus Post-Structuralism: The Identity Crisis in Feminist Theory." *Signs* 13 (1988): 405–36.

Alter, Robert. *The Pleasures of Reading in an Ideological Age*. New York: Simon & Schuster, 1989.

Althusser, Louis. *For Marx*. Trans. Ben Brewster. New York: Random House, 1969.

———. *Lenin and Philosophy and Other Essays*. Trans. Ben Brewster. New York: Monthly Review Press, 1972.

———. "A Letter on Art in Reply to André Daspre." In *Lenin*, 221–27.

Anderson, Perry. *In the Tracks of Historical Materialism*. Chicago: University of Chicago Press, 1984.

Appiah, Anthony. "Tolerable Falsehoods: Agency and the Interests of Theory." In Arac and Johnson, 63–90.

Arac, Jonathan, and Barbara Johnson, eds. *Consequences of Theory: Selected Papers from the English Institute, 1987–88*. Baltimore: Johns Hopkins University Press, 1991.

Aristotle. *The Rhetoric and The Poetics of Aristotle*. Trans. W. Rhys Roberts. Introduction and notes by Friedrich Solmsen. New York: Random House, 1954.

Works Cited

Attridge, Derek, Geoff Bennington, and Robert Young, eds. *Post-Structuralism and the Question of History*. Cambridge: Cambridge University Press, 1987.

Augustine, St. *Confessions*. Trans. R. S. Pine-Coffin. Harmondsworth: Penguin, 1961.

Barber, C. L. *Shakespeare's Festive Comedy: A Study of Dramatic Form and Its Relation to Social Custom*. Princeton: Princeton University Press, 1959.

Barker, Francis. *The Tremulous Private Body*. London: Methuen, 1984.

Barker, Francis, and Peter Hulme. "Nymphs and Reapers Heavily Vanish: The Discursive Con-texts of *The Tempest*." In Drakakis, 191–205.

Barthes, Roland. *The Pleasure of the Text*. Trans. Richard Miller. New York: Hill & Wang, 1975.

Barton, Anne. Introduction to Shakespeare, *The Tempest*. Harmondsworth: Penguin, 1968.

——. "Perils of Historicism." *New York Review of Books*, 28 March 1991, 53–56.

Begley, Adam. "The Tempest around Stephen Greenblatt." *New York Times Magazine*, 28 March 1993, 32–38.

Bell, Daniel. *The End of Ideology: On the Exhaustion of Political Ideas in the Fifties: With a New Afterword*. Cambridge: Harvard University Press, 1988.

Belsey, Catherine. *Critical Practice*. London: Methuen, 1980.

——. "Disrupting Sexual Difference: Meaning and Gender in the Comedies." In Drakakis, 166–90.

——. *The Subject of Tragedy: Identity and Difference in Renaissance Drama*. London and New York: Methuen, 1985.

Bentley, Eric. *The Theatre of Commitment and Other Essays on Drama in Our Society*. New York: Atheneum, 1967.

Berger, Harry, Jr. *Imaginary Audition: Shakespeare on Stage and Page*. Berkeley: University of California Press, 1989.

——. "Miraculous Harp: A Reading of Shakespeare's *Tempest*." *Shakespeare Studies* 5 (1969): 253–83.

Bersani, Leo. *The Culture of Redemption*. Cambridge: Harvard University Press, 1990.

Billington, Michael. Review of Robert Lepage's *Midsummer Night's Dream*. *Guardian* (Manchester), 11 July 1992.

Bloom, Allan. *The Closing of the American Mind*. New York: Simon & Schuster, 1987.

Bloom, Edward, ed. *Shakespeare, 1564–1964: A Collection of Modern Essays by Various Hands*. Providence: Brown University Press, 1964.

Boose, Lynda E. "The Family in Shakespeare Studies; or—Studies in the Family of Shakespeareans; or—The Politics of Politics." *Renaissance Quarterly* 40 (1987): 707–42.

Booth, Stephen. "Syntax as Rhetoric in *Richard II*." *Mosaic* 10 (1977): 87–103.

Booth, Wayne C. "Reply to Richard Berrong." *Critical Inquiry* 11 (1984): 697–701.

Bradbrook, Muriel C. *The Growth and Structure of Elizabethan Comedy*. 1955; rpt. Harmondsworth: Penguin, 1963.

——. *The Rise of the Common Player*. London: Chatto & Windus, 1964.

Bredbeck, Gregory W. *Sodomy and Interpretation: Marlowe to Milton*. Ithaca: Cornell University Press, 1991.

Breight, Curt. " 'Treason Doth Never Prosper': *The Tempest* and the Discourse of Treason." *Shakespeare Quarterly* 41 (1990): 1–28.

Bristol, Michael D. *Shakespeare's America, America's Shakespeare*. London and New York: Routledge, 1990.

——. "Where Does Ideology Hang Out?" In Kamps, 31–43.

Brown, Paul. " 'This Thing of Darkness I Acknowledge Mine': *The Tempest* and the Discourse of Colonialism." In Dollimore and Sinfield, *Political Shakespeare*, 48–71.

Browne, Sir Thomas. *The Prose of Sir Thomas Browne*. Ed. Norman Endicott. New York: New York University Press, 1968.

Bruce, Lenny. *How to Talk Dirty and Influence People: An Autobiography*. Chicago: Playboy Press, 1963.

Brustein, Robert. "A Bottomless Dream." *New Republic*, 16 and 23 September 1985.

Burke, Kenneth. *The Philosophy of Literary Form*. Berkeley: University of California Press, 1973.

——. *A Rhetoric of Motives*. New York: Prentice-Hall, 1950.

Calderwood, James L., and Harold E. Toliver. *Essays in Shakespearean Criticism*. Englewood Cliffs, N.J.: Prentice-Hall, 1970.

Carton, Evan. "The Self Besieged: American Identity on Campus and in the Gulf." *Tikkun* 6, no. 4 (1991): 40–47.

Chambers, E. K. *The Elizabethan Stage*, vol. 3. 1923. Oxford: Oxford University Press, 1951.

Clayton, Thomas. "Shakespeare at the Guthrie: *A Midsummer Night's Dream*." *Shakespeare Quarterly* 37 (1986): 229–36.

Cohen, Walter. "Political Criticism of Shakespeare." In Howard and O'Connor, 18–46.

Coleridge, Samuel Taylor. *Selected Poetry and Prose*. Ed. Elisabeth Schneider. New York and Toronto: Rinehart, 1951.

Cook, Ann Jennalie. *The Privileged Playgoers of Shakespeare's London: 1576–1642*. Princeton: Princeton University Press, 1981.

Cook, Carol. "Straw Women and Whipping Girls: The (Sexual) Politics of Critical Self-Fashioning." In Kamps, 61–78.

Coveney, Michael. Review of Robert Lepage's *Midsummer Night's Dream*. *Observor* (London), 12 July 1992.

Cressy, David. "Foucault, Stone, Shakespeare, and Social History." *English Literary Renaissance* 21 (1991): 121–33.

Crews, Frederick. "Whose American Renaissance?" *New York Review of Books*, 27 October 1988, 68–81.

Culler, Jonathan. *Framing the Sign: Criticism and Its Institutions*. Oxford: Basil Blackwell, 1988.

———. *The Pursuit of Signs: Semiotics, Literature, Deconstruction.* Ithaca: Cornell University Press, 1981.

Cutts, John. *Rich and Strange: A Study of Shakespeare's Last Plays.* Pullman: Washington State University Press, 1968.

Dawson, Anthony B. "The Impasse over the Stage." *English Literary Renaissance* 21 (1991): 309–27.

———. "*Measure for Measure*, New Historicism, and Theatrical Power." *Shakespeare Quarterly* 39 (1988): 328–41.

Dean, Leonard F., ed. *Shakespeare: Modern Essays in Criticism.* Rev. ed. New York: Oxford University Press, 1967.

de Lauretis, Teresa, ed. *The Essential Difference: Another Look at Essentialism. Differences* 1, no. 2 (Summer 1989), special issue.

de Man, Paul. *The Resistance to Theory.* Minneapolis: University of Minnesota Press, 1986.

Dillon, George L. *Contending Rhetorics: Writing in Academic Disciplines.* Bloomington: Indiana University Press, 1991.

Dollimore, Jonathan. "Introduction: Shakespeare, Cultural Materialism, and the New Historicism." In Dollimore and Sinfield, *Political Shakespeare*, 2–17.

———. "Introduction to the Second Edition." In *Radical Tragedy*, xi–lxviii. Hemel Hempstead, Herts.: Harvester Wheatsheaf, 1989.

———. *Radical Tragedy: Religion, Ideology, and Power in the Drama of Shakespeare and His Contemporaries.* Chicago: University of Chicago Press, 1984.

———. *Sexual Dissidence: Augustine to Wilde, Freud to Foucault.* Oxford: Clarendon, 1991.

———. "Shakespeare, Cultural Materialism, Feminism, and Marxist Humanism." *New Literary History* 21 (1990): 471–94.

———. "Subjectivity, Sexuality, and Transgression: The Jacobean Connection." *Renaissance Drama*, n.s., 17 (1986): 53–81.

Dollimore, Jonathan, and Alan Sinfield. "Culture and Textuality: Debating Cultural Materialism." *Textual Practice* 4 (1990): 91–100.

———. "History and Ideology: The Instance of *Henry V.*" In Drakakis, 206–27.

———, eds. *Political Shakespeare: New Essays in Cultural Materialism.* Ithaca: Cornell University Press, 1985.

Drakakis, John. Introduction to Drakakis, *Alternative Shakespeares*, 1–25.

———, ed. *Alternative Shakespeares.* London: Methuen, 1985.

Dryden, John. "An Essay of Dramatic Poesy." In *Essays of John Dryden*, ed. William P. Ker, 1:21–108. New York: Russell, 1961.

Eagleton, Terry. *Criticism and Ideology: A Study in Marxist Literary Theory.* London: Verso, 1978.

———. "The Historian as Body-Snatcher." *TLS*, 18 January 1991, 7.

———. *William Shakespeare.* Oxford: Blackwell, 1986.

Erickson, Peter. "Rewriting the Renaissance, Rewriting Ourselves." *Shakespeare Quarterly* 38 (1987): 327–37.

Evans, Malcolm. "Deconstructing Shakespeare's comedies." In Drakakis, 67–94.

Felperin, Howard. *The Uses of the Canon: Elizabethan Literature and Contemporary Theory.* Oxford: Clarendon, 1990.

Ferguson, Margaret, Maureen Quilligan, and Nancy J. Vickers, eds. *Rewriting the Renaissance: The Discourses of Sexual Difference in Early Modern Europe.* Chicago: University of Chicago Press, 1986.

Fish, Stanley. "Commentary: The Young and the Restless." In Veeser, *New Historicism,* 303–16.

———. *Doing What Comes Naturally: Change, Rhetoric, and the Practice of Theory in Literary and Legal Studies.* Durham: Duke University Press, 1989.

———. "Rhetoric." In Lentricchia and McLaughlin, 203–22.

Foucault, Michel. Afterword, "The Subject and Power." In *Michel Foucault: Beyond Structuralism and Hermeneutics,* ed. Hubert L. Dreyfus and Paul Rabinow, 208–26. Chicago: University of Chicago Press, 1982.

———. *The History of Sexuality.* Vol. 1, *An Introduction.* Trans. Robert Hurley. New York: Random House, 1978.

———. *Power/Knowledge: Selected Interviews and Other Writings, 1972–1977.* Ed. Colin Gordon. New York: Random House, 1980.

———. "Questions of Method: An Interview with Michel Foucault." In *After Philosophy: End or Transformation?* ed. Kenneth Baynes, James Bohman, and Thomas McCarthy, 100–17. Cambridge: MIT Press, 1987.

———. "What Is an Author?" In *Textual Strategies: Perspectives in Post-Structuralist Criticism,* ed. Josué V. Harari, 141–60. Ithaca: Cornell University Press, 1979.

Fox-Genovese, Elizabeth. "Literary Criticism and the Politics of the New Historicism." In Veeser, *New Historicism,* 213–24.

Franklin, Phyllis. "Editor's Column." *MLA Newsletter* 24, no. 1 (1992): 4–6.

Fuss, Diana. *Essentially Speaking: Feminism, Nature, and Difference.* New York: Routledge, 1989.

Gallie, W. B. "Essentially Contested Concepts." *Proceedings of the Aristotelian Society* 56 (1955–56): 167–98.

Geertz, Clifford. *The Interpretation of Cultures: Selected Essays.* London: Hutchinson, 1975.

Goffman, Erving. *Forms of Talk.* Philadelphia: University of Pennsylvania Press, 1981.

Goldberg, Jonathan. *James I and the Politics of Literature: Jonson, Shakespeare, Donne, and Their Contemporaries.* Baltimore: Johns Hopkins University Press, 1983.

———. "The Politics of Renaissance Literature: A Review Essay." *ELH* 49 (1982): 514–42.

Goldman, Michael. *The Actor's Freedom: Toward a Theory of Drama.* New York: Viking, 1975.

Grady, Hugh. *The Modernist Shakespeare: Critical Texts in a Material World.* Oxford: Clarendon, 1991.

Graff, Gerald. "The Nonpolitics of PC." *Tikkun* 6, no. 4 (1991): 50–52.

———. "Other Voices, Other Rooms: Organizing and Teaching the Humanities Conflict." *New Literary History* 21 (1990): 817–40.

——. *Professing Literature: An Institutional History.* Chicago: University of Chicago Press 1987.

——. "The Pseudo-Politics of Literature." *Critical Inquiry* 9 (1983): 597–610.

——. "Teaching Power." Review of Robert Scholes, *Textual Power: Literary Theory and the Teaching of English. Novel* 19 (1986): 179–82.

——. "Teach the Conflicts." *South Atlantic Quarterly* 89 (1990): 51–58.

——. "Teach the Conflicts: An Alternative to Educational Fundamentalism." In *Literature, Language, and Politics*, ed. Betty Jean Craige, 99–109. Athens: University of Georgia Press, 1988.

——. "What Should We Be Teaching—When There's No 'We'?" *Yale Journal of Criticism* 1 (1988): 189–21.

Greenblatt, Stephen. "Culture." In Lentricchia and McLaughlin, 225–32.

——. "Improvisation and Power." In *Literature and Society: Selected Papers from the English Institute, 1978*, ed. Edward L. Said. Baltimore: Johns Hopkins University Press, 1980.

——. Introduction to Greenblatt, *Forms of Power*, 3–6.

——. "Invisible Bullets: Renaissance Authority and Its Subversion." *Glyph* 8 (1981): 40–61. Expanded as "Invisible Bullets: Renaissance Authority and Its Subversion, *Henry IV* and *Henry V*," in Dollimore and Sinfield, *Political Shakespeare*, 18–47.

——. "Kindly Visions." *New Yorker*, 11 October 1993, 112–20.

——. "King Lear and Harsnett's 'Devil Fiction.'" In Greenblatt, *Forms of Power*, 239–42.

——. *Learning to Curse: Essays in Early Modern Culture.* New York and London: Routledge, 1990.

——. *Marvelous Possessions: The Wonder of the New World.* Chicago: University of Chicago Press, 1991.

——. *Renaissance Self-Fashioning: From More to Shakespeare.* Chicago: University of Chicago Press, 1980.

——. "Shakespeare and the Exorcists." In *After Strange Texts: The Role of Theory in the Study of Literature*, ed. Gregory S. Jay and David L. Miller, 101–23. Birmingham: University of Alabama Press, 1985.

——. *Shakespearean Negotiations: The Circulation of Social Energy in Renaissance England.* Berkeley: University of California Press, 1988.

——, ed. *The Forms of Power and the Power of Forms in the Renaissance. Genre* 15 (1982): 1–242, special issue. Norman: University of Oklahoma Press, 1982.

——, ed. *Representing the English Renaissance.* Berkeley: University of California Press, 1988.

Greene, Gayle. "The Myth of Neutrality, Again?" In Kamps, 23–29.

Hewison, Robert. Review of Robert Lepage's *Midsummer Night's Dream. Times* (London), 12 July 1992.

Hexter, J. H. *Doing History.* Bloomington: Indiana University Press, 1971.

Hirsch, Marianne, and Evelyn Fox Keller. *Conflicts in Feminism.* New York: Routledge, 1990.

Holstun, James. "Ranting at the New Historicism." *English Literary Renaissance* 19 (1989): 189–225.

Horwitz, Howard. " 'I Can't Remember': Skepticism, Synthetic Histories, Critical Action." *South Atlantic Quarterly* 87 (1988): 787–820.

Howard, Jean. Review of Jonathan Goldberg's *James I. Shakespeare Quarterly* 35 (1984): 234–37.

Howard, Jean, and Marion O'Connor, eds. *Shakespeare Reproduced: The Text in History and Ideology*. New York and London: Methuen, 1987.

Huizinga, Johan. *Homo Ludens: A Study of the Play Element in Culture*. Boston: Beacon, 1955.

Hunt, Lynn. "History as Gesture; or, The Scandal of History." In Arac and Johnson, 91–107.

Hunter, G. K., and S. K. Hunter, eds. *John Webster*. Harmondsworth: Penguin, 1969.

Ignatieff, Michael. *The Needs of Strangers*. New York: Viking–Elisabeth Sifton Books, 1985.

Jacobi, Derek. "Interview: Derek Jacobi on Shakespearean Acting." *Shakespeare Quarterly* 36 (1985): 134–40.

Jameson, Fredric. *The Political Unconscious: Narrative as a Socially Symbolic Act*. Ithaca: Cornell University Press, 1981.

Jardine, Lisa. *Still Harping on Daughters: Women and Drama in the Age of Shakespeare*. Brighton: Harvester, 1983.

Jay, Martin. *Marxism and Totality: The Adventures of a Concept from Lukacs to Habermas*. Berkeley: University California Press, 1984.

Joyce, James. *Ulysses*. New York: Modern Library, Random House, 1942.

Kahn, Victoria. "Habermas, Machiavelli, and the Humanist Critique of Ideology." *PMLA* 105 (1990): 464–76.

Kamps, Ivo, ed. *Shakespeare Left and Right*. New York: Routledge, 1991.

Kamuf, Peggy. "Replacing Feminist Criticism." *Diacritics* 12 (1982): 42–47.

Kastan, David Scott, and Peter Stallybrass, eds. *Staging the Renaissance: Reinterpretations of Elizabethan and Jacobean Drama*. New York: Routledge, 1991.

Kavanagh, James H. "Ideology." In Lentricchia and McLaughlin, 306–20.

——. "Shakespeare in Ideology." In Drakakis, 144–65.

Kenshur, Otto. "(Avoidable) Snares and Avoidable Muddles." *Critical Inquiry* 15 (1989): 658–68.

——. "Demystifying the Demystifiers: Metaphysical Snares of Ideological Criticism." *Critical Inquiry* 14 (1988): 335–53.

Kermode, Frank. *The Art of Telling: Essays on Fiction*. Cambridge: Harvard University Press, 1983.

——. "Hail to the Chief." *London Review of Books*, 10 January 1991, 6.

——. Introduction to Shakespeare, *The Tempest*. London: Methuen, 1951.

——. *The Sense of an Ending: Studies in the Theory of Fiction*. Oxford: Oxford University Press 1967.

——. "Sensing Endings." In *Narrative Endings*, ed. Alexander Welsh. *Nineteenth-Century Fiction* 33 (1978): 144–58.

Kernan, Alvin B., ed. *Modern Shakespearean Criticism: Essays on Style, Dramaturgy, and the Major Plays*. New York: Harcourt Brace Jovanovich, 1970.

Kinney, Arthur F., and Dan S. Collins, eds. *Renaissance Historicism: Selections from "English Literary Renaissance."* Amherst: University of Massachusetts Press, 1987.

Knapp, Steven, and Walter Benn Michaels. "Against Theory." In *Against Theory: Literary Studies and the New Pragmatism*, ed. W. J. T. Mitchell, 11–30. Chicago: University of Chicago Press, 1985.

Kolodny, Annette. "Dancing through the Minefield: Some Observations on the Theory, Practice, and Politics of a Feminist Literary Criticism." In *The New Feminist Criticism: Essays on Women, Literature, and Theory*, ed. Elaine Showalter, 144–67. New York: Pantheon, 1985.

Kuhn, Thomas S. *The Structure of Scientific Revolutions*. 2d ed. Chicago: University of Chicago Press, 1970.

Kuriyama, Constance. "Marlowe, Shakespeare, and Biographical Evidence." *Shakespeare Newsletter* 38 (1987): 10.

Kushner, Tony. *Angels in America: A Gay Fantasia on National Themes*. Pt. 2, *Perestroika*. London: Royal National Theatre and Nick Hern Books, 1994.

Lanham, Richard. *The Motives of Eloquence: Literary Rhetoric in the Renaissance*. New Haven: Yale University Press, 1976.

Lentricchia, Frank. *After the New Criticism*. Chicago: University of Chicago Press, 1980.

——. *Ariel and the Police: Michel Foucault, William James, Wallace Stevens*. Madison: University of Wisconsin Press, 1987.

——. *Criticism and Social Change*. Chicago: University of Chicago Press, 1983.

Lentricchia, Frank, and Thomas McLaughlin, eds. *Critical Terms for Literary Study*. Chicago: University Chicago Press, 1990.

Lenz, Carolyn, Ruth Swift, Gayle Greene, and Carol Thomas Neely, eds. *The Woman's Part: Feminist Criticism of Shakespeare*. Urbana: University of Illinois Press, 1980.

Lerner, Laurence. "Against Historicism." *New Literary History* 24 (1993): 273–92.

Levin, Richard. "Bashing the Bourgeois Subject." *Textual Practice* 3 (1989): 76–86.

——. "Feminist Thematics and Shakespearean Tragedy." *PMLA* 103 (1988): 125–38.

——. "Ideological Criticism and Pluralism." In Kamps, 15–21.

——. *New Readings vs. Old Plays*. Chicago: University of Chicago Press, 1979.

——. "The Poetics and Politics of Bardicide." *PMLA* 105 (1990): 491–504.

——. "The Problem of 'Context' in Interpretation." In *Shakespeare and the Dramatic Tradition: Essays in Honor of S. F. Johnson*, ed. W. R. Elton and William B. Long, 88–106. Newark: University of Delaware Press, 1989.

Levine, Lawrence W. "William Shakespeare in America." In *Highbrow/Lowbrow: The Emergence of Cultural Hierarchy in America*, 11–82. Cambridge: Harvard University Press, 1988.

Liu, Alan. "Local Transcendence: Cultural Criticism, Postmodernism, and the Romanticism of Detail." *Representations* 32 (1990): 75–113.

Livingston, Paisley. *Literary Knowledge: Humanistic Inquiry and the Philosophy of Science.* Ithaca: Cornell University Press, 1988.

Longhurst, Derek. " 'You Base Football Player!': Shakespeare in Contemporary Popular Culture." In *The Shakespeare Myth*, ed. Graham Holderness, 59–73. Manchester: Manchester University Press, 1988.

Macherey, Pierre. *A Theory of Literary Production.* Trans. Geoffrey Wall. London: Routledge, 1978.

Mack, Maynard. *"King Lear" in Our Time.* Berkeley: University of California Press, 1965.

Macksey, Richard, and Eugenio Donato. *The Structuralist Controversy: The Languages of Criticism and the Sciences of Man.* Baltimore: Johns Hopkins University Press, 1970.

MacLure, Millar, ed. *Marlowe: The Critical Heritage.* London: Routledge & Kegan Paul, 1979.

Mannheim, Karl. *Ideology and Utopia: An Introduction to the Sociology of Knowledge.* Trans. Louis Wirth and Edward Shils. 1936. New York: Harcourt, n.d.

Marcus, Jane. "The Asylums of Antaeus: Women, War, and Madness—Is There a Feminist Fetishism?" In Veeser, *New Historicism*, 132–51.

Marcus, Leah. "Justice for Margery Evans: A 'Local' Reading of *Comus*." In *Milton and the Idea of Woman*, ed. Julia Walker, 66–85. Urbana: University of Illinois Press, 1988.

Marder, Louis M. "Shakespeare Heard 'Round the World.' " *Shakespeare Newsletter* 210 (1991): 31.

Marlowe, Christopher. *The Tragical History of the Life and Death of Doctor Faustus.* Ed. John D. Jump. London: Methuen, 1962.

Marx, Karl. *The Eighteenth Brumaire of Louis Bonaparte.* New York: International Publishers, 1963.

——. *Karl Marx: Selected Writings in Sociology and Social Philosophy.* Ed. T. B. Bottomore. New York: McGraw-Hill, 1956.

McDowell, Deborah. "Recycling: Race, Gender, and the Practice of Theory." In *Studies in Historical Change*, ed. Ralph Cohen, 246–63. Charlottesville: University Press of Virginia, 1992.

McGann, Jerome J. *The Beauty of Inflections: Literary Investigations in Historical Method and Theory.* Oxford: Clarendon, 1985.

Meisel, Perry. *The Myth of the Modern: A Study in British Literature and Criticism after 1850.* New Haven: Yale University Press, 1987.

Miller, Nancy K. *Getting Personal: Feminist Occasions and Other Autobiographical Acts.* New York: Routledge, 1991.

——. "The Text's Heroine: A Feminist Critic and Her Fictions." *Diacritics* 12 (1982): 48–53.

Milton, John. *Milton: Complete Poems and Major Prose.* Ed. Merritt Y. Hughes. New York: Odyssey, 1957.

Moi, Toril. *Sexual/Textual Politics: Feminist Literary Theory.* London: Methuen, 1985.

Montrose, Louis Adrian. "New Historicisms." In *Redrawing the Boundaries: The Transformation of English and American Literary Studies,* ed. Stephen Greenblatt and Giles Gunn, 392–418. New York: Modern Language Association of America, 1992.

——. " 'Shaping Fantasies': Figurations of Gender and Power in Elizabethan Culture." *Representations* 2 (1983): 61–94.

Moore, Don D., ed.. *Webster: The Critical Heritage.* London: Routledge & Kegan Paul, 1981.

Morgann, Maurice. *Morgann's Essay on the Dramatic Character of Sir John Falstaff.* Ed. William Arthur Gill. 1912. Freeport, N.Y.: Books for Libraries, 1970.

Muir, Kenneth, and Samuel Schoenbaum, eds. *A New Companion to Shakespeare Studies.* Cambridge: Cambridge University Press, 1971.

Neely, Carol Thomas. "Constructing the Subject: Feminist Practice and the New Renaissance Discourses." *English Literary Renaissance* 18 (1988): 5–18.

Nelson, Cary. "Against English: Theory and the limits of the Discipline." In *Profession 87,* ed. Phyllis Franklin, 46–52. New York: Modern Language Association, 1987.

Newton, Judith Lowder. "History as Usual? Feminism and the 'New Historicism.'" In Veeser, *New Historicism,* 152–67.

Nightingale, Benedict. Review of Robert Lepage's *Midsummer Night's Dream. Times* (London), 11 July 1992.

Orkin, Martin. *Shakespeare against Apartheid.* Craighall, South Africa: Ad. Donker, 1987.

Page, Malcolm. "Guy Sprung's *Midsummer Night's Dream." Canadian Theatre Review* 54 (1988): 24–28.

Parker, Patricia, and Geoffrey Hartman, eds. *Shakespeare and the Question of Theory.* London and New York: Methuen, 1985.

Paster, Gail Kern. *The Body Embarrassed: Drama and the Discipline of Shame in Early Modern England.* Ithaca: Cornell University Press, 1993.

Patterson, Lee. "Literary History." In Lentricchia and McLaughlin, 250–62.

Pearson, D'Orsay. " 'Unless I Be Reliev'd by Prayer': *The Tempest* in Perspective." *Shakespeare Studies* 7 (1974): 253–82.

Pease, Donald. "Toward a Sociology of Literary Knowledge: Greenblatt, Colonialism, and the New Historicism." In Arac and Johnson, 108–53.

Pechter, Edward. "Bardicide." *London Review of Books,* 13 February 1992, 5–6.

Pechter, William S. *Twenty-four Times a Second: Films and Filmmakers.* New York: Harper & Row, 1971.

Peckham, Morse. *Explanation and Power: The Control of Human Behavior.* New York: Seabury Press, 1979.

Plato. *The Collected Dialogues of Plato, Including the Letters.* Ed. Edith Hamilton and Huntington Cairns. New York: Bollingen Foundation, 1961.

Poovey, Mary. "Feminism and Deconstruction." *Feminist Studies* 14 (1988): 51–66.

Porter, Carolyn. "Are We Being Historical Yet?" *South Atlantic Quarterly* 87 (1988): 743–86.

Quilligan, Maureen. *Milton's Spenser: The Politics of Reading.* Ithaca: Cornell University Press, 1983.

Rabine, Leslie Wahl. "A Feminist Politics of Non-Identity." *Feminist Studies* 14 (1988): 11–31.

Rabkin, Norman. *Approaches to Shakespeare.* New York: McGraw-Hill, 1964

Rawson, Claude. "An Epiphany of Footnotes." *London Review of Books,* 16 March 1989, 17–19.

Ribner, Irving. "Shakespeare Criticism, 1900–1964." In Edward Bloom, 194–208.

Ridler, Anne, ed. *Shakespeare Criticism: 1935–60.* London: Oxford University Press, 1963.

Rorty, Richard. *Consequences of Pragmatism (Essays: 1972–1980).* Minneapolis: University of Minnesota Press, 1982.

——. *Contingency, Irony, and Solidarity.* Cambridge: Cambridge University Press, 1989.

——. *Philosophy and the Mirror of Nature.* Princeton: Princeton University Press, 1979.

Rosenberg, Brian. "Historicizing the New Historicism: Understanding the Past in Criticism and Fiction." *Modern Language Quarterly* 50 (1989): 375–92.

Said, Edward W. *The World, the Text, and the Critic.* Cambridge: Harvard University Press, 1983.

Shakespeare, William. *The Riverside Shakespeare.* Ed. G. B. Evans et al. Boston: Houghton Mifflin, 1974.

Shetawi, Mahmoud F. al-. "Shakespeare in Arabic: An Overview." *Shakespeare Newsletter* 40 (1990): 29.

Shklar, Judith N. "Why Teach Political Theory?" In *Teaching Literature: What Is Needed Now,* ed. James Engell and David Perkins, 151–67. Cambridge: Harvard University Press 1988.

Sidney, Sir Philip. *An Apology for Poetry.* Ed. Geoffrey Shepherd. London: Thomas Nelson, 1965.

Simpson, David. "Criticism, Politics, and Style in Wordsworth's Poetry." *Critical Inquiry* 11 (1984): 52–81.

Sinfield, Alan. "Give an Account of Shakespeare and Education, Showing Why You Think They Are Effective and What You Have Appreciated about Them. Support Your Comments with Precise References." In Dollimore and Sinfield, *Political Shakespeare,* 134–57.

——. *Literature in Protestant England, 1560–1600.* London: Croom Helm, 1983.

Smith, Barbara Herrnstein. "Belief and Resistance: A Symmetrical Account." *Critical Inquiry* 18 (1991): 125–39.

——. *Contingencies of Value: Alternative Perspectives for Critical Theory.* Cambridge: Harvard University Press, 1988.

Smith, Joseph H., and William Kerrigan, eds. *Pragmatism's Freud: The Moral Disposition of Psychoanalysis.* Baltimore: Johns Hopkins University Press, 1986.

Smith, Paul. *Discerning the Subject.* Minneapolis: University Minnesota Press, 1988.

Spencer, Charles. Review of Robert Lepage's *Midsummer Night's Dream. Daily Telegraph* (London), 13 July 1992.

Stanton, Domna. "Language and Revolution: The Franco-American Disconnection." In *The Future of Difference,* ed. Alice Jardine, 73–78. Boston: G. K. Hall, 1980.

Stimpson, Catherine R. "Are the Differences Spreading? Feminist Criticism and Postmodernism." *English Studies in Canada* 15 (1989): 364–82.

———. "Nancy Reagan Wears a Hat: Feminism and Its Cultural Consensus." *Critical Inquiry* 14 (1988): 223–43.

———. "President's Column." *MLA Newsletter* 22 (1990): 2–3.

Stoll, E. E.. *John Webster: The Periods of His Work as Determined by His Relations to the Drama of His Day.* 1905. New York: Gordian Press, 1967.

Stone, Lawrence. *The Family, Sex, and Marriage in England, 1500–1800.* 1964. London: Weidenfeld & Nicholson, 1977.

Taylor, Gary. "Bardicide." *London Review of Books,* 9 January 1992, 7–8.

Tennenhouse, Leonard. "Strategies of State and Political Plays: *A Midsummer Night's Dream, Henry IV, Henry V, Henry VIII.*" In Dollimore and Sinfield, *Political Shakespeare,* 109–28.

Thomas, Brook. *The New Historicism and Other Old-Fashioned Topics.* Princeton: Princeton University Press, 1991.

Tillyard, E. M. W. *Shakespeare's History Plays.* 1944. New York: Collier, 1962.

Veeser, H. Aram, ed. *The New Historicism.* New York and London: Routledge, 1989.

———, ed. *The New Historicism Reader.* New York and London: Routledge, 1993.

Waller, Marguerite. "Academic Tootsie: The Denial of Difference and the Difference It Makes." *Diacritics* 17 (1987): 2–20.

Warren, Roger. *"A Midsummer Night's Dream": Text and Performance.* London: Macmillan, 1983.

Wayne, Don. "Power, Politics, and the Shakespearean Text: Recent Criticism in England and the United States." In Howard and O'Connor, 47–67.

Weber, Samuel. *Institution and Interpretation.* Minneapolis: University of Minnesota Press, 1987.

Webster, John. *The Duchess of Malfi.* Ed. John Russell Brown. Manchester: Manchester University Press, 1977.

Wells, Stanley, ed. *The Cambridge Companion to Shakespeare Studies.* Cambridge: Cambridge University Press, 1986.

Wells, Susan. *The Dialectics of Representation.* Baltimore: Johns Hopkins University Press, 1985.

Werstine, Paul. Review of Jonathan Dollimore's *Radical Tragedy. Shakespeare Quarterly* 38 (1987): 522–24.

Works Cited

West, Cornel. *The American Evasion of Philosophy: A Genealogy of Pragmatism.* Madison: University of Wisconsin Press, 1989.

Whigham, Frank. "Sexual and Social Mobility in *The Duchess of Malfi.*" *PMLA* 100 (1985): 167–86.

White, Hayden. *Metahistory: The Historical Imagination in Nineteenth-Century Europe.* Baltimore: Johns Hopkins University Press, 1973.

Wilde, Oscar. "Phrases and Philosophies for the Use of the Young." In *"The Soul of Man under Socialism" and Other Essays,* ed. Phillip Rieff, 296–98. New York: Harper & Row, 1970.

Williams, Raymond. *Keywords: A Vocabulary of Culture and Society.* Rev. ed. New York: Oxford University Press, 1985.

———. *Marxism and Literature.* Oxford: Oxford University Press, 1977.

Wilson, John Dover. *The Fortunes of Falstaff.* 1943. Cambridge: Cambridge University Press, 1964.

Wilson, Richard, and Richard Dutton, eds. *New Historicism and Renaissance Drama.* London and New York: Longman, 1992.

Worthen, W. B. "Deeper Meanings and Theatrical Technique: The Rhetoric of Performance Criticism." *Shakespeare Quarterly* 40 (1989): 441–55.

Yachnin, Paul. "The Powerless Theater." *English Literary Renaissance* 21 (1991): 49–74.

Index

✦

Abrams, M. H., 163–165
Adams, Douglas, 12
Adorno, Theodor W., 118
Allen, Woody, 104
Alter, Robert, 127–28, 130, 145–47, 148, 175–76n.1
Alternative Shakespeares (Drakakis), 15, 30–31, 133
Althusser, Louis, 52, 58, 71, 152, 161, 169n.3, 176n.5
Anderson, Perry, 50, 78
Antony and Cleopatra, 67–68
"Are the Differences Spreading?" (Stimpson), 9
Aristotle, 133, 134, 173n.2
Ars poetica (Horace), 5
Audiences, 85–86, 95–96
  and materialist criticism, 51–52, 63–64
Augustine, Saint, 173n.2

Barber, C. L., 109, 111, 113, 115, 116, 119, 172–73nn.1–3
Barker, Francis, 61, 148–51, 154, 155, 164

Barthes, Roland, 105, 146
Barton, Anne, 150
Bedford Case Studies in Contemporary Criticism, 49
Begley, Adam, 49
"Belief and Resistance" (B. H. Smith), 139
Bell, Daniel, 156
Belsey, Catherine, 68, 71, 74, 146, 152–154, 170n.5, 176n.5
Bentley, Eric, 139–40
Berger, Harry, 44, 175n.12
Billington, Michael, 174n.6
Blake, William, 12
Bloom, Edward, 15, 19–20, 22, 26, 27
Booth, Stephen, 45
Booth, Wayne, 52
Bradbrook, Muriel, 104
Brecht, Bertolt, 66–67, 139–40
Breight, Curt, 176n.3
Brief and True Report of the New Found Land of Virginia, A (Harriot), 55
Bristol, Michael D., 76, 143, 154–56, 160
Brook, Peter, 112–14

Brown, Paul, 61–63, 67
Browne, Sir Thomas, 172n.4
Bruce, Lenny, 90, 92, 93
Brustein, Robert, 112
Burke, Kenneth, 69, 71, 73, 92, 152
Busino, Orazio, 93–96, 100

Caird, John, 112
Calderwood, James L., 13, 15, 18–19,
    22
Cambridge Companion (Wells), 16
Carousel (Rodgers & Hammerstein), 101
Change, 4
    and continuity, 36–39
    and ideology, 159–60, 163–66,
        177nn.13, 14
    and jargon, 138–41
    and materialist criticism, 28–31, 35
    See also Continuity; Fragmentation of
        criticism; Materialist-humanist
        disagreement
Ciulei, Liviu, 173n.5
Clayton, Thomas, 112
Cleaver, Eldridge, 69
Cohen, Walter, 76
Coleridge, Samuel, 23, 26, 31, 89
Colonialism, 54, 61, 65–67
"Commentary" (Fish), 176n.7
Confessions, The (St. Augustine), 173n.2
Consequences of Pragmatism (Rorty), 160
Contingencies of Value (B. H. Smith), 158
Contingency, Irony, and Solidarity (Rorty),
    11, 128, 162, 163
Continuity, 4, 56–57
    and change, 36–39
    and criticism as social practice,
        139–41
    and distinctions, 4–6
    and fairness, 119–20
    and fragmentation of criticism, 11–12,
        129–30
    in Greenblatt, 79
    vs. heroic transformation, 28–31
    and multiplicity, 118–19
    and new stories, 102–5

and textual autonomy, 6–7
    See also Change; Materialist-humanist
        disagreement
Cook, Ann, 63–64
Crane, R. S., 8
Crews, Frederick, 174n.9
Critical Practice (Belsey), 71, 152
Criticism
    as active, 2–4
    as antagonistic, 68–69
    division of, 87–90
    fragmentation of, 9–12
    function of, 13, 24–28, 47–48,
        127–28, 143–44, 167–68n.1,
        175–76n.1
    as social practice, 10, 140–41, 175n.2
    See also Shakespeare criticism; *specific
        topics*
Criticism and Ideology (Eagleton), 151,
    153–54
Criticism and Social Change (Lentricchia),
    69, 71–73
Cruttwell, Patrick, 168n.5
Culler, Jonathan, 130, 135, 136, 140,
    163, 164, 175n.2
Cultural materialism. *See* Materialist
    criticism

Daniels, Ron, 174n.10
Dean, Leonard, 15–19, 22–23, 25–27
Declaration of Egregious Popish Impostures, A
    (Harsnett), 54
de Man, Paul, 69, 122
de Tracy, Destutt, 157
Diacritics, 36–37
Dillon, George L., 4, 6, 8
Discerning the Subject (P. Smith), 161–62
Doctor Faustus (Marlowe), 91–93
Doing What Comes Naturally (Fish), 139,
    176n.7
Dollimore, Jonathan, 15, 36, 64–69, 76,
    139, 169n.6, 170n.5, 177n.11
Donato, Eugenio, 15
Donne, John, 153, 172n.4
Drakakis, John, 15, 30–35, 38, 46, 133

Index

Duchess of Malfi, The (Webster), 93, 100–103, 172n.5

Eagleton, Terry, 110–11, 116, 146, 151, 153–54, 169n.3, 170n.6, 176n.6
Eighteenth Brumaire, The (Marx), 47, 84, 139, 141, 166
Elizabethan World Picture, The (Tillyard), 31–32
Empson, William, 24, 26–27, 69
End of Ideology, The (Bell), 156
Essentialism, 160, 169n.7
Evans, Malcolm, 13, 167–68n.1

Felperin, Howard, 176n.3
Feminist criticism, 15
    fragmentation of, 9, 10, 129, 169n.6
    marginalization of, 143
    vs. materialist criticism, 36–37, 169n.7
"Feminist Thematics and Shakespearean Tragedy" (Levin), 142
Fish, Stanley, 139, 155, 175n.2, 176n.7
Fitzjeffrey, Henry, 99
Formalism, 51, 56, 79, 95
    Greenblatt on, 28–29, 83–84
    See also Humanist criticism; Postformalism
For Marx (Althusser), 58
Forms of Power, The (Greenblatt), 53, 56
Fortunes of Falstaff, The (Wilson), 56
Foucault, Michel, 52, 62, 64, 70, 78, 86, 93, 170nn.5, 8
Fox-Genovese, Elizabeth, 36
Fragmentation of criticism, 4, 15–16
    and feminism, 9, 10, 129, 169n.6
    as historical constant, 11–12, 129–30
    and indeterminacy, 119
    internalization of, 130–32
    and jargon, 127, 129–32
    necessity of, 34, 127, 147–49, 165–66
    and teaching, 106–7, 121, 165
Framing the Sign (Culler), 130
Frankfurt school, 157
Freud, Sigmund, 39, 81
Functionalism, 78, 161–63, 170n.7

Gallie, W. B., 156
Geertz, Clifford, 169n.4
Gender
    and anxiety, 111–12, 173–74nn.5–7
    and materialist-humanist
        disagreement, 89, 100–102, 171n.3
Godard, Jean-Luc, 99
Goffman, Erving, 136
Goldberg, Jonathan, 60, 63, 64, 67, 68, 176n.6
Goldman, Michael, 109, 172n.1
Graff, Gerald, 34, 52, 75, 120–21, 130, 175n.14
Greenblatt, Stephen, 28–29, 36–38, 49, 53–57, 61, 62, 66, 67, 74, 76–86, 94, 125, 150, 169nn.2, 4, 170nn.5, 6, 8
Greene, Gayle, 143, 144, 156, 159, 166

"Hail to the Chief" (Kermode), 82, 170n.6
Hall, Peter, 174n.10
Hall, Stuart, 176n.4
Hamlet, 39, 130–31
Hammerstein, Oscar, 88–89, 101
Harner, James, 168n.3
Harriot, Thomas, 55
Harsnett, Samuel, 54
Hartman, Geoffrey, 15
Hegel, G. W. F., 151
Henry IV, Part I, 55–57
Henry IV, Part II, 39–45
Hewison, Robert, 174n.6
Hexter, J. H., 65
Hirsch, John, 173n.5
"Historian as Bodysnatcher" (Eagleton), 170n.6
History, 39–45
    and humanist criticism, 20, 168–69n.5
    and materialist-humanist
        disagreement, 97–99
    See also Materialist criticism
History of Sexuality, The (Foucault), 62
Horace, 5
Howard, Jean, 34, 51
How to Talk Dirty and Influence People (Bruce), 90

Huizinga, Johan, 6, 7, 104
Hulme, Peter, 61, 67, 148–51, 154, 155, 164
Humanist criticism, 16–28
    brief anthology introductions in, 17
    consensus in, 14–15, 155–56, 168n.4
    and function of criticism, 24–28
    and ideology, 143–48, 159, 163
    old historicism, 53, 56, 102
    and reality/fiction distinction, 107–9, 172–73nn.1, 2
    and selection, 17–21, 168–69n.5
    textual autonomy in, 18–20, 23, 51, 56
    theoretical awareness of, 30–32
    unity in, 19–23, 27
    See also Fragmentation of criticism; Materialist-humanist disagreement
Hunter, G. K., 99
Hunter, S. K., 99

Idealism. *See* Humanist criticism
"Ideological Criticism and Pluralism" (Levin), 147
Ideology
    Althusser on, 58
    and change, 159–60, 163–66, 177nn.13, 14
    commitment to, 158–63
    and humanist criticism, 143–48, 159, 163
    and Marxism, 152, 176n.4
    and materialist criticism, 148–55, 157–64, 176n.5
    MLA session, 142–45
    and necessity of agreement, 147–48
    Plato on, 157, 177n.8
    vs. pleasure, 145–47, 175–76n.1
    rejection of, 156–58
    and textual autonomy, 145–46, 159, 177n.10
    and theology, 152–54
    See also specific topics
Ideology and Utopia (Mannheim), 152
Ignatieff, Michael, 103
Imaginary Audition (Berger), 175n.12

"Improvisation and Power" (Greenblatt), 171n.8
"Invisible Bullets" (Greenblatt), 170n.7
"Is the One-Volume Anthology Obsolete?" (Weil), 14

James I and the Politics of Literature (Goldberg), 60
Jameson, Fredric, 52, 57–58, 71, 75, 97, 154, 176n.6
Jardine, Lisa, 102
Jargon
    and change, 138–41
    and criticism as social practice, 140–41
    definition of, 126–27
    and fragmentation of criticism, 127, 129–32
    and materialist-humanist disagreement, 127–29
    and preaching to converted, 134–38
    value of, 132–34, 139–40
Jesus, 134
Jonson, Ben, 63, 64
Joyce, James, 83, 84
Julius Caesar, 68

Kafka, Franz, 70
Kahn, Victoria, 143, 158
Kamps, Ivo, 142–43
Kamuf, Peggy, 36–38
Kavanagh, James H., 110–11, 115, 133–34, 137, 138, 174n.9
Kermode, Frank, 82–83, 109, 135, 150, 170n.6, 172n.1, 176n.2
Kernan, Alvin B., 15, 20–21, 168–69n.5
Keynes, John Maynard, 46
King Lear, 54, 67, 106, 107, 114–15
"*King Lear* and Harsnett's 'Devil Fiction'" (Greenblatt), 54
Kitto, H. D. F., 25–26
Knapp, Steven, 115
Knight, G. Wilson, 35, 121
Knights, L. C., 35
Kolodny, Annette, 10
Koren, Edward, 27–28

Index

Kuhn, Thomas, 11, 32, 38, 139, 159

Lanham, Richard, 104, 130–31
Laurier, Angela, 174n.6
Learning to Curse (Greenblatt), 77, 79–83, 85, 170n.6
"Lecture, The" (Goffman), 136
Lenin and Philosophy and Other Essays (Althusser), 152
Lentricchia, Frank, 68–69, 71–74
Lenz, Carolyn, 15, 169n.6
Lepage, Robert, 113, 173n.5, 174nn.6, 10
"Letter on Art" (Althusser), 58
Lever, J. W., 31
Levin, Richard, 63, 67, 142–44, 147–49, 156, 159, 160, 164, 177n.10
Levine, Lawrence, 2
Levine, Michael, 173n.5
Livingston, Paisley, 161
Longhurst, Derek, 2

Macherey, Pierre, 69–70
Mack, Maynard, 114–15, 175n.12
Macksey, Richard, 15
MacLure, Millar, 91
Mannheim, Karl, 152, 158
Marcus, Jane, 36
Marcus, Leah, 177n.10
Mark, St., 166
Marlowe, Christopher, 91–92, 171–72nn.3, 4
"Marlowe, Marx, and Anti-Semitism" (Greenblatt), 82
Marvelous Possessions (Greenblatt), 86, 171n.8
Marx, Karl, 47, 84, 139, 141
Marxism
    and ideology, 152, 176n.4
    and materialist criticism, 52–53, 57, 58, 68, 73, 76
Marxism and Literature (Williams), 85, 97, 157, 163–65
Materialist criticism, 4–5, 49–86
    and anxiety, 110–12, 173–74nn.5–7

audiences in, 51–52, 63–64
    culture and text in, 53–56
    detachment from text in, 66–71, 73–74
    and differences, 33–38, 169n.6
    domestication of, 49–50
    vs. feminist criticism, 36–37, 169n.7
    Greenblatt's role in, 77–86, 170–71nn.6, 7
    growth of, 49, 51–52
    as heroic transformation, 28–31, 35
    and ideology, 148–55, 157–65, 176n.5
    and Marxism, 52–53, 57, 58, 68, 73, 76
    vs. old historicism, 53, 56
    and political action, 69–71, 116–18
    power relations in, 60–66, 73
    recent analysis of, 75–77
    structure and subject in, 50–51
    and textual autonomy, 6
    theory and application in, 57–58
    theory in, 58–60, 169n.3
    "thick description" in, 60, 62–63, 169–70n.4
    value of, 71–75, 170n.5
    See also Fragmentation of criticism; Materialist-humanist disagreement
Materialist-humanist disagreement
    appropriation of stories, 171–72n.3
    and contextualization, 90–93
    and cultural determination, 96–97
    division and unity in, 87–90
    and gender, 89, 100–102, 171n.3
    and history, 97–99
    and jargon, 127–29
    and new stories, 103, 105, 118
    and political action, 99–100
    reversibility of, 32–33, 104–5
    and teaching, 29, 106–7, 120–22, 175n.14
    and textual autonomy, 3, 55–56, 113–15, 174n.10, 175n.12
    and theatrical absorption, 93–97, 172n.4
    and theoretical awareness, 30–31

See also Change; Continuity
McGann, Jerome, 116–18
Michaels, Walter Benn, 115
Midsummer Night's Dream, A, 60, 61, 64,
    107–14
    and anxiety, 110–13, 115,
        173–74nn.5–7
    and jargon, 133–34
Miller, Nancy K., 36–38
Milton, John, 153, 154
Modern Shakespearean Criticism (Kernan),
    15, 20–21, 168–69n.5
Moi, Toril, 36
Montaigne, Michel de, 96
Montrose, Louis Adrian, 60–61, 63, 64,
    67, 111–13, 115, 121, 129, 174n.10
Morgann, Maurice, 57, 59, 144
Moshinsky, Elijah, 173n.5
Motives of Eloquence, The (Lanham), 130

"Nancy Reagan" (Stimpson), 9, 27–28,
    129, 169n.6
Narrativity, 80–82
Needs of Strangers, The (Ignatieff), 103
"Negative Love" (Donne), 153
Nelson, Cary, 13, 168n.1
New Readings (Levin), 67
Newton, Judith Lowder, 36
Nightingale, Benedict, 173–74n.5

O'Connor, Marion, 34
Oklahoma (Rodgers & Hammerstein),
    88–89
Ovid, 158

Page, Malcolm, 173n.5
Paradigms, 11–12, 32, 38, 159
Paradise Lost (Milton), 153, 154
Parker, Patricia, 15
Paster, Gail Kern, 174n.7
Pater, Walter H., 26
Patterson, Lee, 6–8
Pechter, William, 99
Peckham, Morse, 93
Pepys, Samuel, 117

Philosophy and the Mirror of Nature (Rorty),
    158
Philosophy of Literary Form, The (Burke),
    92
Piaget, Jean, 172n.1
Plato, 117, 118, 157, 177n.8
Pleasure of the Text, The (Barthes), 105
*Pleasures of Reading in an Ideological Age,
    The* (Alter), 127, 145
Pluralism, 148
Poetics (Aristotle), 173n.2
"Poetics and Politics of Bardicide, The"
    (Levin), 177n.10
Political action, 69–71, 99–100, 116–18
Political Shakespeare (Dollimore &
    Sinfield), 15, 64, 65, 67, 69, 169n.6
Pope, Alexander, 3
Popular culture, 2
Porter, Carolyn, 76
Portrait of the Artist as a Young Man, A
    (Joyce), 83
Positivism, 6
Postformalism, 28–29, 168n.2
Power, 60–66, 73, 113. *See also* Materialist
    criticism
Power/Knowledge (Foucault), 93
Pragmatism, 170n.7
"Problem of 'Context' in Interpretation,
    The" (Levin), 147
Professing Literature (Graff), 130
"Psychoanalysis and Renaissance
    Culture" (Greenblatt), 81
Pursuit of Signs, The (Culler), 135, 175n.2

Quilligan, Maureen, 68

Rabkin, Norman, 13, 15, 21–23, 26
Radical Tragedy (Dollimore), 66–67
Rawson, Claude, 118
Renaissance Self-Fashioning (Greenblatt),
    37, 53–54, 57, 61, 66, 70, 83, 94
Resistance to Theory, The (de Man), 122
"Resonance and Wonder" (Greenblatt),
    77
Rhetoric (Aristotle), 133

Rhetoric of Motives, A (Burke), 152
Ribner, Irving, 22, 27, 35
Richard II, 45
Ridler, Anne, 15, 23–26
Rise of the Common Player, The
  (Bradbrook), 104
Rodgers, Richard, 88–89, 101
Romanticism, 98, 99, 172–73n.2
Rorty, Richard, 11, 75, 128, 158, 160,
  162, 163, 165, 167n.2, 177n.14
Ryle, Gilbert, 169n.4

Said, Edward, 69
Scholes, Robert, 75
Scientific model, 12, 167n.2
Scientific realism, 161
Sejanus (Jonson), 63, 64
Self-referentiality. *See* Textual autonomy
Sense of an Ending, The (Kermode),
  172n.1
"Sensing Endings" (Kermode), 135
Sexual/Textual Politics (Moi), 36
"Shakespeare and the Exorcists"
  (Greenblatt), 82, 125
Shakespeare and the Question of Theory
  (Parker & Hartman), 15
Shakespearean Moment, The (Cruttwell),
  168n.5
Shakespearean Negotiations (Greenblatt),
  79
Shakespeare criticism
  function of, 13, 24–25, 47–48,
    167–68n.1
  future of, 46–47, 166
  and history, 45–46
  increase in, 13–14, 23–24, 168n.3
  non-European, 168n.2
  vs. Shakespeare's plays, 2–3, 6
  See also Fragmentation of criticism;
    Humanist criticism; Materialist
    criticism; Materialist-humanist
    disagreement
"Shakespeare in Ideology" (Kavanagh),
  110
Shakespeare Left and Right (Kamps), 143

Shakespeare Reproduced (Howard &
  O'Connor), 34
Shakespeare's America (Bristol), 76, 154,
  160
Shakespeare's plays
  vs. criticism, 2–3, 6
  definition of, 1
  ongoing vitality of, 1–2, 167–68n.1
  as *pananthropos*, 22
  " 'Shaping Fantasies' " (Montrose),
    60–61, 111–12
Shaw, Glen Byam, 114
Sheppard, Samuel, 98
Shetawi, Mahmoud F., al-, 168n.2
Sidney, Sir Philip, 173n.2
Simpson, David, 52
Sinfield, Alan, 15, 36, 64, 65, 67, 69, 76,
  169n.6
Smith, Barbara Herrnstein, 132, 139,
  158
Smith, Paul, 161–62, 176n.4, 177n.13
Socrates, 130
Spall, Timothy, 173n.5
Sprung, Guy, 173n.5
Stanton, Domna, 169n.6
Stein, Gertrude, 88
Stimpson, Catherine, 9, 27–28, 37, 129,
  169n.6
Stone, Lawrence, 101
"Subjectivity, Sexuality, and
  Transgression" (Dollimore), 139
Symposium, The (Plato), 117

Teaching
  and fragmentation of criticism, 106–7,
    121, 165
  and materialist-humanist
    disagreement, 29, 106–7, 120–22,
    175n.14
  subjective factors in, 122–25
"Teaching Power" (Graff), 75
Tempest, The, 61, 63, 65–66, 150, 176n.3
Tennenhouse, Leonard, 60, 63, 67
Textual autonomy, 6–9, 51, 56
  and continuity, 6–7

vs. detachment from text, 66–71,
  73–74
and ideology, 145–46, 159, 177n.10
and jargon, 128
and materialist-humanist
  disagreement, 3, 55–56, 113–15,
  174n.10, 175n.12
and selection, 18–19, 20, 23
and theater, 2–3, 175n.12
Three Guineas (Woolf), 171n.3
Tillyard, E. M. W., 31–32, 44, 56, 102
Toliver, Harold, 13, 15, 18–19, 22

Ulysses (Joyce), 84
Uses of the Canon, The (Felperin), 176n.3

Waller, Marguerite, 36
Warren, Roger, 113, 115, 175n.12
Weber, Samuel, 175n.2
Webster, John, 93, 98, 100–103, 172n.5
Weil, Herbert, 14, 106–7

Wells, Stanley, 16, 168n.4
Wells, Susan, 101
Werstine, Paul, 76
"What Is an Author?" (Foucault), 86
Whigham, Frank, 101
White, Hayden, 8, 32–33
White Devil, The (Webster), 98
Wilde, Oscar, 104
Williams, Raymond, 46–47, 50, 79, 83,
  85, 97, 156, 157, 163–65
William Shakespeare (Eagleton), 110
"William Shakespeare in America"
  (Levine), 2
Wilson, John Dover, 56
Wimsatt, W. K., 79–80
Woman's Part, The (Lenz et al.), 15,
  169n.6
Woolf, Virginia, 171n.3

Yachnin, Paul, 99